Eric Clapton FAQ

Series Editor: Robert Rodriguez

Eric Clapton FAQ

All That's Left to Know About Slowhand

Happy 41st Birthday
Love Dad

David Bowling

Backbeat
Books

An Imprint of Hal Leonard Corporation

Published in 2013 by Backbeat Books
An Imprint of Hal Leonard Corporation
7777 West Bluemound Road
Milwaukee, WI 53213

Trade Book Division Editorial Offices
33 Plymouth St., Montclair, NJ 07042

The FAQ series was conceived by Robert Rodriguez and developed with Stuart Shea.

Printed in the United States of America

Library of Congress Cataloging-in-Publication Data is available upon request.

ISBN 978-1-61713-454-8

www.backbeatbooks.com

To Josef Casimir Hofmann and Thomas Edison

Contents

Introduction

When I started this project, I googled the name Eric Clapton. I received 10,400,000 responses. It was not 10,400,401 or 10,399,999 but a nice round number. No matter how you look at it, that's a lot of information about one person. There is more to come, as his career shows no signs of slowing down.

Amazon also had 650 books dealing with him in some manner or other, and that is not counting compilation or omnibus-type volumes. All this calls for the question, is another book about Eric Clapton really necessary?

The answer, up until this point, has always been yes. There has been an insatiable urge by millions of his fans for more and more knowledge about the man, his life, and his music. I feel it's a combination of the type of society in which we live and the magnitude of the career he has carved out for himself.

He has been a fixture on the music scene for half a century. The Yardbirds, Cream, Blind Faith, and Derek and the Dominos are all testament to his talent and creativity. If he had retired in his mid-twenties after folding Derek and the Dominos, he would have left a lasting imprint on the music world. It turned out he was just warming up, as his solo career now spans four decades.

Eric Clapton is still alive and well and adding to his legacy and bank of information. He continues to be active in the studio and on the road. He released his latest studio album, *Old Sock*, in 2013. He has already scheduled a number of concerts for 2013 that may well have been completed by the time this book is published. He is constantly adding to the information files about his life. His own book *Clapton: The Autobiography* and Pattie Boyd's tell-all autobiography just whetted the appetite for more information, as they are only the tip of the iceberg.

FAQ books are a gathering together of just that. They are not all-inclusive, nor are they biographies in the normal sense of the word. I have divvied his career into different components, so in a sense they are a number of mini biographies centered around different parts of his professional life. While this led to some repetitiveness in places, I felt it was a good way to present the material.

I also decided to go a little further afield and present some of the people who have meandered through his life and even some who influenced it but had passed away before he was born. They are important components to his life and thus his story.

No one fan knows everything or every fact about Eric Clapton, and I realize there are people whose knowledge is much vaster than mine. So we are back to a gathering of pertinent, and hopefully interesting, information in one place.

While this is a book based on the presentation of facts, at times I have tried to make it more accessible and folksy, if you will, by using a more interactive style such as is used in reviews.

Clapton's story is constantly changing, and any person, whether a public figure or not, creates quite a history during his or her lifetime. I am confident others could write about his life from a different perspective and create an entirely different book. If you are so inclined, I say have at it, as there is always room for more.

In the final analysis, if this book entertains or educates you in some way, it will have been a success and a worthwhile endeavor. Above all, as you turn the pages, enjoy.

Who, Me?

It was an average day in 2010 when the phone rang, and much to my amazement, it was not a telemarketer. It was Robert Rodriguez asking if I had any interest in writing the Eric Clapton book for Backbeat Books' FAQ series.

It seemed like an exciting idea at the time. What I didn't consider was the time and effort that would go into accomplishing my simple yes to his question.

I have been aware of Clapton since his time with the Yardbirds. We are of the same generation, although he does have a few years on me. I became a fan during his time with Cream and have followed his career since that time. I was not obsessive about Clapton but rather about his music as I have a complete run of his singles and albums in my collection, including most of his work with other artists. When I began researching the man and all he entailed, I was stunned at how much was out there. It was reduce, reduce, and reduce.

I had just completed a series of reviews about each of his studio albums, so I had listened to them fairly recently. There was a lot of material, however, that had not graced my stereo system in years, and so I became a veritable Eric Clapton roadie in my record room, as singles, live albums, and collaboration efforts were continually blasting from my speakers. It was a virtual trip down memory lane as his career just about spans my lifetime of listening to and collecting music. It was a trip worth taking for my own sake.

I realized I could have added more material to the story and introduced additional chapters almost ad infinitum, but there always comes a point when you say enough is enough. It's like a term paper in school where you add, delete, adjust, but eventually there comes a point where you must have the resolve to say I have done my best and submit the finished product with hope and a little faith as well. I finally reached that point.

In My White Room

The closer I got to my submission date, the more I burrowed into my computer/record room, which is indeed white. There are a number of people to thank for this project and some whom it will affect in the future.

To my wife Susan, who, against her inclinations, did not disturb my piles of "stuff" that were accruing at an alarming rate in my little hideaway. She has also humored my passion for collecting vinyl records, which now number in the tens of thousands, and has only skimmed one or two out into the backyard when the impulse became too much to overcome.

To my grandparents, Guy and Edith Fish, who, although born in the late 1890s, established a love of music within my soul. It may not have been music they could relate to at the time, but it was music nevertheless. They also gave me a small allowance each week plus the ability to do odd jobs, allowing me to begin purchasing music.

To Herioux's Music Store in downtown Woonsocket, Rhode Island. It was a small mom-and-pop operation that is long gone and forgotten by most, but it was there I spent many Saturday mornings flipping though the latest releases. The first record I ever bought was from that store. "The Little Old Lady from Pasadena" by Jan & Dean still holds a place of honor in my collection. Support your local record stores, as they are the heart and soul of the music industry. They make music personal, which is an important component of the experience.

To Rob Rodriguez, who gave me that first call and provided guidance through the process. Check out his FAQ books, *Fab Four FAQ* and *Fab Four FAQ 2.0*.

To the Hal Leonard Performing Arts Publishing Group and Backbeat Books, including publisher John Cerullo, who took a flyer on a person who had never written a full-length book.

To my daughters Stacey and Amy, who when they were growing up always thought my music collection was cool and now in adulthood have settled into a supportive if bemused outlook concerning my passion. They will like the book no matter what the outcome, and it's important to have people like that in your life.

Finally to Grandmaster T, Rockin' Rylan (with an L), Charismatic Camden, and Bubba Chubs; my grandchildren, more commonly known as Tyler, Rylan (still with an L), Camden, and Ashley. They are the next generation of music lovers. I have no idea what their musical tastes or journeys will be like, but I do know one of them will inherit a great music collection.

Hellhound on My Trail

The Delta Blues

T he primordial ooze of the Louisiana bayous has produced any number of rare and dangerous creatures but none so exotic as the group of primarily black musicians who were born around the turn of the twentieth century. They were a generation or two removed from slavery, and their parents still worked the dirt farms of the South. They would make, acquire, borrow, and steal their instruments and play on street corners and in smoke-filled honky-tonks, only being paid by passing the hat around for donations. Those talented and lucky enough would record their songs on old shellac 78s, which were called race records and would receive no play on mainstream radio stations. They endured and created the blues.

The blues, or the Delta blues, were raw, primitive, sexual, and passionate. Black rhythms from the Delta would support lyrics about life's trials, death, religion, and culture. The instruments were acoustic, and the best of the early blues artists were some of the most technically adept musicians to ever walk this earth.

And so God created the Delta blues, and it was good.

Robert Johnson

Much of the life of Robert Johnson remains shrouded in mystery. There are two authenticated pictures of him that have survived. His music sold poorly during his lifetime even among the black audience at which it was aimed. Very little of his music remains as very few 78 rpm records were released during his lifetime and one more after his death. His complete recorded catalog consists of only forty-one tracks, and that includes a number of alternate takes. Yet today he is regarded as one of the seminal figures of American music, and artists such as Eric Clapton, Peter Green, Keith Richards, and a host of others worship at his musical altar.

Robert Johnson began his musical journey on May 8, 1911, in Hazlehurst, Mississippi, as the son of Julia Dodds and Noah Johnson. He accompanied his mother as she spent the next couple of years

Robert Johnson was *the* influence on Eric Clapton and
the generations of blues artists that have followed him.
Author's collection

employed as a migrant worker and living the rough and tumble life in
various labor camps. When he was three years old, he was left at the home
of Charles Spencer, where for the next four years he lived with Spencer's
wife, mistress, and assorted children. He was reunited with his mother in
1914, in Robinsonville, Mississippi, where she married Willie Willis in 1916.

Johnson's interest in music began to blossom as a teenager, and he
became proficient on the Jew's harp and harmonica. After marrying and
losing his sixteen-year-old wife in childbirth during 1929, his life changed
forever when blues legend Son House moved into town. Johnson trailed
behind House and cohort Willie Brown as they performed their brand of raw
blues in local bars and saloons. He crossed paths with Charley Patton, who
did not think much of his still developing guitar skills. As the Depression
deepened, he returned to his birth town of Hazlehurst to search for his
father, earn a living, marry Colletta Craft, practice his guitar skills, and if
legend has it correct, keep an appointment with the devil at the crossroads.

Highways 61 and 49 intersect at the crossroads in Clarksdale, Mississippi,
and it was there that Robert Johnson sold his soul to the devil in exchange
for the ability to play the guitar as few people have ever been able to do.
While this legend has been changed, enhanced, and twisted through the
years, the Robert Johnson who returned to Robinsonville several years

later proved to be one of the most adept and creative guitar players in blues history. Even Son House quickly realized that Johnson was now the master. Whether it was the pact with the devil or his constant practicing in his hometown, the stage had been set for one of the most influential blues players in American history to assume his throne.

He established his home base in Helena, Arkansas, and for the rest of his short life he traveled the juke joint circuit, playing with many of the premier bluesmen of the day and leaving his mark on them; they would in turn pass it on to others.

He would only record two times during his lifetime. The first was in San Antonio in November 1936 and the second was in Dallas in June 1937. A little over a year later he was dead.

The twenty-nine different songs he left behind form a powerful legacy and a jumping-off point for the thousands of blues and rock musicians who would follow him. He took a primitive art form and while remaining true to its roots, fleshed it out and passed it along to the next generation. His place in the evolutionary process of the blues and American music remains secure.

His original releases were all on the Vocalion label, and these old brittle 78s are now some of the rarest and most treasured in music history and bring huge prices from music fanatics and collectors.

1936
- "Kind Hearted Woman"/"Terraplane Blues" (Vocalion 03414)
- "30-20 Blues"/"Last Fair Deal Gone Down" (Vocalion 03445)
- "(I Believe I'll) Dust My Broom"/"Dead Shrimp Blues" (Vocalion 03475)
- "Rambling on My Mind"/"Cross Road Blues" (Vocalion 03519)
- "Come On in My Kitchen"/"They're Red Hot" (Vocalion 03563)
- "Walking Blues"/"Sweet Home Chicago" (Vocalion 03601)

1937
- "From Four Till Late"/"Hell Hound on My Trail" (Vocalion 03623)
- "Malted Milk"/"Milkcow's Blues" (Vocalion 03665)
- "Stones in My Passway"/"I'm a Steady Rollin' Man" (Vocalion 03723)
- "Stop Breakin' Down Blues"/"Honeymoon Blues" (Vocalion 04002)
- "Little Queen of Spades"/"Me and the Devil Blues" (Vocalion 04108)

1938
- "Preaching Blues"/"Love in Vain" (Vocalion 04630)

If you do not have the time, money, or inclination to collect these old pieces of shellac, his entire forty-one-track catalog was issued in the classic box set *The Complete Recordings,* which was released by the Columbia label in 1990.

When you listen to his music today, his passion and intense attitude are still present. Also of note is how much he packed into a few minutes. All of his material was written with the 78 rpm format in mind, and none of his songs exceed three minutes in length. While his material has been covered by hundreds of artists, very few are able to get it right.

Robert Johnson's music is not for the faint of heart as it is a primitive and ominous ride through the mind of a hard-living blues genius. But if you stay with it and pay attention, it will be well worth the price of admission.

Charley Patton

No one person can lay claim to being the originator of the blues but if you had to place the mantle on someone it would probably be Charley Patton.

Charley, or sometimes spelled Charlie, Patton was born in Hinds County, Mississippi, circa 1891. Only one picture of him remains, but legend has it he was part African American and part Native American. He was a child at the end of the post–Civil War South, and his music reflected multiple cultures and influences. While he was deeply rooted in the black rhythms of his surroundings, he also incorporated such disparate sounds as early country, or hillbilly as it was known; traditional folk music; and even elements of white vaudeville music.

Patton was a traveling man who lived a hard life. He was probably an alcoholic and was prone to violence. He married on eight different occasions and was a difficult man to get along with. He almost died in 1933 when his throat was slit in Holly Ridge, Mississippi. Through it all he remained a popular attraction on the early honky-tonk and blues circuit. Likewise, many of his releases met with commercial success as "race records," which were aimed exclusively at the black market of the day.

He did meet and play with many of the leading blues musicians of his era. Since he was their senior he was given respect, and his bottleneck style of playing and his impassioned singing were copied, changed, and ultimately incorporated into the evolution of the blues. Robert Johnson, Howlin' Wolf, Muddy Waters, Son House, and hundreds of musicians who would follow can trace elements of their sound and style to him.

Patton's entire recording career consisted of four recording sessions between 1929 and 1934. I find his recordings even more primitive than those of Robert Johnson. His vocal style is almost unintelligible upon occasion, and it overpowers his guitar at times. Though he was considered one of the premier guitar technicians of the era, his disciples would be much more technically adept.

If you want to hear the recorded blues near the beginning, you need to hear many of the songs he recorded during his first sessions in Richmond, Indiana. "Mississippi Boweavil Blues" is the blues at its basic foundation. "Screamin' and Hollerin' Blues" is just that, and more accomplished vocalists would hone the style presented here. A lot of people have sung the blues, but "Lord I'm Discouraged" is an example of a man who lived the blues and is able to put his heartbreak and hurt into words and music.

His 1929 and 1930 recording sessions in Grafton, Wisconsin, find him at the height of his powers. The 1929 sessions include Henry Sims giving support with some southern fiddle playing, which provides an odd and effective base for Patton's guitar sound and vocal. The 1930 tracks find the legendary Son House and Willie Brown adding their guitars to that of Patton's. Thousands of blues recordings to come would pick up on this primitive guitar interplay.

His last recording session took place in New York City in 1934, shortly before his death from a heart attack. He would cut twenty-six sides between January 30 and February 1. I can't help but think he recorded just about every song in his repertoire, and as such it is more hit or miss than his other sessions.

If you want to explore the legacy of Charley Patton and have some funds to invest, and by that I mean quite a bit of money, I would recommend his 2001 seven-disc box set, *Screamin' and Hollerin' the Blues: The Worlds of Charley Patton*. This is the best compilation of his material that I have heard, as the Revenant label has done an extraordinary job of remastering and enhancing the sound quality. Paramount records were famous for the poor quality of their releases as their old 78s hiss and crackle even when in good condition. The set is an excellent look into the evolution of Patton's music and the elements that would be gathered and enhanced by his disciples. The extra bonuses are the Paramount recordings of Son House, Willie Brown, and Lonnie Johnson.

Charley Patton's fame and legacy are secure among serious blues and music enthusiasts, but to the general music-buying public it has been superseded by the likes of Robert Johnson, Muddy Waters, and those whose own legacies have directly influenced many of the music legends of the sixties and beyond.

There can be little doubt that Charley Patton is near ground zero for the American blues. His early recordings are primitive even by twenties and thirties standards, but they remain some of the most influential in American music history.

Son House

Eddie James "Son" House Jr. entered the world March 21, 1902, in Riverton, Mississippi. He was born into a devout Christian household and felt the call of ministry, preaching his first sermon at the age of fifteen. In his twenties a music calling proved stronger than the church, and he learned to play the guitar before setting off on a career that would elevate him to the top of his new profession and solidify his fame as an influential American blues performer.

In 1928–1929, he would spend time at Parchman Farm Penitentiary for killing a man in self-defense. Luckily for him the final thirteen years of his sentence were commuted. What was truly amazing was that unlike many of his twenties and thirties blues counterparts, he lived well into his eighties.

Son House was a close friend to Charley Patton as he constantly toured primarily with him and Willie Brown. He would also serve as a second guitarist for a number of his recordings. He acted as a mentor to Robert Johnson for a time but ultimately would be surpassed by his former student in guitar virtuosity.

His Baptist ministry would influence him for the rest of his music career. His live shows were wild musical sermons as he pounded his guitar and played it in various positions. They were emotional presentations and suited for the dance hall as his music was based on repetitive rhythms and howling vocals, which would demand an audience response. He was more powerful in a live setting than on record, especially with the technology of the day. In some ways he was one of the first rock 'n' rollers, at least in spirit, as he was the forerunner of Pete Townshend's windmilling style and Jerry Lee Lewis pounding away with abandon on his piano.

House cut nine sides for the Paramount label in 1930, but they sold virtually no copies. Songs such as "My Black Mama," "Preachin' the Blues," and "Dry Spell Blues" remain some of the rarest records in history. He did not record again until Alan Lomax brought his three-hundred-pound recording machine to the Delta in 1941–1942 and recorded nineteen tracks by House for the Library of Congress.

His definitive release today is titled *The Complete Library of Congress Sessions, (1941–1942)*. He brings to life the raw emotion of his vocals and his slide guitar technique along with sidekicks Willie Brown and Joe Martin. He whales away on "Delta Blues," "Pony Blues," and "American Defense." Listen for the railroad noise in the background.

Son House would fade from the music scene as many of his contemporaries passed away, but his legacy remained as one of the original wild men of American music.

Memphis Minnie

Who says only men can play the blues?

Lizzie Douglas was born on June 3, 1897, in Algiers, Louisiana. She was one of the few blueswomen to play the guitar and sing, as most females were just vocalists.

Make no mistake that Lizzie, who became known as Memphis Minnie, lived the hard blues life just like her male counterparts. She ran away at thirteen and began playing the guitar in nightclubs and even joined the circus for a short time. Her songs were about life from a female perspective, which was unusual in the honky-tonks of the south. Illicit love, cheating men, life's difficulties, and sexual lyrics made her music both relevant and interesting.

She had one of the best voices of the pre–World War II blues singers. When you listen to her recordings, it is immediately apparent that you are hearing a superior vocalist. Her lyrics are clearly understood; the tone is superior and the presentation dramatic. That voice graced a large catalog of recordings.

One of her greatest contributions was her experimenting with an electric guitar sound in 1942, which paved the way for the generations of blues artists who would follow.

Her second major contribution was her move to Memphis and the fusion of the blues with a country sound. The blues have undergone a number of

These old 78s by the blues masters have become highly collectable. *Author's collection*

transformations during the last century, and her foray into the heartland of country music was an important step in this process.

The best example of her work is *Queen of Country Blues: 1929–1937*, which is a five-disc, 124-track CD box set. Her music sounds much more contemporary than many of her blues companions from the era. Songs such as "Hoodoo Lady," "Bumble Bee Blues," "Me and My Chauffeur Blues," and the fun-filled "I'm Gonna Bake My Biscuit," plus 120 others, represent her talent well.

Memphis Minnie many times remains an afterthought in the evolution of the blues, which may be because of her sex, but she was an excellent vocalist/guitarist who pushed the boundaries of her chosen profession, and that is what the blues are all about.

There were thousands of musicians who called the blues their own in the years prior to the Second World War. Many just faded into the mists of time, but a few left a lasting imprint on the musical landscape. Their disciples would spread across the United States, but the hub of the post–Delta blues era would center in Chicago.

2

The Mojo Travels North

Sweet Home Chicago

he year 1948 found millions of former soldiers settling into civilian life. The economy was good, and factories were booming. Tens of thousands of rural Americans were moving to the cities of the North. Against that backdrop, a seemingly insignificant shellac 78-rpm record was released by the Aristocrat Label as number 1305. "(I Feel Like) Going Home/I Can't Be Satisfied" by Muddy Waters briefly appeared on the rhythm and blues charts of the day and disappeared. It would turn out to be one of the most influential releases in American music history as Muddy Waters electrified his guitar by plugging it into an amplifier. The blues would be forever changed and the road to rock 'n' roll was now open.

Many of the Delta bluesmen would travel the dusty roads north with the sprawling metropolis of Chicago as their destination. Little did they realize that a new generation of blues players was waiting for them with not only guitars in hand but also bass, drums, piano, and even saxophones, which had all been "plugged in." Their primitive rhythms and stories would be enhanced and changed through the power of amplification. It would allow their style of music to be recorded in ways they could not have imagined and attain a commercial popularity that would have been beyond their expectations just a short time before.

Many of the old bluesmen never made it to Chicago, and their legacy is confined to old juke joints and rare 78-rpm records. Their music has been collected and released on CDs, a format they could not have envisioned. Some did make it, fewer still became commercially successful, and a very few would become legendary and change the course of the musical landscape.

Howlin' Wolf

The twentieth president of the United States, James Garfield, was shot in the back by Charles Guiteau July 2, 1881, and died a little over two months later. His vice president, Chester Arthur, would assume the presidency, serve with little distinction, be denied his own party's nomination to serve another term, and quickly become one of America's forgotten presidents. Today very few Americans know anything significant about Chester Arthur.

It is not known how many children were named after him, but one would achieve more popularity and lasting fame than the old president.

Chester Arthur Burnett entered this world June 10, 1910, in the Mississippi town of White Station, about a quarter century after his namesake's demise. How a Southern, future Hall of Fame bluesman came to be named after a white, Northern politician is not known and in the long run did not matter as his grandfather would tell the young boy stories about behaving or the wolf would come and get him. Little Charles Arthur took the nickname "Howlin' Wolf" and set off to live a life that would resonate through music history.

He would be estranged from his mother all of his life; first for not wanting to work on their farm and finally for playing the devil's music. He would live with an uncle and at age thirteen with his father, who had left his mother when he was a young child. By the time he was twenty, he had met Charley Patton, who taught him to play the guitar.

If there was ever an intimidating presence onstage, it was Howlin' Wolf. He was well over six feet tall and usually weighed in the range of 275–300 pounds. His gruff vocals and physical presence made him a dominant and at times terrifying performer.

He learned his craft the same way as many of his Delta contemporaries by continually playing on street corners, small clubs, and bars. Many times he crossed paths with the likes of Robert Johnson, Son House, Johnny Shines, Charley Patton, and Sonny Boy Williamson II.

The five-year period 1948–1953 would set the foundation for Howlin' Wolf's commercial success and popularity. He would have his own radio show in West Memphis, Arkansas, which allowed him to promote himself. He always had the ability to attract the top blues talent to his bands, mainly because he paid well and on time. In 1948, he formed his first great band, consisting of guitarists Willie Johnson and Matt "Guitar" Murphy, harmonica player Junior Parker, and drummer Willie Steele. Nineteen fifty-one found the legendary Sam Phillips signing him to a recording contract. Finally, in 1953, guitarist Hubert Sumlin joined his band and would play for Wolf for the rest of his career. *Rolling Stone* magazine would honor Sumlin as #65 on their list of the 100 Greatest Guitarists of All Time.

Howlin' Wolf's first two albums are essential for understanding the blues. *Moanin' in the Moonlight*, released in 1959, gathered twelve previously released songs and issued them in LP format. The music is elemental, powerful, and dark. Highlights include the title track "I Asked for Water (She Gave Me Gasoline)," which was based on Tommy Johnson's "Cold Drink of Water Blues," and the immortal "Smokestack Lightning," which is one of the historic blues songs. *Rolling Stone* would rank the album #153 on their list of the 500 Greatest Albums of All Time. *Howlin' Wolf Sings the Blues*, also known as the Rocking Chair album, was released in 1962. It is a virtual all-star lineup of early Chicago blues songs as "The Red Rooster," "Spoonful," "Back Door Man," and "Shake for Me" are all found here.

The good news for modern blues aficionados is that both albums were rereleased on one CD titled *Howlin' Wolf/Moanin' in the Moonlight*. Why they were issued in reverse order I have no idea. I prefer this release to his many compilation albums as it presents his music in the manner originally intended. If you want an introduction to his music, this is the place to start.

If you would like to explore his early legacy a little deeper, I would recommend any or all of the following. "Saddle My Pony" and "Worried All the Time" are both from 1948 Memphis and catch him in his evolutionary period between the Delta and Chicago. The first is stark and primal, while the second features the piano work of Ike Turner. "Howlin' Wolf Boogie" matches the title well as Willie Johnson's guitar lines drive the song along. "Oh Red," recorded in 1952, finds him expanding his musical horizons by adding brass to the mix. "My Last Affair" is an excellent early example of his expertise at a slow blues song. If you want to move to the late fifties, "I Better Go Now" is another fine example of a Howlin' Wolf band at its best driven by Sumlin's guitar.

Howlin' Wolf not only helped to establish the Chicago blues but lived to reap some of the rewards. He would travel to England in 1971 and record one of the great blues albums of the era with some of the best musicians around, but that's a story for another day.

Muddy Waters

The Mississippi River meanders over twenty-three hundred miles through the center of the United States, and the area known as the Mississippi Delta only encompasses a small portion of it. Quaint counties named Panola, Sunflower, Tallahatchie, and Yazoo contain some of the most fertile soil in America. This native soil would not only be used to grow crops but would produce a crop of musicians including Charley Patton, Robert Johnson, Howlin' Wolf, John Lee Hooker, Big Bill Broonzy, and McKinley Morganfield, who would take the nickname Muddy Waters.

Muddy Waters was born on or about April 4, 1915, and would be ranked the #17 Greatest Artist of All Time by *Rolling Stone*. Raised by his

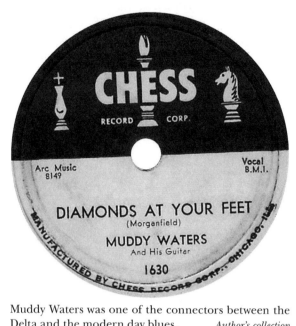

Muddy Waters was one of the connectors between the
Delta and the modern day blues.   *Author's collection*

grandmother from an early age after the death of his mother, he would
travel from his birthplace of Jugs Corner, Mississippi, which is located in
Issaquena Country, to the big city and become known as the Father of the
Chicago Blues.

By the age of seventeen, he was performing at local parties and clubs and
developing his unique slide guitar style. At twenty-five, he was running his
own juke joint. Alan and John Lomax brought their recording equipment
to Stovall, Mississippi, in 1941, hoping to record Robert Johnson again for
the Library of Congress, not realizing he had died. Instead, they recorded
Muddy Waters. They returned in 1942 for another session. By the time he
left for Chicago in 1943, Waters left behind two wives, one girlfriend, and
two children.

His early gigs in the windy city were opening for Big Bill Broonzy.
Broonzy was tremendously influential in his own right, but his sound just
missed the brass ring. His foundation was country blues, which evolved
into a folk/blues fusion. He may have started in Mississippi, but he was one
of the early traveling men of blues. He spent two years in Europe serving
in the military during World War I. He arrived in Chicago during the
1920s and traveled to New York City during the thirties. His close to three
hundred compositions encompassed music from the cities, the country, and

the Delta. He would constantly take traditional folk songs and transform them. He allowed Muddy Waters to be his opening act when he arrived in Chicago. The audiences were drunk, enthusiastic, and above all very loud. Waters began playing the electric guitar in order to be heard. One can only wonder how life would have been different for Broonzy if he had followed a similar path.

The fifties would find Waters at the height of his early popularity. His 1953 band consisting of harpist Little Walter Jacobs, guitarist Jimmy Rogers, drummer Elga Edmunds, and pianist Otis Spann was one of the best in history and helped to expand the blues idiom. His releases consistently charted on the national rhythm and blues charts. The sixties would find his popularity on the wane as soul music and the beginnings of modern R&B began to grow in popularity. He would continue to record and enjoy a late career renaissance.

His early LP releases for the Chess label remain the best examples of his early work. Of course, if you are a purist and have money and time on your hands, you can look for his old 78s. In some ways they remain the perfect vehicle for understanding the early blues. If you just want the music, the following are recommended, and all have been reissued in CD form.

The Best of Muddy Waters (Chess LP 1427, issued 1958). As with many of his contemporaries, Muddy Waters's first album was a compilation of his hit material. Ten of the twelve tracks were issued from 1947 to 1951 and the final two in 1954. The sound is not the best as it was taken from the original tapes and sometimes I think directly from the 78s themselves, but that is part of its charm. The Chicago blues were not meant to be scrubbed clean.

The tracks include "I Just Want to Make Love to You," "Long Distance Call," "Louisiana Blues," "Honey Bee," "Rolling Stone," "I'm Ready," "Hoochie Coochie Man," "She Loves Me," "I Want You to Love Me," "Standing Around Crying," "Still a Fool," and "I Can't Be Satisfied." If you want to understand the Chicago blues, this is a place to start. The foundation of American and British blues can be found here.

Muddy Waters Sings Big Bill Broonzy (Chess LP 1444, issued 1960). Muddy Waters entered the studio with bassist Andrew Stephenson, pianist Otis Spann, harpist James Cotton, guitarist Pat Hare, and drummer Francis Claxton and recorded an album of material by his old friend who died two years before the album was released.

This is a more structured release than his first compilation album as his sound had begun to evolve and mature. It is interesting to hear him take Broonzy's acoustic material and interpret it on his electric guitar. It is a fine support band, but this is a release that revolves around Waters. Standout songs include "Southbound Train," "When I Get to Thinking," "Just a

Dream (On My Mind)," "Mooper's Blues," and "Hey Hey." It may be a short affair at around thirty minutes, but it is time well spent.

Muddy Waters at Newport 1960 (Chess LP 1149, issued 1960). This release remains the best and certainly the most interesting of his early live material. Waters was well into his forties when he brought his band to the Newport Jazz Festival and took center stage on July 3, 1960. While bassist Andrew Stephenson, guitarist Pat Hare, and drummer Francis Clay are along for support, it is longtime pianist Otis Spann who provides the foundation for his vocals. In fact, this concert remains one of the better documents of Spann's prowess.

This is probably one of the slicker recorded concerts of his career. The rough edges, which he would return to later in his career, have been erased. This is particularly apparent on his "Got My Mojo Working Part 1 and Part 2." Elongated versions of "Soon Forgotten," "I Got My Brand on You," and "Tiger in Your Tank" give both him and the band room to stretch and are much preferred over their originally recorded counterparts. Other performances include "Hoochie Coochie Man," "Baby Please Don't Go," "I Feel So Good," and "Goodbye Newport Blues." This album remains a fine introduction to Muddy Waters in his prime.

The sixties and early seventies would find Waters constantly touring and recording, but his popularity would succumb to a new generation of rock, soul, and blues musicians. It would not be until his release of *Hard Again* for the Blue Sky label in 1977 that he would return to the limelight. By that time his influences had moved from small Chicago nightclubs to a worldwide stage as thousands of musicians and the elite blues players would trace their origins to him.

Willie Dixon

William James Dixon began his life like many other Delta and Chicago bluesmen of the day. He took his first breath in Vicksburg, Mississippi, on July 1, 1915. He spent many of his teenage years on various prison farms where he was exposed to the blues. By the time he was twenty-two years old, he had grown to six and a half feet tall while tipping the scales at close to 250 pounds. He had been a member of the Gospel Quartet, the Jubilee Singers, and had won the novice heavyweight division of the Illinois Golden Gloves Championship. More importantly, he had begun writing poems and putting them to music.

He arrived in Chicago during the late thirties and quickly became a part of the Five Breezes vocal group with Leonard Caston, Joe Bell, Jimmie Gilmore, and Willie Hawthorne. It was more of a pop/rhythm and blues group similar to the Mills Brothers and the Ink Spots. After the war, he continued his involvement with vocal groups; first with the Four Jumps of Jive and then the Big Three Trio, who managed to obtain a recording contract with the Columbia label.

The late forties found him signing with the Chess label, and this relationship would last into the early sixties. During that time he would emerge as one of the major influences of not only the Chicago blues but European blues as well, and also become an important connector to rock 'n' roll.

He would continue to play and record himself, but he gradually became a full-time producer and arranger for the label. More important were the songs he wrote. They would be recorded by many of the leading artists of his generation and the following generation of musicians as well. His catalog of original compositions remains one of the most impressive in blues history.

Some of his better-known compositions with the most famous versions are listed below.

- "Back Door Man": Howlin' Wolf, the Doors, the Grateful Dead, the Shadows of Knight, and the Blues Project
- "Bring It on Home": Sonny Boy Williamson II, Led Zeppelin, and Van Morrison
- "Built for Comfort": Howlin' Wolf
- "Close to You": Muddy Waters, Stevie Ray Vaughan, and the Doors
- "Diddy Wah Diddy": Bo Diddley, the Remains, and Bruce Springsteen
- "Don't Go No Farther": Muddy Waters, the Doors, and B. B. King
- "Eternity": the Grateful Dead
- "Evil (Is Going On)": Howlin' Wolf, Derek and the Dominos, Canned Heat, Faces, the Steve Miller Band, and Captain Beefheart
- "Groanin' the Blues": Eric Clapton
- "Hoochie Coochie Man": Muddy Waters, the Shadows of Knight, Allman Brothers, Alexis Korner, Eric Clapton, Jimi Hendrix, and the New York Dolls
- "Howlin' for My Darlin'": Howlin' Wolf and George Thorogood
- "I Ain't Superstitious": Howlin' Wolf, the Yardbirds, the Grateful Dead, and the Jeff Beck Group
- "I Can't Quit You Baby": Led Zeppelin and John Mayall
- "I Got My Brand on You": Muddy Waters and Alexis Korner
- "I Just Want to Make Love to You": Muddy Waters, the Animals, the Kinks, the Yardbirds, the Grateful Dead, the Rolling Stones, Tom Petty, and the Alex Harvey Band

- "I'm Ready": Muddy Waters and Aerosmith
- "I Want to Be Loved": Muddy Waters and the Rolling Stones
- "Let Me Love You Baby": Stevie Ray Vaughan, the Jeff Beck Group, Muddy Waters, and B. B. King
- "Little Baby": Howlin' Wolf, the Rolling Stones, and the Blues Project
- "Little Red Rooster": the Rolling Stones, Howlin' Wolf, and the Yardbirds
- "Mellow Down Easy": Little Walter, Paul Butterfield Blues Band, and ZZ Top
- "My Babe": Elvis Presley, Bo Diddley, and the Spencer Davis Group
- "My Babe Is Sweeter": Little Walter and Fleetwood Mac
- "Pain in My Heart": the Rolling Stones, Otis Redding, and the Grateful Dead
- "The Seventh Son": Johnny Rivers, Sting, Mose Allison, Bill Haley, and Long John Baldry
- "Shake for Me": Howlin' Wolf and Stevie Ray Vaughan
- "Spoonful": Howlin' Wolf, Muddy Waters, Cream, Ten Years After, and Etta James
- "The Same Thing": Muddy Waters, the Allman Brothers, the Band, and the Grateful Dead
- "You Can't Judge a Book by Its Cover": Bo Diddley, Eric Clapton, the Yardbirds, the Rolling Stones
- "You Shook Me": Muddy Waters, the Jeff Beck Group, and Led Zeppelin

If you want a quick introduction to the music of Willie Dixon and the Chicago blues in general, a good place to start is *Chess Box by Willie Dixon*. While at thirty-six tracks it only provides a taste of his music, it does provide a good introduction.

The tracks are the original releases and not covers. Such songs as "Little Red Rooster" by Howlin' Wolf, "Seventh Son" by Willie Mabon, and "My Babe" by Little Walter are the essence of the blues. In addition, there are five tracks by Dixon himself. "Weak Brain, Narrow Mind," "Violent Love," "Crazy for My Baby," "29 Ways," and "This Pain in My Heart" proved that he could also perform with the best of the early blues artists. He also plays a mean bass. The best part is that used copies of this release can be found at a very reasonable price on many Internet websites.

Willie Dixon may not have been a star of the magnitude of Howlin' Wolf or Muddy Waters, but his influence would outlive them through his catalog of compositions. His songs continue to be interpreted and reintroduced to new generations of music fans.

Leonard and Phil Chess

Lejzor and Fiszel Czyz were not born anywhere near the Mississippi Delta. If fact they were born in Motal, Poland, in 1917 and 1921, respectively. By 1928, their family had migrated to the United States, adopted the name Chess, and settled in Chicago, Illinois, which set them on a path to influence the course of American music.

In 1947, they purchased the Macomba Club, which provided a hands-on introduction to the Chicago music scene. Leonard quickly purchased a stake in the Aristocrat Label. By 1950, he and his now invested brother Phil owned the label, and they quickly changed the name to Chess.

This originally small, independent label would help change the music scene, as it would sign many of the leading blues artists of the day. Big Bill Broonzy, Willie Dixon, Lowell Fulsom, Dale Hawkins, Howlin' Wolf, John Lee Hooker, Memphis Slim, Little Milton, Little Walter, Sonny Boy Williamson II, and Muddy Waters all made the Chess Label their recording home during the 1950s. When you add in early rock 'n' rollers Chuck Berry and Bo Diddley, you have one of the most important and influential independent labels, rivaling Sam Phillips's Sun Records.

The Chess brothers may have been an odd duo in the studio, but they provided the vehicle for the early blues to reach the record-buying public. They had an innate ability to sign artists who would be commercially successful and the knowledge to run a successful company that would make both of them millionaires before it was all done.

Chicago proved to be a place where many of the early blues artists settled and honed their sound. It would become a temporary home for the blues as the music form would quickly ripple outward, even beyond the confines of the country itself.

3

The Midnight Special Hops the Pond

Early British Blues

I t is unknown what thirteen-year-old Eric Clapton was doing when Muddy Waters first stepped onto English soil in 1958. Whether it was chasing girls, practicing the guitar, or any other typical early teenage activity, he had no way of knowing that the British blues and his life would be forever changed.

American blues had reached the British shores during World War II, courtesy of American G.I.'s who had brought the music of the Southern Delta with them. Old shellac 78s began to circulate on a limited basis. Big Bill Broonzy would tour during the mid-fifties, introducing his fusion of folk and urban blues. British artists of the day, while far from the blues musically, would add many of its tunes to their repertoire.

Chris Barber would form his first jazz band in 1949. His focus would be traditional jazz with some Dixieland thrown in for good measure. As time passed, musicians such as Cyril Davies and Alexis Korner began performing blues numbers between his sets. While he would not add a blues guitarist to his band until the mid-sixties, Barber would be instrumental in setting up tours for some of the leading American blues artists of the day, including Waters. It also did not hurt that the great Northern Ireland blues singer Ottilie Patterson would join his band during the mid-fifties and marry him several years later.

Fans who purchased tickets to Muddy Waters's series of concerts were expecting American-based acoustic blues. Muddy Waters was playing a lot of things during this period, but acoustic blues was not one of them. Waters had been playing electric blues for almost a decade, but it was an epiphany for English blues fans. His wild and loud performances electrified (pun intended) blues aficionados of England. A generation of future musicians was listening, and they would fuse his sound with their own and claim the results for themselves. Music would never be the same.

Alexis Korner

One of my college friends was a hard-core Alexis Korner fan. I, on the other hand, was listening to the Rolling Stones, Cream, Led Zeppelin, and the like. Little did I realize that my friend was providing me with a history lesson in the evolution of the blues.

Alexis Korner can be considered the godfather of the British blues. While playing with the Chris Barber Jazz Band during the mid-fifties, he met Cyril Davies. Their love of the blues would forge a friendship that led them to open their own club. The London Blues and Barrel House Club would become a mecca for early British blues. It would also be a training ground for dozens of aspiring musicians.

His early career would culminate with the founding of Blues Incorporated with Davies. While they would eventually part ways due to Davies's desire to play traditional blues, this largely commercially unsuccessful group would be the foundation on which John Mayall, Brian Jones, Eric Burdon, Rod Stewart, Paul Jones, Eric Clapton, and others would build their sound.

The best preservation of their legacy can be found on *R&B from the Marquee*, which catches Korner, Davies, and vocalist Long John Baldry at their pinnacle. Recorded in June 1962, it also catches the British blues at the end of its formative stage. Supporting the three stars were sax player Dick Heckstall-Smith, pianist Keith Scott, bassist Spike Heatley, and drummer Graham Burbridge. The album is a basic course in the early British blues. Davies provides the vocals on five tracks including three by Muddy Waters, "I Got My Brand on You," "I Wanna Put a Tiger in Your Tank," and "Hoochie Coochie," all of which show his love of a traditional blues sound.

Long John Baldry, on the other hand, was a wailer, and his lead vocals can be heard on "I Thought I Heard That Train Whistle Blow," "How Long, How Long Blues," and "Rain Is Such a Lonesome Sound." They all show him moving in a different direction.

Through it all, Korner proves he has the blues down pat as his guitar playing intertwines with Davies's harp, which would make any Chicago blues musician stand up and take notice.

Korner would be the great connector in British blues. He would take the Delta and Chicago sound and move it to the edge of rock 'n' roll. He was never able to grasp the commercial brass ring himself, but he passed the torch to the Rolling Stones, the Yardbirds and dozens of other bands that used his music as a stepping-stone.

Cyril Davies

If Alexis Korner was the king of the early British blues, then Cyril Davies can be considered its crown prince.

Early photographs of Davies give no hint of his future. He seems more like a schoolteacher than a future blues artist. Yet lurking inside was one of the purest blues artists England would ever produce.

Davies also cut his teeth playing with Chris Barber. He was an early convert to the blues and by the mid-fifties was mimicking the Delta blues on his Grimshaw 12-string guitar while running the Barrel House Club with sidekick Alexis Korner.

Ultimately, Davies had two things against him. He was at heart a blues purist. When Blues Incorporated began moving away from a traditional sound, he promptly left and formed the Cyril Davies Blues Band with drummer Cario Little, bassist Rick Brown, pianist Nicky Hopkins, and guitarist Bernie Watson, and if you ever want to hear one of the great early blues guitarists, this is the man.

Davies's early work was essential and influential, but his unwillingness to adapt his sound confined him and his legacy to the very early British blues and prevented it from expanding beyond that point.

The other limiting factor of his career was his life span, which was very short.

The best example of his music is the obscure single release "Country Line Special" by Cyril Davies and His Rhythm and Blues All Stars. By this time he had transitioned from the guitar to the harmonica and quickly became its leading British proponent.

Davies remains a seminal if somewhat forgotten figure in the evolution of the British blues. He helped to expose a unique American musical form to his country. A generation of musicians would embrace his introduction and take it to places he could not have imagined.

The early sixties had set the stage for Eric Clapton, who was coming of age, listening, and above all practicing.

4

Those Cotton Fields Back Home

4

Whatever Happened To

Robert Johnson

If Robert Johnson really did make a deal with the devil, he got the short end of the stick as payment came due at the age of twenty-seven. Fellow bluesman Sonny Boy Williamson had advised Johnson never to drink from an open bottle. Johnson, who was playing an extended engagement at a club near Greenwood, Mississippi, became involved with a woman at the time and ignored this advice. He was most likely poisoned by strychnine. He would die a couple of days later on August 16, 1938.

As much of his life has been shrouded in mystery, so was his death and burial. There are three sites that purport to be his final resting place.

He was most likely buried in an unmarked grave in the Mount Zion Missionary Baptist Church Cemetery near Morgan City, Mississippi, not far from where he died. A cenotaph is a monument placed for a person whose remains are elsewhere, so this as his final resting place is not a foregone conclusion. The Columbia label paid for a two-thousand-pound monument listing all of his songs.

A second gravestone marker was placed in the Payne Chapel Cemetery near Quito, Mississippi. It simply says; "resting in the blues." Since the cemetery's owner paid for the stone, it remains the least likely place.

The third entrant in the Robert Johnson grave sweepstakes is located in Little Zion Cemetery, which is north of Greenwood. The gravedigger's wife has pointed to a place under a pecan tree as Johnson's final resting place. Sony music paid for this third monument.

Only two authenticated pictures of Johnson have been found, and his body of recorded work remains very small. Still, he is revered as one of the founders of the blues. He was inducted into the Blues Hall of Fame in

1980, the Rock and Roll Hall of Fame in 1986, and posthumously received a Grammy Lifetime Award in 2006.

"I went down to the crossroad, fell down on my knees. I went down to the crossroad, fell down on my knees. Asked the Lord above, 'Have mercy now save poor Bob if you please.'" Lyrics taken from "Cross Road Blues," recorded November 27, 1936.

Son House

As World War II and the American landscape began to change, the career of Son House began to wane. He finally disappeared and became a forgotten figure.

The early sixties blues revival led to his rediscovery. He was found living in Rochester, New York, working for the New York Central Railroad. His twenty-year railroad career came to a quick end as he appeared at the 1964 Newport Folk Festival and for the next decade toured throughout the United States and Europe.

Son House toured and recorded for another decade and became a well-respected link to the past. He retired for the final time in 1974 and passed away at the wise old age of eighty-six. He is buried in the Mount Hazel Cemetery in Detroit. The city's blues society erected and paid for his tombstone.

Charley Patton

The Holly Ridge Cemetery in Holly Ridge, Mississippi, is a stark place that forms the background for the final resting place of Charley Patton.

He would never achieve wide commercial success or acclaim during his lifetime. He was a man of the road who only recorded a few times during his time on earth. He died of heart problems at Heathman-Dedham Plantation on his forty-second birthday, April 28, 1934. The newspapers of the time made no mention of his passing. His only known photograph adorns his tombstone. His epitaph reads, "The foremost performer of Early Mississippi blues whose songs became cornerstones of American Music." Amen!

Memphis Minnie

Memphis Minnie may have been a traveling woman, but she stopped long enough to marry three times and all to blues guitarists. First came Joe McCoy, then Casey Bill Weldon, and finally Ernest Lawlers, with whom she recorded over two hundred sides. She finally retired to Memphis in 1957.

Lawlers passed away in 1961. Memphis Minnie spent her last years in a nursing home and died on August 6, 1973.

She now resides in the New Hope Baptist Church cemetery, in Wallis, Mississippi. Bonnie Raitt paid for her tombstone, which reads, "The hundreds of sides Minnie recorded are the perfect material to teach us about the blues. For the blues are at once general, and particular, speaking for millions, but in a highly singular, individual voice. Listening to Minnie's songs we hear her fantasies, her dreams, her desires, but we hear them as if they were our own."

Willie Dixon

Willie Dixon outlived most of his contemporaries, finally passing away on January 29, 1992. He was active to almost the end of his life, with his album *Hidden Charms* winning a 1989 Grammy Award.

He was always a smart businessman and established his own publishing company, Ghana Music, in 1957. Even at that early date, he realized that his songs needed protection. In many ways his legacy will never die as the five hundred or so songs he composed will continue to be reinterpreted by future generations of artists.

He continued to tour in the United States and Europe and became respected by many of the leading bluesmen of the day. He was inducted into the Blues Foundation Hall of Fame in 1980 and the Rock and Roll Hall of Fame as an early influence in 1994.

If you are ever passing through Alsip in Cook County, Illinois, and come across Burr Oak Cemetery, stop and look for the willow trees. It is there you will find the final resting place of Willie Dixon.

Philip and Leonard Chess

The Chess Brothers continued to expand their roster and vision throughout the sixties. The history of both the blues and rock 'n' roll can be found on their colorful old 78s and 45s.

In 1955, they started the Argo label for jazz and pop releases. Radio stations at the time limited the number of releases they would play from one label, and so the Chess brothers found an easy way for their artists to gain more exposure.

Leonard's health began to fail during the late sixties, and they sold the label for $6.5 million in 1969. While that is still a lot of money today, it was an extraordinary amount in the late sixties. Unfortunately, money does not equal health, and Leonard Chess died on

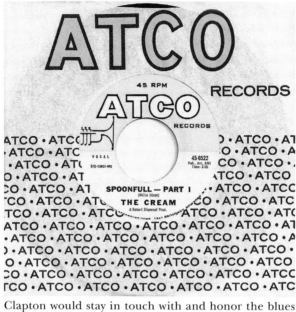

ATCO RECORDS

45 RPM

ATCO Records

VOCAL

SPOONFULL — PART I
(Willie Dixon)
THE CREAM
A Robert Stigwood Prod.

45-6522
Pub., Arc, BMI
Time: 2:25

Clapton would stay in touch with and honor the blues
heritage throughout his career.   *Author's collection*

October 16, 1969, at the age of fifty-two. He is buried under an unassuming
stone in Westlawn Cemetery in his adopted home of Chicago.

Both Leonard and Philip were inducted into the Blues Hall of Fame in
1995 as nonperformers. Leonard was also inducted into the Rock and Roll
Hall of Fame.

Sometimes, however, money and age due work out well. Philip Chess
retired to Arizona in 1972 and as of this writing is still alive and forty years
into his retirement, having outlived virtually all of the old bluesmen who
recorded for his label.

Howlin' Wolf

Howlin' Wolf passed away on January 10, 1976, and was put to rest in Oak
Ridge Cemetery, Hillside, Illinois. Rumor has it that Eric Clapton donated
the gravestone.

He continued to record and tour until near the end of his life. In
1971, he and longtime guitarist Hubert Sumlin traveled to London to
record an album with some of the cream of second-generation British
blues players and musicians. *The London Howlin' Wolf Sessions* were a critical
and commercial success and featured such artists as Eric Clapton, Steve

Winwood, Charlie Watts, Ian Stewart, Ringo Starr, and Klaus Voormann, among others.

Howlin' Wolf was inducted into the Blues Hall of Fame in 1980 and the Rock and Roll Hall of Fame in 1991 as an early influence. The Rock and Roll Hall of Fame honored three of his songs among the 500 Songs That Shaped Rock 'n' Roll. "Smokestack Lightning" (1956), "Spoonful" (1960), and "The Red Rooster" (1962) are permanently enshrined in the mecca of American rock music. The U.S. Postal Service issued a stamp in his likeness on September 17, 1994, as a part of their blues series.

Howlin' Wolf was one of the few bluesmen of his generation to become financially secure. His wife Lillie managed his career for years and handled his finances and provided a stable home environment. She remained active by appearing at various blues events until her death in 2001. She was buried next to her husband.

Muddy Waters

Muddy Waters's career flourished during the 1970s. He won six Grammy Awards during the decade, all for Best Ethnic or Traditional Folk Recording. *They Call Me Muddy Waters* (1971), *The London Muddy Waters Session* (1972), *The Muddy Waters Woodstock Album* (1975), *Hard Again* (1977), *I'm Ready* (1978), and *Muddy "Mississippi" Waters Live* (1979) all introduced him to a new generation of fans and cemented his legacy.

He was elected to the Blues Foundation Hall of Fame (1980), the Rock and Roll Hall of Fame (1987), and was honored with a Grammy Lifetime Achievement Award (1992). Like his old friendly rival, he was honored by the U.S. Postal Service with a twenty-nine-cent stamp that bore his likeness. "Rollin' Stone" (1950), "Hoochie Coochie Man" (1954), "Mannish Boy" (1955), and "Got My Mojo Working" (1957) were all honored by the Rock and Roll Hall of Fame among the 500 Songs That Shaped Rock 'n' Roll. *Rolling Stone* named him the seventeenth greatest artist of all time.

His gravestone is unimposing, unlike his legacy, which remains one of the most important in blues/rock music.

Alexis Korner

Alexis Korner lived hard, played hard, and died hard. A heavy smoker all of his life, he succumbed to lung cancer on January 1, 1984. He was cremated, with his ashes scattered at his home in Wales.

Korner never achieved the popularity of many of the musicians who cashed in on his blues sound. He did, however, have a colorful and varied career. He left Blues Incorporated in 1966; formed C.C.S. (Collective Consciousness Society) in 1970, which produced the hit single "Whole Lotta Love"; and then formed Snape in 1973 with Boz Burrell, Mel Collin, and Ian Wallace, formerly of King Crimson. In 1981, he became a member of Rocket 88 with such stalwarts as Ian Stewart, Jack Bruce, and Charlie Watts.

In the midst of his group experiences, he found time to become a noted broadcaster, interviewer, and historian. He also flourished as one of the grand old men of the British blues, despite his young age. He was honored on his fiftieth birthday at a gala concert featuring Eric Clapton, Dick Heckstall-Smith, Paul Jones, and Zoot Money. *The Party Album* is a live chronicle of the concert and forms a fitting epitaph of his career.

Cyril Davies

Cyril Davies may have been a talented musician and seminal British blues figure but when it came to genetics, he received the short end of the stick. He died at the age of thirty-one on January 7, 1964.

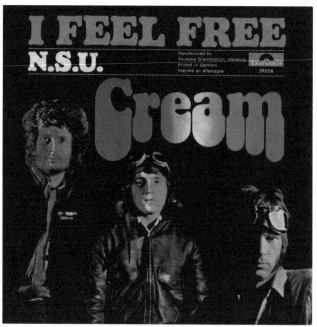

It is doubtful that the early Delta blues masters could have envisioned where Eric Clapton and his generation would take the sound they invented.   *Author's collection*

After splitting with Korner and Blues Incorporated, he formed the Cyril Davies All-Stars in 1962. They recorded a few tracks with Davies, which can be found on a number of anthology albums.

The cause of his death is not definitely known. Leukemia, pleurisy, and lung cancer have all been mentioned as possibilities. The giant and very complete website *Find a Grave* (findagrave.com) is still seeking information about his final resting place at this writing.

Chris Barber

Chris Barber was born on April 17, 1930. That may seem like a long time ago, but Chris Barber and his band are still on the road. Trumpeter Phil Halcox, who retired on July 16, 2008, played with Barber for fifty-four years, having joined his band in 1954. It is thought to be the longest continuous relationship in modern music.

His lasting legacy insofar as the blues is concerned was his recognition of a new music form. Barber allowed some of his musicians to explore and perform it and was adaptable to their ideas. He later served as a concert producer who brought many noted American blues artists to the British Isles. While he has played jazz music all of his life, it was these early contributions to the formation of the British blues that cemented Barber's legacy.

The stage was set! The blues had traveled from the bayous of the Mississippi Delta to the inner city of Chicago, and traveled thousands of miles to Great Britain. A generation of young English musicians was coming of age, and they had immersed themselves in this new musical form. They were about to change and twist the sound, while taking it in many directions. One of the most talented, Eric Clapton, was about to take the stage.

5

I'm Gonna Leave Here Running

Growing Up Clapton

Reginald Cecil Clapton met and fell in love with Rose Mitchell. They married without much fanfare in February 1927. This seemingly insignificant marriage would set in motion the birth of one of the legendary musicians of the rock era. They would quickly have two children, but Reginald would die of consumption in 1932. His early death prevented him from seeing his grandson develop into one of the greatest guitarists in history. It would be a decade before Rose remarried. She finally walked down the aisle again ten years later with Jack Clapp.

Patricia Molly Clapton was born to Reginald and Rose in 1929. She spent her early teenage years growing up in wartime Britain. A fateful meeting with Canadian serviceman Edward Walter Fryer left the fifteen-year-old Patricia pregnant. He would return to his native country and Canadian wife before she gave birth. Eric Patrick Clapton was born on March 30, 1945.

Rose and Jack would take Patricia and Eric into their home. The young Eric grew up thinking Patricia was really his sister. She would move out and marry soldier Frank MacDonald and then move to Canada and Germany. They made a visit when young Eric was nine, and the cat was let out of the bag as he found out that she was really his mother. It was a traumatic and seminal point in his life.

Life with his grandparents was a primitive affair. There was no plumbing, and so the toilet was outside in a shed. Eric would undergo a couple of sponge baths during the week but on weekends would take a real bath at his Aunt Audrey's house. There was also no electricity, and at night gas lamps would provide light.

In 1956, young Eric attended St. Bede's Secondary Modern School. While he was never a distinguished scholar, his time at the school would have passed uneventfully except for him meeting schoolmate John Constantine. Constantine came from a fairly well-off family, and while the other boys were running around and playing sports, the two friends were ensconced in the house playing Constantine's 78 rpm records. Elvis Presley's "Hound Dog" was the big hit of the summer, but it was the blues that opened up a new world for the young Clapton.

Somewhere in his early teens young Eric immersed himself in the blues. He may have liked Elvis, but he fell in love with Robert Johnson and other practitioners of the Delta and Chicago blues. He received his first guitar at age thirteen. It was a used instrument with steel strings. Learning to play the guitar would be an imposing task for any thirteen-year-old, and the strings almost made him give up several times.

At age sixteen, Eric graduated to a 100 Electric Double Cutaway Clone (a Gibson ES-335 Clone), and serious practicing began in earnest. He owned an old German recorder and would tape blues songs. He would then mimic the guitar work. A year later, he had improved enough to venture out into the musical world.

6

This Train Is Bound for Glory

Early Groups

Eric Clapton and Dave Brock

ave Brock was born August 25, 1941, which made him close to four years older than Eric Clapton. He received a banjo at age twelve and gradually switched to the guitar. He was an early appreciator of Fats Domino, which led him to some of the early blues artists.

While a young Eric Clapton was struggling with his steel-stringed guitar, Brock was coming of age in Feltham, Middlesex. While he was becoming an adept guitarist, when he reached eighteen he got a real job. First, he worked as a capstan setter and then as an animator for Larkin Studios. Gradually, he began playing music in the evenings at various clubs.

Rather than forming a formal group, he engaged in busking with a number of friends. Busking is performing for pay in public but without a formal contract or promise of pay. The most common type of busking is found on street corners, where musicians play for tips. Usually their guitar case or some like container is left open with the hope of contributions. The second type of busker plays in clubs with the hope of being paid by the patrons. This is the type of busking at which David Brock became proficient.

He would have a rotating cast of friends who would accompany him. Keith Relf, Mike Slattery, Jeff Watson, and a young Eric Clapton would all be his partners. Hundreds of artists, both American and British, would begin their careers in this manner. Joan Baez, Jimmy Page, Jimmy Buffett, Judy Collins, Joni Mitchell, Paul Simon, Bob Dylan, and many more would play for pay at the beginning of their career.

Brock and Eric Clapton would never formalize their relationship, but their performing as a duo enabled Clapton to get his first taste of live performances and begin to develop the ability to play with another person.

Many times when a major star has a professional relationship early in his or her career, the other person disappears from music history. Not so with David Brock. He would form the short-lived Dharma Blues Band and then the Famous Cure. He would spend time busking around Europe before returning to the developing psychedelic scene in England.

Brock and old friend Mike Slattery would meet bassist John Harrison and form a new group. Drummer Terry Ollis plus friends Nick Turner and Michael Davies would also join. Nick Turner would name the band after clearing his throat, which was known as Hawking. It may not be pretty, but the shortened form became Hawkwind.

Dave Brock may not have climbed to the mountaintop like his main former busking partner, but he was able to make a very good living.

The Roosters

Thousands and probably tens of thousands of bands were formed in Great Britain and the United States during the sixties. A very select few would go on to lasting fame and fortune. A small percentage would become semifamous due to a lucky hit song but would quickly fade away.

Most communities have a band or two that make a part-time living from performances at bars, weddings, and birthday parties. Most such bands come together for a time, rehearse, never earn a dime, never perform, and then disappear into the mists of time.

There have been several groups that have taken the name the Roosters. There is a Japanese punk rock group with a constantly changing lineup. Soul star Jerry Butler was a member of the Roosters but changed the named to the Impressions, which was in retrospect an excellent idea. There was a late sixties Roosters based in L.A. who had a near hit with "Love Machine" issued on the Philips label. Future Bread member James Griffin wrote the song, and it is labeled a Snuff Garrett production.

The British Roosters came into being in early 1963 at the Prince of Wales Pub in New Malden when guitarist Tom McGuinness met fellow guitarist Eric Clapton. The meeting occurred because McGuinness's girlfriend had been a classmate of Clapton's at Art College. McGuinness allowed Clapton to audition for his group, and he passed with flying colors.

The Roosters consisted of vocalist Terry Brennan, drummer Robin Mason, and piano player Ben Palmer, in addition to the aforementioned guitarists. The group did not have a bass player. The hidden key in this short-lived band was Palmer, who would become Clapton's lifelong friend and would accompany him on his Greek venture, which is another story.

The Roosters would only last from January to August. They practiced incessantly but played live sparingly and then in small upstairs rooms in small pubs. Still, Eric Clapton was a real band member for the first time and was learning his craft.

The British Roosters may not have recorded nor played to large crowds, but they have gone down in rock 'n' roll history as one of the training grounds for Eric Clapton.

Casey Jones and the Engineers

Mississippi John Hurt is recognized for immortalizing the American railroad man in song. John Luther "Casey" Jones (1863–1900), worked all his life for the railroad system in the United States. His fatal claim to fame came as the engineer of Cannonball Express passenger train that was traveling seventy-five miles per hour toward a stalled freight train. Instead of jumping from the train and saving himself, he remained at the controls and managed to slow the train to thirty-five miles per hour. While it still plowed into the other train, all the passengers were saved. Casey Jones was killed instantly.

Brian Casser would use this story to name his second band. His first group, Cass and the Casanovas, was popular in the Liverpool music scene 1959–1960. Unfortunately for him the other three members of the group decided to carry on without him and unceremoniously dumped him from his own band. He would go on to manage the Blue Gardenia Club in London.

By 1963, the music scene and the Beatles were exploding in London. Casser thought it would be a good time to form another band, and so Casey Jones and the Engineers were born. He recruited bassist Dave McCumisky and drummer Ray Stock but was in need of two guitarists. Tom McGuinness and Eric Clapton were two guitarists in need of a band.

Clapton's time with the group would be very short. He would last for seven performances and depart due to the pop nature of the band. Still, it would provide him with his first taste of touring.

The young Eric Clapton was unemployed again and waiting for the phone to ring. Ring it did, and this time Keith Relf was at the other end of the line.

7

I Hate to Leave You, Baby

Whatever Happened To

Edward Walter Fryer

It is unknown if Eric Clapton's father ever realized that his son was one of the most talented guitarists to ever walk this earth. If he did, it was never mentioned to anyone. His life would be shrouded in mystery after returning to his native Canada at the end of the Second World War. He had several wives, who produced three children. Eva Jane, Sandra, and Edward Jr. are all half brothers and sisters to Eric Clapton. Only Eva has been forthcoming about the relationship.

There is little doubt that some of Clapton's musical ability runs through Fryer. He would sing and play the piano before entering the army and continued to moonlight while he was stationed in England. He may not have been famous or extremely talented, but the genetic code was in place.

He died on May 15, 1985, in a veteran's hospital in Ontario from leukemia. His sole possession was a sailboat; other than that he was penniless. He was cremated, and his ashes were scattered in the water from his beloved boat.

Dave Brock

Hawkwind came together in 1969 and played their first live gig at a local talent night at the All Saints Hall in Notting Hill. Their long jam of the Byrds' "Eight Miles High" led to a recording deal with the Liberty label.

Their debut album was released in 1970, and was produced by Dick Taylor, who had been a short-term member of the embryonic Rolling Stones for five months in 1962. He formed the Pretty Things is 1963 and continues to lead that group to the present day. *Hawkwind* (the album) received critical praise if not commercial popularity and set the tone for their career.

While it was based in the psychedelic music of the era, the space-rock sound for which they would become famous was already present. Brock had already emerged as the leader and chief songwriter and had begun to develop his skills on various keyboards.

Their second album, *In Search of Space,* was released in 1971 and became Dave Brock and Hawkwind's breakout release. It reached #18 on the British album charts. They had now settled into the type of spacey rock that would dominate their career.

Their popularity was solidified in 1972. Brock recruited guitarist Ian Fraser "Lemmy" Kilmister and drummer Simon King, and they formed a solid foundation on which he would build his and Hawkwind's signature sound. Lemmy left the group in 1975 and became a founding member of Motorhead.

Hawkwind, with Lemmy and King, performed at the legendary Roundhouse in London as a part of the Greasy Truckers Party. They shared the stage with Man and Brinsley Schwarz. A live album featuring the three artists would be released to commercial success. Hawkwind reworked a song from the performance and released it as a single. "Silver Machine" climbed to #3 on the British single charts. It would be the single that kept on ticking; it was reissued in 1978, reaching #34, and again in 1983, reaching #67.

Hawkwind would have dozens of personnel changes, but Dave Brock would be the constant. On October 21, 2000, he organized a reunion of twenty former members for a thirtieth anniversary concert at Brixton Academy. Now over four decades as the leader of the group, he is still on the road and released his latest album, *Blood on the Earth,* on June 21, 2010.

Dave Brock has had a long and prolific career, releasing twenty-five studio, nine live, thirteen compilation, and thirty-three albums of archival material (give or take). His sound may have ranged far from that of his old busking partner, but Dave Brock has carved out a career of his own making.

Tom McGuinness

Tom McGuinness stayed with Casey Jones for a little while after Eric Clapton left but soon departed for the same reason, as he was not comfortable with the pop sound.

He quickly landed on his feet as he received a call from Manfred Mann to become the group's bass player. They had a number of hits in the United States, but their popularity in the USA paled next to that in their home country. He played on such hit songs as "Do Wah Diddy Diddy," "Sha La La," "Pretty Flamingo," and "Just Like a Woman." McGuinness eventually took over lead guitar duties and stayed with the group until 1969. He also formed a lasting musical relationship with lead singer Paul Jones.

McGuinness next formed McGuinness Flint after leaving Manfred Mann. Hughie Flint was a former drummer for John Mayall. Other members of the group were keyboardist Dennis Coulson, guitarist Benny Gallagher, and bassist Graham Lyle. Gallagher and Lyle were responsible for much of the music and would go on to form a successful duo. The group produced two huge hits in England, "When I'm Dead and Gone" reaching #2 on the singles charts and "Malt and Barley Blues" climbing to #5.

A number of McGuinness Flint albums have been reissued on CD. While the group was grounded in a rock/blues sound, there are also elements of jazz and acoustic folk. Their major early problem was producing their sound live. The band would gradually lose its commercial appeal and disintegrate in 1975.

Tom McGuinness and Paul Jones would form "the Blues Band" in 1979 with slide guitarist Dave Kelly. The band has been together for over three decades and continues to tour mainly in Europe.

Jones and McGuinness formed a second band in 1991. The Manfreds were composed of former members of Manfred Mann minus Mr. Mann himself. Such stalwarts as Mike Hugg and Mike D'Abo are associated with the group, which played a combination of classic Manfred Mann material and the blues. Tom McGuiness continues to perform with this group, giving him the best of both worlds.

McGuinness's musical journey may not have the acclaim or popularity of that of old bandmate Eric Clapton, but he has traveled many of the same roads.

Brian Casser

Brian Casser, who became Casey Jones, never gained any lasting fame and is best known as a footnote in the early career of Eric Clapton.

After Clapton and then McGuinness left the group, Casey Jones and the Engineers experienced some hard times in their native country. Thousands of bands were springing up in reaction to the Beatles' success, making for a very crowded field. Gigs were difficult to obtain, and recording contracts were even harder to come by.

Casser decided to transplant his band to Germany, which was immersed in the music of the British Invasion but had few groups in residence. He changed the name to Casey Jones and the Governors and quickly produced a hit song. The Governors included lead guitarist David Coleman, who had the distinction of replacing Eric Clapton; rhythm guitarist Roger Cook; drummer Peter Richards; and bassist Jim Rodford.

"Don't Ha Ha" was issued on the Bellaphon label and quickly climbed the German singles charts. It was based on the old Huey Smith song "Don't You Just Know It." They would not repeat this triumph and so resorted to playing such standards of the day as "Mickey's Monkey," "Too Much Monkey Business," "Dizzy Miss Lizzy," and Larry Williams's "Slow Down." Success was fleeting, as by 1966 the group would dissolve.

Casey Jones and the Governors released two albums of somewhat raw and simple British pop. The music is still available on CD and is worth a listen for the historical interest.

A final note that has nothing to do with Eric Clapton. The Beatles were a support act for Casser in 1960. Rumor has it Casser suggested they take the name Long John and the Silver Beatles. While they did use Silver Beatles for a while, they later shortened it to the Beatles. Brian Casser came close to grabbing the brass ring for naming the Beatles.

8

I'll Give You Everything and More

Replacing Top Topham

T he Yardbirds are now safely ensconced in the Rock and Roll Hall of Fame in Cleveland, Ohio. They have been recognized as one of the innovative groups in rock history. Their music, primarily through their creative guitar sound, was groundbreaking and extended the limits of rock and modern blues.

Still, no matter what their musical legacy, it is the trio of guitarists who played lead for the group that has given them lasting fame. *Rolling Stone* ranks Eric Clapton #4, Jimmy Page #9, and Jeff Beck #14 on their list of the 100 greatest guitarists of all time. No other band in rock history can brag that they produced three Rock and Roll Hall of Fame guitarists.

Original Members Chris Dreja and Jim McCarty still tour and record as the Yardbirds with a rotating cast of musicians. *Live at B. B. King Blues Club* is an excellent example of the latest incarnation of the Yardbirds. Dreja and McCarty were joined by lead guitarist Ben King, vocalist John Idan, and harpist Billy Miskimmon for a live broadcast on XM Satellite Radio. The nineteen-track show is a combination of old classics and new material. While it is a new group for the most part, they bring energy to "Heart Full of Soul," "Shapes of Things," "Over Under Sideways Down," and "For Your Love."

While the classic Yardbirds are remembered for Clapton, Page, and Beck, they actually had four lead guitarists during the 1960s. Many people forget that it was Top Topham who was the group's first guitarist.

"Yardbirds" can be defined as hoboes hanging around a railway yard waiting for a train to take them to their next location. They would hide themselves on the train without paying and travel from location to location. These out-of-work hoboes would provide the name for one of the classic rock groups of the sixties.

Keith Relf and Paul Samwell-Smith were playing together in the Metropolitan Blues Band in 1962. A year later, the band took in singer/

harmonica player Keith Relf, drummer Jim McCarty, and lead guitarist Top Topham from another Richmond band called Suburbiton R&B. Smith and McCarty had played together while in school. The newly formed group changed their name to the Yardbirds. One of their earliest gigs was backing traditional blues legend Cyril Davies at Eel Pie Island.

They quickly moved on to the legendary Crawdaddy Club in Richmond, Surrey, England. When the Rolling Stones left their gig as the resident band at the club, the Yardbirds replaced them.

The main problem for the band at this time was the age of Top Topham. He was fifteen when the band was formed, and as their popularity increased, they were playing five to six nights a week. Topham was a promising art student, and his parents frowned on his nighttime activities. The rest of the group members were several years older than Topham, and his parents were pressuring him to leave the group despite him earning more than both of them.

Topham finally gave in to their pressure and left the band in the fall of 1963. His replacement was another art student named Eric Clapton.

Clapton had been a member of several groups, but the Yardbirds were a more serious affair as they were already getting well-paying gigs. Clapton quickly integrated himself into the group as the lead guitarist and helped the band's reputation as a blues/rock band to grow. Their and Clapton's dream job would occur two months after Clapton's debut.

Sonny Boy Williamson II was planning to tour Great Britain, and like many American blues artists who traveled to Europe, he was looking for backing bands. The Animals and the Yardbirds would both serve in that capacity at various stops on the tour.

Aleck Ford was born sometime near the turn of the twentieth century. The exact date of his birth has never been determined. Early in life he took his stepfather's last name of Miller and so performed as Aleck Miller until the early forties. He was beginning to become popular, so he changed his name to Sonny Boy Williamson to cash in on the reputation of the Delta bluesman of the same name. He always claimed that he was the first Sonny Boy, but music history has added II to his name to distinguish him from the accepted original.

He had attended a Yardbirds concert when in London for the American Folk Blues Festival tour. After the tour ended, he stayed on for a series of small club dates. When he brought his stage act to the Crawdaddy Club on December 8, 1963, the Yardbirds were on hand to provide the instrumental backing.

The resultant album, *Sonny Boy Williamson and the Yardbirds*, was originally intended to be a Sonny Boy Williamson release, but it would go down

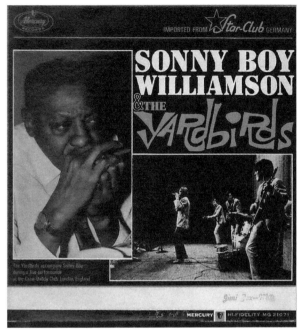

The early Yardbirds with Eric Clapton were only too
happy to back Sonny Boy Williamson when he toured
England.   *Author's collection*

in history as some of the earliest Yardbird and Eric Clapton music ever
recorded.

This was a traditional blues album consisting of nine Sonny Boy
Williamson compositions. It also featured a developing Eric Clapton, There
were no fuzz tones, wah-wah pedals, or feedback. It was just one of the
future best guitarists in history learning his craft.

Sonny Boy Williamson was not in good health and would pass away less
than two years later. Still, there are flashes of brilliance. "Pontiac Blues" is
sixties Delta blues at its near best. "Mister Downchild" features some nice
harp playing by Sonny Boy, but it is Clapton's guitar playing that sells the
track. "Do the Western" also finds Clapton in blues mode.

The real treat from this club date did not surface for decades. In 1993,
the Yardbirds' four-CD box set *Train Kept A-Rollin': The Complete Giorgio
Gomelsky Productions* was released on the Charly label. It included not only
extra tracks by Williamson but also the six-song set by the Yardbirds that
had been recorded prior to Williamson's set. This set is also included on the
box set *The Yardbirds Story: The Complete Recordings 1963–1967.*

At this stage of their career, the Yardbirds relied on blues standards
for their live performances. This suited Clapton just fine, as he was a blues

purist in 1963. They played "Smokestack Lightning," "You Can't Judge a Book by Its Cover," "Let It Rock," "I Wish You Would," "Who Do You Love," plus Keith Relf's "Honey in Your Hips." Even though he had only been with the group for two months, it is Clapton's guitar that is the centerpiece of these recordings. Now almost fifty years after the fact, his talent was readily apparent, and it would quickly come to the forefront as the centerpiece of a group that had taken the first steps toward induction into the Rock and Roll Hall of Fame.

9

I'll Give You Diamonds Bright

The Yardbirds Featuring Eric Clapton

E ric Clapton had settled in as the lead guitarist of the Yardbirds. Late 1964 found the group ready to release their first album. Not many bands would even consider releasing a live album as their debut, but the Yardbirds were anything but normal.

Five Live Yardbirds was issued December 4, 1964. It had been recorded at a March 13, 1964, performance at the Marquee Club in London. While it did not make a big commercial impact, it did establish the group as a force to be reckoned with.

The music on *Five Live Yardbirds* is raw and powerful. The sound is somewhat limited by the recording equipment of the day, but it represents a piece of the mid-sixties Yardbirds and serves to enhance the experience. If you want to hear early Eric Clapton and the Yardbirds at their best, just grab a copy of this album and turn the sound up as loud as you can stand it.

At this point, Clapton shared the instrumental spotlight with Keith Relf's harp. This can be frustrating at times since while Relf was a very good

Long after the fact, the Yardbirds would receive all sorts of honors including a first day cover.

Author's collection

A prime example of the haphazard manner in which albums by the Yardbirds were thrown together.

Author's collection

harp player, even at this early stage in his development it can be seen that Clapton was a special musician.

There is a lot of straight electric blues, but at times they come close to a rock sound. Chuck Berry's "Too Much Monkey Business" is rock and would look ahead to a style that would ultimately drive Clapton from the band.

"Smokestack Lightning" may be the best song. This old Howlin' Wolf tune was one Eric Clapton could play in his sleep. This may be the definitive version, and that includes the original.

The last four tracks included three Bo Diddley compositions and together form one of the best sections of live playing in sixties English blues history. "Pretty Girl," "Here 'Tis," and especially "I'm a Man" find a young, happy, and energetic Eric Clapton just playing with abandon. He was relatively unknown at the time, and there were no expectations for him to live up to. The phrasing of "I'm a Man" remains brilliant nearly half a century later.

The 2003 reissue came with a number of bonus tracks. There were five tracks from a December 8, 1963, performance at the Crawdaddy Club. Songs such as "You Can't Judge a Book by Looking at the Cover," "Let It Rock," "I Wish You Would," "Who Do You Love," and "Honey in Your Hips" may not have the tightness of the original release, but they present a starting place for the group and show how much they had improved in a few months. The last five tracks are obscure singles releases. The studio version of "Good Morning Little Schoolgirl" pales next to the live performance, but John Lee Hooker's "Boom Boom" is a lost gem.

Five Live Yardbirds remains a significant historical album. Not only does it trace the recorded beginnings of Eric Clapton's journey to stardom, it also presents the London club scene of the mid-sixties in all its vitality.

Everything was well with the Yardbirds. Their first album was behind them, and they were developing a reputation as a first-rate live band. Their gigs were increasingly financially successful, and their popularity was expanding. Enter Graham Gouldman!

Gouldman had played in a number of bands in the early sixties: the High Spots, the Crevattes, the Planets, the Whirlwinds, and finally the Mockingbirds, who received a recording contract from Columbia. The label promptly rejected his composition "For Your Love." The song eventually made its way to the Yardbirds manager, Giorgio Gomelsky, who brought it to the attention of the band. Shortly afterwards, the Mockingbirds were the warm-up band for the Yardbirds, who played the song to a thunderous reception.

"For Your Love" was released in February 1965 and became the Yardbirds commercial breakthrough. It reached #3 on the English singles charts and #6 in the United States. It would be their biggest American hit, selling in excess of a million copies and earning the band a gold record award. The main problem was that Eric Clapton hated the song. He felt it was too popish and not enough blues. It would precipitate his leaving the group.

Nearly a half-century after its release, Clapton was right that it is not a blues song. It was,

Cassettes are quickly disappearing from the musical landscape, but, for several decades, they were a format of choice. *Author's collection*

however, one of the unique and innovative rock songs of the mid-sixties. Its odd cadence and subtle guitar playing by Clapton have held up well through the years. It has always been ironic that a truly great song drove Eric Clapton out of the Yardbirds.

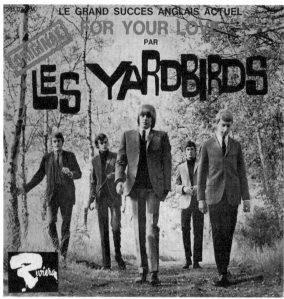

"For Your Love" was the song that initiated Clapton leaving the band.   *Author's collection*

10

It Hurts So Bad for Us to Part

Departure

E ric Clapton was out, and Jeff Beck was in. All in all it was a fair trade for the Yardbirds, although it may not have seemed so at the time. In many ways, Beck was the more innovative guitarist during his time with the group. His use of feedback, distortion, and fuzz tones in the mid-sixties was groundbreaking.

There were hard feelings before, during, and after his departure. This is very apparent on *For Your Love*. The album was released in the United States July 5, 1965. It was a U.S. release only and was put together to cash in on the

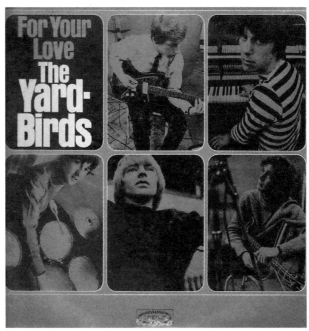

The Yardbird material just kept on coming.

Author's collection

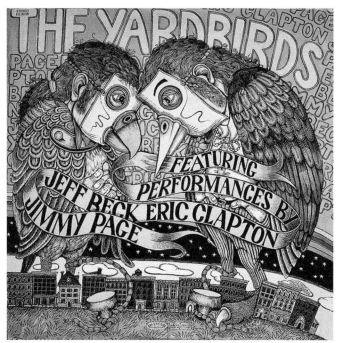

Clapton's time as a member of the Yardbirds was short but extremely influential. The band's catalog of music has been reissued dozens of times.   *Author's collection*

Yardbirds' big hit of the same name. It was issued to support their first American tour and reached #96 on *Billboard*'s album charts.

Clapton is the lead guitarist on eight of the eleven tracks, yet is not pictured on the album cover or mentioned anywhere in the liner notes. Jeff Beck, who provided the guitar work for "I'm Not Talking," "I Ain't Done Wrong," and "My Girl Sloopy," was now the man. At the time, many people would have assumed that Beck played on all the tracks.

The production leaves a lot to be desired even when compared to other recordings of the day. There is a real tinny quality that today detracts from the listening experience but also gives it an authenticity of British rhythm and blues.

The music is consistently excellent and was far different from much of what was being issued in 1965. Clapton's guitar playing combined with Keith Relf's harp sounds fused rock and blues in a unique way.

Clapton is really at home with the old blues numbers. "Good Morning Little School Girl," "I Ain't Got You," and "Putty in Your Hands" all demonstrate early flashes of his brilliance. Clapton's feeling aside, "For Your Love" remains a superb performance.

Clapton would again be ignored on the U.S. release *Having a Rave Up*. He was not pictured or mentioned on the album despite being the lead guitarist on side two's four tunes.

The album was another patchwork affair, and the Clapton tunes had all been previously released in Britain as part of their first live album. While it remains a somewhat odd release in the Clapton catalog, it does present him at his early best. The most interesting tracks are his live version of "I'm a Man" and Jeff Beck's studio version on the first side. The contrast in styles and Clapton's ability to improvise outside the confines of the studio were very apparent even at this early stage of his career.

While it has nothing to do with Eric Clapton, if you are going to listen to the live tracks, you might as well listen to the Jeff Beck ones as well. The top ten American single "Heart Full of Soul" features some great early fuzz tone. "Train Kept A-Rollin'" was Beck's coming-out party, proving he was the equal of the departed Clapton in talent if not in style.

Having a Rave Up is early and important rock 'n' roll. It would be the Yardbirds' best-selling and highest-charting album in the United States. *Rolling Stone* placed it among their 500 Greatest Albums of All Time. It remains an important step in the evolution of rock music. Without the Yardbirds with Eric Clapton, the future of the guitar and rock music would have followed a different road.

An early solo release by Keith Relf.   *Author's collection*

I Really Hate to Leave You, Baby

Whatever Happened To

Top Topham

W hen the Yardbirds were inducted into the Rock and Roll Hall of Fame in 1992, there were seven musicians mentioned, including three of the greatest guitarists ever to walk this earth. Paul Samwell-Smith, Chris Dreja, Jim McCarty, Jeff Beck, and Jimmy Page were onstage. Eric Clapton was working on his *Unplugged* project and unable to attend. His family represented the deceased Keith Relf. Yet one of the founding members of the group was not mentioned.

It was Top Topham and Keith Relf who had the original idea to form the Yardbirds. The timing was just wrong for the fifteen-year-old. His parents were adamant about not letting the promising teenage art student become a professional musician. He bowed out in favor of another art student named Eric Clapton. The great question remains what would the future of the Yardbirds have been had he stayed in the group. Topham has stated that he would have left, as did Clapton, when they veered away from a traditional blues sound. However much we may speculate, his age kept him from sharing the stage at the Rock and Roll Hall of Fame with the people with whom he formed the group.

Topham would go on to a successful, if intermittent, art career, particularly as a dealer, but would always be drawn back to music.

He formed a musical relationship with the erratic blues musician Duster Bennett and played with him on his 1969 live album, *Bright Lights*. Bennett's future releases became more and more and more eclectic but were always interesting. He died in an auto accident on March 26, 1976, after playing a gig with American blues artist Memphis Slim.

Topham's association with Bennett led to his being hired as a session guitarist for the Blue Horizon label. He released a solo album in 1970 titled

This may be a reissue, but it pictures a young Clapton learning his craft.

Author's collection

Ascension Heights. The original vinyl release is extremely rare and fetches in excess of $100. The easiest and best place to find this album and other Topham material from his time at Blue Horizon is the 2008 CD *Complete Blue Horizon Sessions.* It contains the twelve tracks from the original vinyl release plus seven rare bonus tracks.

The material veers from a blues foundation at times, traveling into jazz and rock territory. Topham's only single for the label, "Christmas Cracker/ Cracking Up over Christmas," is an odd holiday piece from the early seventies. The treasure of the album is the live version of "Hop House" from a BBC session. It shows what a talented guitarist Topham had become by 1970.

He hooked up with old Yardbirds bandmate Jim McCarty from 1988 to 1990. Their recorded material is currently out of print and difficult to find.

Top continues to play and tour. In 2005, he joined the reconstituted Yardbirds onstage for the first time in over thirty-five years. Now how about a call from the Rock and Roll Hall of Fame?

Keith Relf

Keith Relf had an active, if short-lived, career after the demise of the Yardbirds. He produced the album *Pearls of Amber* by the acoustic trio Amber. Amber consisted of Julian McAllister, Mac MacLeod, and Roy Cooper. MacLeod's Sitar work makes the album worth a visit today. Relf was also associated with the band Medicine Head, who would become a duo for most of their existence. They even produced a hit single in 1973, when "One and One Is One" reached #3 on the British charts.

Relf's grand post-Yardbirds project was the formation of Renaissance in 1969. He brought along old bandmate Jim McCarty plus keyboardist Jim Hawken, bassist Louis Cennamo, and his sister Jane Relf as an additional vocalist. The group reflected his vision of fusing rock, folk, and classical music into one form. They released two albums before Relf and all the group members quit except for his sister and Cennamo, who recruited new members to keep the group going. By 1971, they were gone as well, but the group carried on with all-new members.

During the seventies, Renaissance was fronted by vocalist Anne Haslam and continued to explore Relf's original vision. They released a number of commercially successful albums in the United States including *Scheherazade and Other Stories, Live at Carnegie Hall,* and *Novella.*

Relf moved on to produce the only album by the psychedelic rock group Saturnalia. *Magical Love* was released in February 1973, and despite being English in origin is a nice slice of a San Francisco–type sound that was in vogue at the time. The original and rare vinyl release came complete with a twenty-eight-page book about cosmology and a 3-D cover. Band members included dual vocalists Adrian Hawkins and Aletta Lohmeyer, guitarist Red Roach, bassist/keyboardist Richard Houghton, and drummer Tom Compton.

Relf's next project was as a member of the hard-rock band Armageddon. He had produced an album by the group Steamhammer, and when they broke up he co-opted guitarist Martin Pugh and old Renaissance bassist Louis Cennamo along with drummer Bobby Caldwell into his new band. Their only, self-titled album release was typical hard rock of the day. It contained just five tracks, but three clocked in at over eight minutes and a medley at eleven-plus minutes. Armageddon played live only two times during their existence.

Keith Relf decided to gather his old Renaissance bandmates and form a new group, which he named Illusion. McCarty, Hawkins, Cennamo, and his sister all agreed to the reunion and were joined by guitarist John Knightsbridge plus drummer Eddie McNeil.

On May 14, 1976, while rehearsing, Keith Relf was electrocuted, dying of heart failure at the age of thirty-three. He was buried in East Sheen at Richmond Cemeteries, Richmond, Greater London, England. His wife April and son Danny represented him at his Rock and Roll Hall of Fame induction ceremony.

Chris Dreja

Way back when, Stephen Dreja introduced his brother Chris to Top Topham. They first played together in public with Duster Bennett and a very young Jimmy Page. They would both be founding members of the Yardbirds and while Topham would quickly leave the group, it would become the ongoing center of his life.

Chris Dreja originally played rhythm guitar to Clapton's and Beck's lead. When bass player Samwell-Smith quit the group in 1966 and old friend Jimmy Page joined, he switched to the bass guitar.

The Yardbirds disintegrated in 1968 as only Page and Dreja remained. The group had contractual obligations for several concerts in Scandinavia, so Page and Dreja were given permission to recruit new musicians to form the New Yardbirds to fulfill those commitments. Page recruited singer Robert Plant and drummer John Bonham. Dreja, in one of the worst decisions in rock history, withdrew from the new band to become a photographer. Bass player John Paul Jones replaced him. Page changed the name of the band to Led Zeppelin, and the rest is music history of the highest caliber. If you look at the picture on the reverse side of the first Led Zeppelin album, you will find a Chris Dreja photograph, which was the closest he came to hard-rock immortality.

Old bandmates Dreja, McCarty, and Smith formed Box of Frogs in 1983. Why they didn't just take the Yardbird name is beyond me. John Fiddler from Medicine Head was recruited as the vocalist. They even coerced Jeff Beck to provide some guitar work on their self-titled 1984 debut album. The release was well received in the United States, and the band received tour offers. The three former Yardbirds decided not to tour. That decision caused Jeff Beck, who would have toured with the group, and John Fiddler to withdraw in disgust. Their second and last album, *Strange Land*, was a patchwork affair as it employed a host of outside musicians including guitarist Steve Hackett, vocalist Graham Parker, and guitarist Jimmy Page.

In 1992, the lights came back on for the Yardbirds. Chris Dreja and Jim McCarty recruited bass player Rod Demick and resurrected the Rock and Roll Hall of Fame band. Vocalist John Idan would join soon after and remain with the group until 2009.

Birdland was released in 2003 and featured seven compositions, mostly by Dreja and McCarty, plus eight remakes of old Yardbirds tunes including "Shapes of Things," "Over, Under, Sideways, Down," and "Happening Ten Years Time Ago."

Probably the best representation of the new Yardbirds is their 2007 release, *Live at B. B. King Blues Club.* Ben King had taken over as the lead guitarist, and he brought a new and modern direction to the group's sound.

The show's and the CD's nineteen tracks are a combination of the old and new. They blast out of the gate with "Train Kept A-Rollin'" and maintain the energy level throughout the show. Hits such as "For Your Love," "Heart Full of Soul," and "Over, Under, Sideways, Down," are revisited. John Idan's vocals fit these old classics well, and Billy Boy Miskimmin's harmonica playing gives them an authenticity.

Chris Dreja has now been a member of the reconstituted Yardbirds about three times as long as the original group existed and has emerged as its unquestioned leader. At this time, it is probably mortality that will ultimately decide the fate of the group.

Paul Samwell-Smith

Paul Samwell-Smith's musical journey began as a teenager in 1959 when he became the lead guitarist for the Country Gentlemen. The group included Jim McCarty and was primarily an instrumental band. School bands rarely last, and the Country Gentlemen went their separate ways upon graduation. Samwell-Smith joined the short-lived Strollers as their bass player, which became his instrument of choice.

He was a founding member of the Yardbirds, but three years of constant touring wore him down, and he departed in 1966. Despite his bass playing and occasional compositions, it was his work as a producer that would influence the rest of his life.

Samwell-Smith coproduced their 1966 album *The Yardbirds*, which is better known as the *Roger the Engineer Album.* It was released in the United States under the name of its hit single, "Over, Under, Sideways, Down."

While he was part of the Box of Frogs and the Yardbirds reunion in 1983, it was as a producer that he earned his living. He began by producing a series of singles for various artists. The most interesting was for former Manfred Mann vocalist Paul Jones. "And the Sun Will Shine"/"The Dog

Presides" featured himself on bass, Jeff Beck on guitar, and for some inexplicable reason Paul McCartney playing the drums.

His long-term relationship with Cat Stevens produced a series of hit albums in the United States and not only made Stevens a star but also made Samwell-Smith a producer in demand. He produced *Mona Bone Jakon; Tea for the Tillerman*, which *Rolling Stone* named the 206th greatest album of all time; *Teaser and the Firecat*, which produced such hit singles as "Morning Has Broken" "Moonshadow," and "Peace Train"; the #1 *Catch Bull at Four; Buddha and the Chocolate Box;* and *Back to Earth.*

Samwell-Smith went on to work with such artists as Jethro Tull, Carly Simon, Renaissance, Murray Head, Chris DeBurgh, Illusion, the Amazing Blondels, and many others. He was also involved with the films *Harold and Maude* and *Postcards from the Edge.*

While he was not a performing part of the Yardbirds return in 1992, Samwell-Smith was involved behind the scenes. He was active in the music industry as of 2010.

Jim McCarty

I'm sure there are other artists who have been a part of more groups during their careers than Jim McCarty but he is probably near the top of the list. The Yardbirds (twice), the Country Gentlemen, Shoot, Box of Frogs, Renaissance, the Topham-McCarty Band, Illusion, Stairway, Pilgrim, the British Invasion All Stars, and the Jim McCarty Band, among other, have all been graced with Jim McCarty as a member.

When he left the Yardbirds, he began training himself as a guitarist and developing his vocal skills. In 1973, he became the lead vocalist of Shoot. Their album *On the Frontier* is one of the lost gems of the early seventies. Its raw sound belies the sophistication of its production. The harmonies are tight, and the use of various instruments including a Dobro is unique. Guitarist Dave Greene, bassist Bill Russell, drummer Craig Coccinge, steel guitar and Dobro player B. J. Cole, pianist Jim Trout, plus some horns and a violin all add up to an album worth tracking down.

Keith Relf's death during the Renaissance Illusion reunion, especially for his sister Jane and former bandmate McCarty, was catastrophic, but they decided to continue with the band. Two albums were released, the first being 1976's *Out of the Mist* followed by a second, self-titled release. The content was now more lyrical than improvisational, probably due to the loss of Relf. The group toured at least twice, once with Dory Previn and again with Brian Ferry. McCarty, bassist Louis

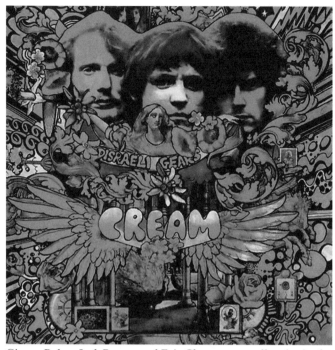

Ginger Baker, Jack Bruce, and Eric Clapton were all active in the British music scene of the early 1960s. They had no idea at the time how fate would bring them together.   *Author's collection*

Cennamo, vocalist Jane Relf, and keyboardist John Hawken reunited again in 2001 and released *Through the Fire* but did not tour.

Jim McCarty embraced a number of musical styles, from the blues/rock of the Yardbirds to the classical-influenced Renaissance. He really went in a different direction when he and former Renaissance/Illusion buddy Louis Cennamo decided to start what can best be described as a New Age band, Stairway, which issued five albums 1987–1995. *Aquamarine* (1987), *Moonstone* (1988), *Chakra Dance* (1989), *Medicine Dance* (1992), and *Rain Dreaming* (1995) form the catalog of one of the more unusual stops in the career of Jim McCarty.

Beginning in 1995, he was a member of multiple bands with many different albums in the works. Sometimes I can't help but think he may not have known who he was in the recording studio with at the time. The British Invasion All-Stars released a self-titled album in 2002, which included a revamped version of the old Yardbird tune "Shapes of Things." In 2000, he traveled to Memphis, Tennessee, to work with Richard Hite. The result was the *McCarty Hite Project* released that same year. If that weren't enough, he formed the group Pilgrim with Tanya Matchett, John Richardson, and Carmen Wilcox. The results of this project were *Gothic Dream* (1996) and *Searching for the Dreamland* (2000). Then there were his two solo releases; *Two Steps Ahead* (2003) and *Sitting on Top of Time* (2009).

The gem of all these releases was an album recorded forty years ago. *Live + Direct* by Renaissance was recorded live at the Fillmore West in 1970 when they supported Paul Butterfield in concert. This was the first Renaissance lineup with Keith Relf, and it is a presentation of the original musical vision of the group.

Today, Jim McCarty remains a vital part of the reformed Yardbirds. In addition, he continues to explore other musical opportunities.

Graham Gouldman

So what happened to the guy who wrote "For Your Love" and inadvertently drove Eric Clapton from the Yardbirds? Everything turned out fine, thank you very much.

Eric Clapton complained that "For Your Love" was a pop song, and that was because Gouldman was primarily a pop composer. Some of his early compositions were "Bus Stop" and "Look Through Any Window" for the Hollies, "No Milk Today" and "Listen People" for Herman's Hermits and "Heart Full of Soul," which was another hit for the Yardbirds.

Like many of his British contemporaries, he learned his craft through membership in a number of long-forgotten bands. The High Spots, the Crevattes, the Planets, the Whirlwinds, the Mockingbirds, and High Society were some of the bands Gouldman was part of during his formative years. The interesting aspect to all this was that he was writing hit songs for other artists, but his own groups at this stage in his life would never have a popular song.

His first big break came in 1968, when he served as the replacement bass player for Wayne Fontana and the Mindbenders, whose "Game of Love" and a "Groovy Kind of Love" had been huge hits. Guitarist Eric Stewart was also a member of the group at that time.

Gouldman next became a staff songwriter for Kasenetz/Katz, who were responsible for the bubble-gum phase of music in the United States. In 1969, he wrote a song titled "Sausalito (Is the Place to Go)" and somehow ended up as the lead singer for the Ohio Express, who scored a minor hit with the song in September 1969.

Meanwhile, back in England, Eric Stewart had joined with drummer Kevin Godley and keyboardist Lol Crème, who had played together in the Magic Lanterns, to form Hotlegs. They had one hit, "Neanderthal Man."

Gouldman joined the group as the bass player and was present when they changed their name to 10cc.

10cc became Gouldman's lifetime avocation. They would always be more popular in their native country than in the United States. Their commercial success included three #1 singles and five top ten albums. They are best remembered in the USA for their two seventies hit singles, "I'm Not in Love" and "The Things We Do for Love."

Gouldman has spent three terms as a member of 10cc; 1972–1983, 1992–1995, and 1999 to the present. During his only extended interlude, he formed a pop duo with Andrew Gold called Wax. They released four albums, but wide commercial success always just eluded them.

As of August 2010, 10cc featuring Graham Gouldman continues to tour. It has been a long and successful career for an old pop songwriter.

12

You Got a Boy-Child Coming

Bluesbreakers Spring 1965

John Mayall was born into a musical family on November 29, 1939, in Macclesfield, England. His father constantly played jazz records in the home, and by age twelve John was strumming the guitar and ukulele plus playing some boogie-woogie on the piano.

He formed his first group while in school in 1956, with friend Peter Ward. The Powerhouse Four used a number of local musicians and played some gigs before breaking up due to graduation.

John Mayall entered the armed forces at the age of eighteen and served a tour of duty in Korea. After leaving the service, he got a job working in an art studio. He formed the Blues Syndicate in 1962 with drummer Hughie Flint. They were a basic rhythm and blues outfit that played local clubs in the Manchester area.

In early 1963, he moved to London and began working as a draughts-man. He began assembling a new band that would ultimately take the name Bluesbreakers. The first incarnation of what would become one of the most famous blues bands in history was Mayall playing keyboards and harmonica, guitarist Bernie Watson, bassist John McVie, and on drums old schoolmate Peter Ward, who was quickly replaced by Martin Hart.

By April 1964, the group had signed a contract with the Decca label. The first of a hundred or so personnel changes had occurred as now the band were a quartet comprised of Mayall, McVie, guitarists Roger Dean, and drummer Hughie Flint. They released the single "Crawling up the Hill"/"Mr. James." While it was commercially unsuccessful, it would be the first in a seemingly endless number of recordings John Mayall would release over the next almost half century.

On December 7, 1964, the Bluesbreakers recorded their gig at Klook's Kleek R&B Club in West Hampstead, London. That performance was released in March 1965 as *John Mayall Plays John Mayall*. Another single, "Crocodile Rock," was also released

John Mayall first became impressed with Eric Clapton by hearing the flip side of the Yardbirds' "For Your Love" single. Mayall considered Clapton's guitar virtuosity on "Got to Hurry" some of the best he had heard, and when Clapton left the Yardbirds, Mayall came calling. The opportunity to join what he considered a true blues band was an offer Clapton couldn't ignore, so he officially became a part of Mayall's band. It is ironic that the song and single that led to his leaving the Yardbirds would have a flip side that allowed him to join a group that would help him take a big step on his journey to fame and guitar immortality.

Both Mayall and Clapton gained from the relationship. Mayall began playing to bigger crowds as word circulated that Clapton had joined the group. Clapton found a place to practice his craft. The only person not happy by the addition was guitarist Roger Dean, whom Mayall fired to make room for Clapton. Dean would be one of a long list of famous and not-so-famous musicians Mayall would fire through the years.

Shortly after Clapton's joining the band, they received one of their first big breaks when they were invited to perform on the *Ready, Steady Go Live* television show. Mid-June found them sharing the stage with the Who, the Spencer Davis Group, Long John Baldry, and a host of others at the Uxbridge Blues and Folk Festival. They then embarked on a series of one nighters.

However, trouble was brewing for Eric Clapton and John Mayall. Clapton was young, tired of the road, and a little bored, which is not a good combination as far as commitment is concerned. He and a group of friends decide to play their way around the world, and Clapton left without even informing Mayall.

13

You Told Me You Was High Class

It's Greek to Me

Ah, to be in your early twenties with the world at your feet. Eric Clapton had provided lead guitar for two well-known British bands and elevated himself to the position of one of the better up-and-coming guitarists in rock music. What does one do with that type of reputation at such a young age? The answer was a road trip.

He did not so much leave John Mayall's band as disappear from the group. He and a group of friends piled into an old vehicle and decided to play their way around Europe. This initiated the birth of one of the more obscure Eric Clapton bands.

The Glands consisted of guitarist Eric Clapton, pianist Ben Palmer, drummer Jack Milton, sax player Bernie Greenwood, bassist Bob Ray, and vocalist John Bailey. Every once in a while, they would call themselves the Greek Loon Band.

They traveled to Germany and Yugoslavia but finally settled in Athens, Greece. They auditioned at a local nightclub to be the opening act for the Juniors. No one had heard of the Yardbirds, John Mayall, or Eric Clapton. They were hired for their ability to play material by the Rolling Stones, Chuck Berry, and the Everly Brothers. Their pay was room and board, which was quite a comedown for Mr. Clapton. Their drummer had the good sense to depart and was replaced by a local musician named Makis Saliaris.

The Juniors were involved in a car accident on October 18, 1965. Group leader and manager Thanos Sogioul was killed and guitarist Kara Kadas injured, so he could not play. Clapton stepped in as the guitarist so they would not lose their job at the Igloo Club.

He began playing Yardbird material, and as word circulated that the famous Eric Clapton was playing locally, attendance increased dramatically at the club. The owner quickly realized he had a goldmine under contract.

The band was penniless and so in October 1965 resorted to selling their equipment to buy tickets back to England. Clapton managed to save his guitar but left his amplifier behind. No doubt the band members kissed the ground of their native country when they arrived home.

Eric Clapton now had to decide what to do next as he was unemployed and bandless for the first time in a number of years.

14

The Hoochie Coochie Man Arrives

Clapton Is Almost God

Meanwhile, back in the United Kingdom, John Mayall was not a happy man. October had rolled around, and he had yet to find a permanent replacement for Clapton. He was not happy with the behavior of bass player John McVie and so fired him. McVie was replaced by ex-Graham Bond Organization bassist Jack Bruce where drummer Ginger Baker also resided for a while. Worse was the decline in attendance at their live shows due to Clapton's absence.

Finally in November, Mayall selected Peter Green as Clapton's permanent replacement. He considered Green the first guitarist competent enough to fill Clapton's big shoes. Green's glory would be short-lived, however, when Clapton returned to England, minus his amplifier, from his Greek adventure. All was forgiven, and Mayall welcomed Clapton back into the group with open arms. This meant that Peter Green was quickly fired after one of the shortest stints as a lead guitarist in a major band.

Changes would continue for the Bluesbreakers. Bruce was a member only from November to December 1965. He priced himself beyond what Mayall was willing to pay and was replaced by the returning McVie. What this short period of time did accomplish was the introduction of Eric Clapton and Jack Bruce, whose history together and not together would last the rest of their lives.

With Clapton in tow, Mayall managed to re-sign with the Decca label. It proved a fortuitous event for Mayall, Clapton, Decca, and the world of music. Mayall decided to utilize Clapton's participation as much as possible and released an album under the title *Bluesbreakers: John Mayall with Eric Clapton*. It reached #6 on the U.K. album charts.

This is the album Clapton always wanted to make while with the Yardbirds. It has become recognized as one of the essential blues albums in history and would propel Clapton to superstar status worldwide. His smooth and energetic solos helped to define the fusion of rock and blues

This album made Clapton a household name in some music circles. *Author's collection*

and propelled the guitar as an instrument into the modern age. Much has been written about Clapton's genius in using his Les Paul Gibson guitar with a Marshall amplifier; it created such a different sound that it opened up the world of guitar playing to all sorts of new possibilities.

When listening to this album today, the focus remains directly on Clapton's guitar as Mayall's vocals are adequate at best. Bassist John McVie and drummer Hughie Flint are a competent rhythm section and provide a solid foundation for Clapton's searing solos.

The twelve tracks from the original release are a combination of Mayall compositions and blues classics. "Have You Heard" contains a perfect guitar solo. The old Mose Allison tune "Parchman Farm" is just under two and a half minutes of blues bliss. Even the Ray Charles classic "What'd I Say" succumbs to Clapton's virtuosity. Of particular note is "Ramblin' on My

Mind," originally by blues legend Robert Johnson, which contains Clapton's first recorded lead vocal. He was finally able to kick back and emulate the old blues masters he revered so much.

All was not well in paradise, however, as E. C. was doing a little moon-lighting. In March, he went into the studio with drummer Pete York, bassist Jack Bruce, vocalist/keyboardist Steve Winwood, harmonica player/vocalist Paul Jones, and old friend pianist Ben Palmer. They decided to call them-selves Powerhouse.

The group was never meant to be a long-term project. Three tracks, "Crossroads," "Steppin' Out," and "I Want to Know," were released on a compilation album titled *What's Shakin'* in the United States and *Good Time Music* in the United Kingdom. The songs are credited to Eric Clapton and the Powerhouse in the album credits.

The album is available on CD and is well worth seeking out. Tracks by the Lovin' Spoonful, the Paul Butterfield Blues Band, Tom Rush, and Al Kooper make it an interesting and worthwhile body of work.

Eric Clapton has maintained that the group recorded a fourth slow blues song, but it has never surfaced.

The only person really unhappy with Powerhouse was John Mayall. Whether Clapton was fired or quit really did not matter, as he had received an offer from Ginger Baker to form a new band. What has always amazed me is that John Mayall asked Peter Green to return as Clapton's replacement again. He must have been a smooth talker, as Green readily accepted his offer a second time.

15

I Finally Learned My Lesson

Whatever Happened To

Peter Green

Born Peter Allen Greenbaum on October 29, 1946, he was one of those people born to be a guitarist. *Rolling Stone* placed him #38 on their list of the 100 Greatest Guitarists of All Time.

He began his professional career as part of Peter Barden's group known as Peter B's Looners. This instrumental group not only proved to be a training ground for Green, but it introduced him to drummer Mick Fleetwood. The group would change its name to Shotgun Express and briefly feature vocalist Rod Stewart before dissolving in 1967.

Green's developing guitar prowess brought him to the attention of John Mayall. While his first stint in the Bluesbreakers lasted less than a week due to Clapton's return, Green rejoined in mid July 1967.

Green's first recording for John Mayall was the single "Parchman Farm," which was the B-side to "Key to Love." While the song failed to chart, it showed the beginning of Green's ability to produce a unique sound through the bending of the strings while he played.

The only Bluesbreakers album to feature Green as the lead guitarist was *A Hard Road*. It featured two of his original compositions, "The Same Way" and "The Supernatural," which contained an extended guitar solo and an early use of feedback. This track established Green as one of the premier British blues guitarists. The rest of the album is uneven at best, and Mayall at this point in his career was only an average vocalist. I can't help but think that if Green had been less restrained, he would have emerged as a huge star, as had happened to Clapton the previous year. Still, Green emerged with an enhanced reputation. The album was a hit, reaching #10 on the British album charts.

Though several well-known bands were in his near future, a long
and successful solo career also awaited.   *Author's collection*

By April 1967, the Bluesbreakers consisted of Mayall, Green, bassist John
McVie, and new drummer Mick Fleetwood. Fleetwood's stint only lasted two
months before he was fired by Mayall. Green followed his old bandmate and
formed a new band. In September, John McVie followed, and the nucleus of
Peter Green's Fleetwood Mac was in place. John Mayall landed on his feet
guitar-wise when he invited Mick Taylor to join the Bluesbreakers.

Green added Jeremy Spencer as a second guitarist, and they released
their first single, "I Believe My Time Ain't Long"/"Rambling Pony," in
November 1967. The single did not chart, but their first album released
three months later reached #4 on the British charts and established the
group as a premier rock/blues band.

While their debut would be the highest-charting album of the Peter
Green years, they remained a commercial force on the English charts. *Mr.
Wonderful* reached #10 in August 1968, and *Then Play On* ascended to #6
in September 1969. Both helped the group to expand their fan base to
Europe. The same could not be said for the United States, as their *English
Rose* release failed to chart.

Beyond their album releases, it was a string of popular singles in their native country that further established Peter Green's and Fleetwood Mac's popularity.

"Black Magic Woman" was written by Green and reached the English top forty in the spring of 1968. Santana would record the definitive version, which allowed Green to collect royalties for decades. They returned to the top forty in July 1968. "Need Your Love So Long"/"Stop Messin' Round" continued their blues/rock explorations.

They added Danny Kirwan as a second guitarist in the fall of 1968, which would ultimately begin a change for Fleetwood Mac in a pop direction. Kirwan proved to be the perfect foil for Green. Their first work together produced the instrumental single "Albatross," which topped the British charts and went top five in such countries as the Netherlands, Norway, Sweden, Switzerland, and Ireland. The song explored two chords in creating a dreamy and haunting sound.

The band and Green finally received some recognition in the United States when the single "Oh Well" reached #55 in America.

Sometime in the spring of 1970 while in Munich, Germany, Green took LSD at a commune party. He would never be the same. It led to years of institutionalization and eventually a virtual disappearance from the music industry. There have been rumors that Kirwan was at the same party. Whether this was true or not, he exhibited the same symptoms as Green. Within a few years he was homeless. While Green eventually recovered, the same cannot be said for Kirwan.

Green's last effort with Fleetwood Mac was the top ten single "The Green Manalishi." It was inspired by a dream. When the other members of Fleetwood Mac refused to give away all their money, he left the group. Little did he realize at the time, but Christine McVie and finally Stevie Nicks and Lindsay Buckingham were waiting in the wings and would take his former group to a commercial success he could not have begun to imagine.

For the next decade-plus he managed to create music despite recurring schizophrenia, electroconvulsive therapy, and hospitalizations. His solo albums *In the Skies* (1979) and *Little Dreamer* (1980) both reached the British top forty. After releasing *Kolors* in late 1983, he vanished from the public eye to live a hobo-like existence.

It was not until 1997 that he would return to full-time performing. His Peter Green Splinter Group with friend and guitarist Nigel Watson plus an assortment of other musicians was well received. They released nine studio albums during their existence. The gem of the bunch and the most difficult to find, *Me and the Devil,* released in 2001, was a three-CD limited-edition box set. It is the CD of Robert Johnson covers that shows the enduring guitar brilliance of Peter Green. He continues to perform as a solo artist.

In 1998, Green, Danny Kirwan, and Jeremy Spencer were inducted, with the five well-known members of Fleetwood Mac, into the Rock and Roll Hall of Fame.

Ben Palmer

Ben Palmer has the distinction of playing in three separate groups with Eric Clapton. He was the pianist in the Roosters, Powerhouse, and the Glands, with whom he shared the grand travel adventure with Clapton.

When Clapton left the Bluesbreakers for the last time, he did not forget the friend of his youth. He convinced label owner Robert Stigwood that Palmer was capable of being Cream's road manager. Little did Stigwood realize that Palmer had no experience in this area. At one of Cream's first gigs, he just dropped the band off and didn't bother to make sure the instruments were set up, which did not please drummer Ginger Baker. He would grow into the position and serve the band well.

Everyone needs lifelong friends, and Ben Palmer and Eric Clapton have been that with each other. Today, Palmer spends time working as a woodcarver in Wales.

John Mayall

By June 1967, John Mayall had been blessed by having two of the greatest guitarists in rock history as part of his Bluesbreakers. Eric Clapton and Peter Green had both left voluntarily once and been fired once. I don't think any other musician can make the claim of having fired two of *Rolling Stone*'s guitarists that were ranked in the top forty on their list of the 100 Greatest Guitarists of All Time.

Mayall's search for a new guitarist ended when he selected Mick Taylor. While the Rolling Stones were in Taylor's future, he continued the trend of exceptional musicians to front Mayall's backing band. It was Taylor's expertise that helped Mayall finally break through to an American audience as his 1968 release, *Barb Wire*, finally made a dent on the American charts, checking in at #59.

Mayall reached his American commercial peak, chartwise, in 1969–1971, when albums such as *Empty Rooms, U.A.A. Union,* and *The Turning Point* all entered the top forty.

During the early seventies, he shifted his vision in a fusion direction. The live *Jazz-Blues Fusion* featured jazz trumpeter Blue Mitchell and saxophonist

Clifford Solomon. His next release, *Moving On,* had Fred Jackson joining sax player Ernie Watts plus flutist Charles Owens and a reed section. These two releases remain excellent and unique stops in the Mayall catalog.

Relocated in the United States, Mayall continued to release albums into the early eighties. but his commercial appeal was on the wane. A fire destroyed his California home in 1979, resulting in the loss of his music memorabilia and his collection of vintage pornography dating back to the Victorian era.

He began his comeback in 1982 when he reunited with now former Rolling Stone Mick Taylor and bassist John McVie for a series of performances in the United States and Australia.

Mayall assembled one of his better lineups in 1984. Another superb guitarist, Coco Montoya, took over on lead and was joined by a second guitarist, Walter Trout. Bassist Bobby Hayes and drummer Joe Yuele accompanied them.

By the turn of the millennium, Mayall was recognized as the grand old man of the British blues.

Mayall celebrated his fortieth anniversary in 2001 by releasing the album *Along for the Ride.* It attracted such stalwarts as Gary Moore, Steve Cropper, Steve Miller, Billy Gibbons, Chris Rea, and over a dozen others. He celebrated his seventieth birthday with a charity concert at Kings Dock Arena in Liverpool. He was joined onstage by former guitarists Mick Taylor and Eric Clapton.

While he has talked about retirement as he has passed his 76th birthday, Mayall continues to record and tour. He released *Tough* in 2009. He has never won a Grammy award and is not a member of the Rock and Roll Hall of Fame.

16

It's Getting Near Dawn

Fresh Cream

G inger Baker was born into this world on August 19, 1939, in Lewisham, South London. As a young teenager he hoped to become a professional racing cyclist. That ambition was abandoned when he left home at the age of sixteen to tour with the Storyville Jazz Men. He would go on to play for Acker Bilk, Terry Lightfoot, and Alexis Korner. and gain fame as a member of the Graham Bond Organization, who had also played with Korner.

Baker became known for his wild and frenetic playing. He would attack his drum set with both hands, creating a thunderous sound. His use of two bass drums was unique and greatly enhanced his sound.

Jack Bruce was born May 14, 1943, in Glasgow, Scotland. Music was a part of his life from a very young age, and he won a scholarship for cello and music composition at the prestigious Scottish Academy of Music and Drama. While attending school, he began moonlighting in a jazz band. His school disapproved and issued an ultimatum of either the jazz band or his education. Bruce promptly left school.

His first steady gig was as the double bass player in the Murray Campbell Big Band. By 1963, he had joined organist Graham Bond, drummer Ginger Baker, and sax player Dick Heckstall-Smith in Alexis Korner's Blues Inc. When that group folded, Bruce and Baker joined Bond in his self-named band. John McLaughlin was the guitarist for a short time, and old bandmate Smith joined after his departure.

The main problem for the Graham Bond Organization was the relationship between Bruce and Baker, which, to put it mildly, was not good. They sabotaged each other's equipment and openly fought onstage. Bruce finally had enough and left the band after two tumultuous years.

He served a short stint in John Mayall's Bluesbreakers, where he caught the attention of the returning Clapton. He left for a better monetary offer from Manfred Mann.

Back before Cream were superstars. That would quickly change.   *Courtesy of Robert Rodriguez*

The history of rock music changed when Ginger Baker attended a Bluesbreakers concert in Oxford in June 1966. He approached Clapton after the show and suggested they form a new band. Clapton was ready for a change and asked Bruce to leave Manfred Mann and become the bassist. He was unaware of the animosity that existed between Bruce and Baker. This lack of knowledge would come back to haunt Cream and Clapton in the very near future. It has always been an interesting facet of Cream's formation that Bruce and Baker agreed to be members of the same group again given their history. Whatever their feelings, they made the right decision both commercially and artistically as the chemistry between the three musicians would be some of the best in music history.

The original idea was to form a pure and traditional blues trio, but it quickly gave way to a rock/blues fusion sound that was unique in rock music at the time. They had the idea of naming themselves Sweet 'n' Sour Rock 'n' Roll, which may have been one of the worst names ever considered for a major rock band. They finally settled on Cream, and they were indeed considered the cream of the crop among musicians. A little self-serving, but thus is history born, and the future would prove the name accurate.

They went into secret rehearsals, but word began to leak out about the formation of the impending supergroup, which led to Clapton's firing by Mayall. That did really not matter at this point. Their reputations preceded them, and Robert Stigwood quickly signed them to a recording contact.

They would record for Reactions Records in the United Kingdom and in the United States for Atco, which was a subsidiary of Atlantic.

They made their first stage appearance at the Twisted Wheel on July 29, 1966. Two days later, they took the stage at the Sixth Annual Windsor Jazz & Blues Festival for their first full-blown concert. Performing under their three names, they offered a set of traditional and improvisational blues tunes due to the fact they had little or no original material ready.

Cream convened in London from July through October 1966 to record their first album. The first release from these sessions was the single "Wrapping Paper/Cat's Squirrel." It proved to be a low-key affair and a moderate success, reaching #34 on the British singles charts but not seeing any chart action in the United States. Ginger Baker later said that he and Clapton hated the song and that Jack Bruce was responsible for its release as a single. Whether this is true or not, the song did not appear on their first album. "Wrapping Paper" did have the distinction of being the first composition by Jack Bruce and Pete Brown to see the light of day.

Cream's long-awaited debut was released in December 1966. The reputations of the three musicians had assured its success before its release. It was an instant hit and reached #6 on the British album charts. It would take

A young Cream looks ahead. The road would quickly take its toll.   *Courtesy of Robert Rodriguez*

a little longer in America and only climb to #39. The album would have staying power, however, and remain on the charts for over ninety weeks.

The first time I heard *Fresh Cream* was while attending a party at a friend's house. Over four decades later, I can still remember the lead track, "I Feel Free," blasting out of the speakers and my world coming to a stop at least in a musical sense. That world immediately expanded as the Beach Boys and Roy Orbison competed for time on my turntable.

Jack Bruce cowrote four of the songs and Ginger Baker two more. Eric Clapton did not take a writing credit for any of the songs, but the album bears his imprint with covers of five traditional blues tunes. These songs also formed the foundation of his introduction to an American fan base. Jack Bruce had emerged as the lead vocalist for the group mainly due to Clapton's lack of confidence in his own vocal skills. He did step forward and provide the lead vocal for the old Robert Johnson tune "Four Until Late."

The inclusion of songs by Robert Johnson, Muddy Waters, Willie Dixon, and Skip James were testament to Clapton's desire to remain within a blues framework. Ironically, it was his unique guitar improvisations that quickly moved Cream's sound from traditional to blues fusion and in the process firmly establish that fusion as a recognized musical style. Other musicians had explored this territory previously but none so successfully, intimately, or commercially up until that time, as had Clapton and Cream.

Willie Dixon's "Spoonful" was left off the American release, and "I Feel Free" was not issued on its U.K. counterpart. While the songs were very different, they remain two of the stronger tracks to emerge from the initial recording sessions. "Spoonful" was a guitar coming-out party for Clapton. It was the first of a number of Cream tracks that would validate the "Clapton Is God" moniker and worship that was developing at the time. I doubt that this is the type of music Willie Dixon had in mind when he penned the tune, but he would have appreciated the guitar virtuosity and ingenuity.

"I Feel Free" was issued as a single in England, and it was the practice of many English and European artists to leave singles off of their albums as opposed to America where a successful single and resultant radio airplay many times helped to create album sales. The song would reach #11 in England but inexplicably would fail to chart in the United States. It was more psychedelic than bluesy, and Clapton provided a pivotal brief solo that tied it all together.

Ginger Baker's "Toad" also made its debut. The song's history reached back to his time with the Graham Bond Organization, but this was the first time it had been recorded and released. His famous drum solo was present, but the track's five-minute length only hinted at the path it would travel in the future.

A radio ad prompting listeners to give Cream a try. Eventually millions responded.
Courtesy of Robert Rodriguez

Another Clapton extravaganza was the Muddy Waters tune "Rollin' and Tumblin'," which at 4:42 gave him a little room to stretch out. This old blue tune can be traced back to harmonica player Noah Lewis, who recorded it as a part of Gus Cannon's Jug Stompers in 1928. It was a good example of an old blues number being changed over the years and the actual writing credits becoming confused. The Yardbirds would release a version on their *Little Games* album with Relf/Page/Dreja/McCarty listed as the composers.

A concert with Atco label mates Vanilla Fudge. Cream is long gone but Vanilla Fudge is still around.

Author's collection

Another early Clapton performance of note was "I'm So Glad," which had been written and recorded by Skip James in the 1930s. It would become a staple of their live show.

Rolling Stone would rank it #101 on their list of the 500 Greatest Albums of All Time.

March 1967 found the group settling into a weeklong stay in Murray the K's *Music in the Fifth Dimension* show in New York City. They toured the United States to universal praise from the press and larger and larger audiences. They also rapidly became known for their improvisational skills, of which Clapton was the star.

Before leaving the United States for home, they made an extended stop at Atlantic Studios in New York City to record their next album. Felix Pappalardi stepped in as producer. He proved a good match for the group and would produce their final three studio albums.

Summer found the band back in England. where they shared the stage at the Seville Theatre in early July with the Jeff Beck Group and John Mayall's Bluesbreakers. One can only imagine what was going on backstage.

Late summer would find them back in the United States with an extended stay at the legendary Fillmore West. The release of their second album was on the horizon, which would propel Cream and Eric Clapton to the top of the rock world.

17

Meet Me at the Crossroads

Heavy Cream, or Clapton Is God

*D*israeli *Gears* was released in the United Kingdom November 2, 1967, and in the United States on December 9. It was enclosed in one of the great album jackets of the psychedelic era.

The album is now recognized as one of the defining releases of the late sixties. The American blues of the Delta and Chicago, which had crossed the Atlantic Ocean, had returned home in a much-altered form. It had emerged as British blues meets American psychedelic rock, and Eric Clapton and Cream were its leading practitioners.

The odd album title was conceived out of a conversation focusing on one of Ginger Baker's favorite topics. Clapton was thinking about buying a racing bicycle and had a number of questions for Baker since he was the expert. Roadie Mick Turner overheard the conversation and mentioned it should have Disraeli gears instead of *derailleur* gears. Clapton and Baker were amused that he had substituted the name of the nineteenth-century British prime minister. The album's working title had simply been *Cream*, but it was changed to cash in on the joke, and so one of the pivotal albums in rock history received a name. One can only wonder what Benjamin Disraeli would have thought about his name being better known to modern generations for this album than for his extensive political accomplishments.

The cover art was unique and innovative and remains instantly recognizable to rock fans today. Australian Martin Sharp was an acquaintance of Clapton from the time they lived in the same apartment building in Chelsea. He would create the artwork for their next release as well. His relationship with Clapton extended to the writing area, as he cowrote "Tales of Brave Ulysses" and the single "Anyone for Tennis."

Felix Pappalardi began his run as Cream's producer with this album. How much influence he had on the group will always be debatable, but the fact remains that he was the producer for two of the better and more enduring albums in music history. He and his wife Gail composed "Strange Brew"

Probably the strangest single of Cream's career.

Author's collection

Probably the strangest single of Cream's career with a Japan issued picture sleeve.   *Author's collection*

with Clapton, and he also contributed his talent as a session musician when needed. Pappalardi would go on to a successful, if somewhat short, producing and performing career after his time with the band ended.

The album also marked the beginning of Clapton's association with engineer Tom Dowd. He would also work with Dowd while with Derek and the Dominos plus during his solo career as well.

The first thing that strikes a person is the shortness of *Disraeli Gears*, clocking in at 33:39, and the brevity of each track. Only "Sunshine of Your Love" at 4:10 exceeded the four-minute mark, and five of the eleven tracks are under three minutes. This would be in direct opposition to their live performances, where the improvisational skills of the band would elongate the songs to ten and sometimes close to twenty minutes.

The second noticeable feature was that Eric Clapton's name was more prominent in the credits than on their first album.

He wrote three of the tracks and arranged two more. In addition, his vocals became more frequent and pronounced. While Jack Bruce was still the main vocalist, Clapton sang lead on two of the songs and was a supporting presence on several more.

The Bruce/Brown composition "Sunshine of Your Love" was the most memorable track and today is one of the songs that represents the era itself. While he did not compose it, Clapton provided a series of short notes and solos that convinced me and a generation of aspiring musicians they would never be able to play the guitar, or at least to play it well. I have seen Eric Clapton play this song live several times through the years, and for him it is effortless. This short performance would go a long way toward cementing his legacy especially in the United States. This was the band's breakout song in the United States as it reached #5 on the singles charts and received massive radio airplay.

"Strange Brew"/"Tales of Brave Ulysses" had already been released as a single in the United Kingdom, reaching the top twenty. Both songs had been cowritten by Clapton, who also provided the lead vocal on the A-side. It was a confidence builder that his voice was strong enough to produce a hit single. Both songs are a blues/psychedelic rock fusion, and while Clapton's playing is somewhat restrained, it is also memorable.

Arguably Cream's most popular song. Clapton made the guitar work sound effortless.   *Author's collection*

The bluesiest tracks are the final three. Jack Bruce and Peter Brown went in a blues direction with "Take It Back," and it was a good fit for the tracks that surrounded it. Clapton stayed true to his blues roots with his translations of Arthur Reynolds's "Outside Woman Blues" and the all-too-short and traditional "Mother's Lament."

Disraeli Gears would be reissued in a number of forms over the years, but the 2004 *Deluxe Edition* contains the original album, out-takes, demos, and some live performances, which brings the album full circle.

Some highlights include the previously unreleased "Blue Condition" with a Clapton vocal. "SWLABR" was the flip side of "Sunshine of Your Love" single and contains some more excellent work by E. C. There is a shorter live version included as well. "Strange Brew" and "Tales of Brave Ulysses" are played live back to back from a June 3, 1967, broadcast on the BBC. There is also a three-song blues set broadcast October 29, 1967, on the BBC 1. "Born Under a Bad Sign," "Outside Woman Blues," and "Take It Back" are a fine way to spend eight and a half minutes of your life. It you want some rare Eric Clapton and Cream, this is an album for you.

Disraeli Gears would have a lasting impact upon rock music. It would reappear on the *Billboard Magazine* Hot 200 several times.

Clapton had already reached cult status before the album's release. In February 1968, the band began a tour of the United States at the Fillmore

The single was good, but the extended live versions were the essence of Cream.   *Author's collection*

Auditorium. This was followed by a four-night gig at the Avalon Ballroom in San Francisco, where they shared the stage with the MC5 and the Stooges. By the time the tour was finished, Eric Clapton had become a guitar god on this side of the Atlantic as well.

Despite the commercial success, the sold-out concerts, and the adulation, all was not well with Cream. Egos were running wild, and the old animosity between Baker and Bruce had begun to resurface. These problems were especially apparent onstage, as Baker, Bruce, and sometime Clapton would try to outperform each other. Clapton commented once that it got so bad he actually stopped playing and the other two did not notice.

In the midst of all the controversy, one of the most unusual singles in their history was released. "Anyone for Tennis" is basically a pop tune and an odd one at that. It originally appeared in the film *The Savage Seven*. The Cream name would be the main selling point as it reached #36 in the United Kingdom. American fans were a little more discerning, as it stalled at #64.

Finally in July, Clapton had had enough. He was tired of being the go-between in the Baker/Bruce relationship or lack thereof. Baker has also had enough as his hearing was beginning to be affected due to the volume of their live concerts. They announced that Cream would disband after their current U.S. and forthcoming U.K. tour dates.

Bruce, Clapton, and Baker had been in the studio intermittently for almost a year, (July 1967–April 1968), working on their next album under the guidance of Pappalardi, who would become a virtual fourth member in the studio, adding some organ work, viola, and assorted brass that gave their music a fuller sound.

The double album *Wheels of Fire* was released in July 1967. It consisted of one studio disc and one live, which was recorded at the Fillmore West in San Francisco. It would be the pinnacle of their commercial success, topping the American charts for a month and becoming the first double album in music history to receive a Platinum award for sales.

In a number of countries, *Wheels of Fire* was released as a double album and was split into single releases as well. The U.K. *Live at the Fillmore* cover featured a negative image of the studio version. In Japan, the studio version was black and gold foil, and the live version was black on aluminum foil. Australian copies were laminated versions of the Japanese release. The number of variations has kept collectors busy for decades.

A couple of other interesting U.S. chart facts. The album also reached #11 on the rhythm and blues charts, which given the material was a real stretch. The album that finally replaced it at #1 was the Doors' *Waiting for the Sun*, which is a good fit. The album it replaced at the top of the charts was

For several years, Cream was constantly touring.   *Courtesy of Robert Rodriguez*

The Beat of the Brass by Herb Albert and the Tijuana Brass, which certainly does not fit and is as far away from Cream as it gets.

The jacket was the second in a row by Martin Sharp, and it was another superb effort, worth finding in its original vinyl form just for the cover. It would win the New York Art Director's prize for Best Album Art of 1969.

Eric Clapton did not take any writing credits on *Wheels of Fire*. Maybe he was already withdrawing from the group, but for whatever reason he limited himself to finding two old blues cover songs. "Sitting on Top of the World" and the Albert King signature tune "Born Under a Bad Sign" were the type of songs that Clapton was so adept at transforming into his own creations. Clapton later revealed that the Atlantic label had pressured the group to record "Born Under a Bad Sign" as Albert King was a label mate of the group and they thought it would be good publicity for him. Asking Eric Clapton to cover any song, especially a guitar-based blues piece, to gain popularity for the original artist always has an element of chance. "Born Under a Bad Sign" proved to be one of the more popular songs on the album, and it became a staple of their live act. I am an Albert King fan, but when this song comes to mind, I think Eric Clapton.

The two discs chronicled the schizophrenic nature of Cream's studio work versus their live shows. The nine studio tracks were tight and controlled, ranging in times from 2:53 to 4:58. The production had become slicker than on their first two albums, and extra instruments made their appearance courtesy of producer Pappalardi. Many of the tracks had a fuller sound, with some elements of orchestration present. Except for the two blues covers, the rest of the material was more psychedelic in style.

On the other hand, when listening to the live disc, the four long live tracks were raw, improvisational, and exhausting in a good way.

The enduring song for the second album in a row would be another Bruce/Brown composition. "White Room" featured one of the smoother vocals of Bruce's career, and the dramatic opening is an immediate attention grabber. Despite this, it is Clapton's wah-wah sound that gives the song a unique foundation and makes it memorable. It became a top ten single in the United States.

Ginger Baker and his writing partner Mike Taylor were responsible for three of the studio tracks, and they proved Baker could be a competent composer when given the opportunity. Sometimes I think they should have made use of his composing skills a bit more, as they were closer to the original vision of the group than was the Bruce/Brown duo's. Having said that, you certainly can't argue with success.

"Passing the Time," "Those Were the Days," and the underrated "Pressed Rat and Warthog" are all nice relics of the era. When you add in a couple

more Bruce/Brown compositions, "Deserted Cities of the Heart" and "Politician," you have the makings of one of *Rolling Stone*'s 500 Greatest Albums of All Time, and that's only the first disc.

The live disc begins with a modest four-minute performance of "Crossroads." What it lacked in length it made up for in intensity. The second of Clapton's solos has been honored as one of his best, which means it is very good indeed. It's tough to outplay Robert Johnson on one of his own compositions, but on March 16, 1968, E. C. came very close.

Another song that was shortened to fit the single format. Clapton continues to play the song live today.

Author's collection

This leads to a sixteen-minute version of Willie Dixon's "Spoonful." This track is probably one of the most accurate pictures of Cream live as it is a group affair with Clapton weaving his guitar artistry in and out.

"Toad" was elongated to over sixteen minutes and contains *the* drum solo of Ginger Baker's career, which means one of the best in rock history. Drummers have been influenced by this track for years. I get exhausted listening to it and cannot image a human being playing it live in one take.

The longer live disc is an acquired taste. It does contain a number of treats, but I have found that allowing some time between listens adds to the enjoyment.

Eric Clapton remained busy with short outside projects as his career with Cream came to a close. He took his Les Paul into the studio with George Harrison and the Beatles to play lead on his "While My Guitar Gently Weeps." He also lent a hand on Harrison's solo effort *Wonderwall Music*. Clapton would be a lifelong friend of Harrison, and the relationship would survive illness, addictions, and even wives. He would organize a memorial concert in memory of Harrison after his death.

Wheels of Fire was a part of rock history as Cream embarked on their final tour.

18

Worked All Summer, Worked All Fall

The U.S. tour limped to close at the Rhode Island Auditorium November 4, 1968. The group arrived late without realizing the town had a curfew law. They played "Spoonful" and "Toad" and called it a night. I don't know what I was doing that night, but as a native Rhode Islander I was only about ten miles away.

Cream reached the end of the road at the Royal Albert Hall in London with concerts November 25 and 26, 1968. Thousands of fans were turned away as the two shows sold out in minutes. The performances were average at best but due to the historic nature of the event were filmed by the BBC. They have since been released on DVD. I find the music technically adept, but the fire and energy is missing. The opening acts were Yes and Taste, which featured a young and upcoming guitarist, Rory Gallagher.

Clapton celebrated his newfound freedom by participating in the Rolling Stones project *Rock and Roll Circus*. It was originally recorded as a TV special but was never released. Artists such as John Lennon, the Who, and Jethro Tull also took part in one of the strangest projects of the rock era. A completely out of it Brian Jones is barely able to function.

Clapton became a member of the one-off group put together just for this production. The others included lead guitarist Eric Clapton, John Lennon as the vocalist and rhythm guitarist, drummer Mitch Mitchell of the Jimi Hendrix Experience, violinist Ivry Gitlis, background vocals by Yoko Ono, and a rare turn on bass by Keith Richards. They recorded a cover of the Beatles' "Yer Blues" plus an instrumental jam, making it the shortest tenure of service for any Eric Clapton band.

These tracks remained unreleased until 1995, when the whole production was released as both a CD and a DVD. It was one of those lost/missing productions that had attained a mythic status through the years. The finished product quickly made it clear why it sat on the shelf for twenty-seven years. Still, if you are a fan of the Rolling Stones, Lennon, or Clapton, it is an essential addition to your collection.

Meanwhile, Cream had planned to release a final double album but finally decided to just walk away. *Goodbye* was released in March 1969, which was well after the group's demise.

The album was a haphazard affair basically assembled by producer Pappalardi. It consisted of three studio and three live tracks. Oddly, it was the only Cream album to reach #1 in their home country. Glen Campbell's *Wichita Lineman* kept it from #1 in the United States.

While not of the caliber of their three previous studio releases, it does contain several excellent tracks. "Badge" was a dual composition by Clapton and George Harrison, who provided supporting vocals and rhythm guitar. It would further cement their friendship and working relationship.

The three live tracks were recorded at the Forum in Inglewood, California, in October 1968. A nine-minute performance of "I'm So Glad" is the definitive version of this old Skip James tune as Clapton leaves behind this calling card of just how good a guitarist he had become. "Politician" and "Sitting on Top of the World" are given credible workouts and were welcome at the time of their release, as fans did not know how much material the band had stored away in the vaults.

While it is by far the weakest of the four studio albums, the bits and pieces are excellent reminders of the overall genius of Cream.

19

Another Spoonful

Reunions and Regurgitations

T he lights stayed out for Cream for close to a quarter of a century. In 1993, they were voted into the Rock and Roll Hall of Fame, and despite a great deal of initial reluctance they finally agreed to play together at the induction ceremony.

Their set consisted of "Sunshine of Your Love," "Crossroads," and "Born Under a Bad Sign." I have seen the performances, and the opening notes of "Sunshine of Your Love," which were heard for the first time in twenty-five years, were electric. Cream played it safe, and the performances were technically adept and smooth but did not contain a great deal of energy.

The result of this performance together was some conversation about a number of limited reunion concerts, but nothing came of it, and the hopes of fans disappeared as the years passed. Clapton seemed to have been the most resistant as he was constantly busy with his solo career. Amazingly, Bruce and Baker, like moths to the flame, actually worked together again in BBM with guitarist Gary Moore.

The lights finally went back on, at least for a little while, thirty-five years after Cream's last concert. Clapton figured it was now or never as both of his old bandmates were having physical problems. Bruce had undergone a liver transplant, and Baker had worsening arthritis in his hands.

The reunion was limited to two venues. The first was four concerts, May 2, 3, 5, and 6, 2005, at Royal Albert Hall, where they had played their final concerts. Clapton picked the venue, and it was a fitting place to bring the group full circle and in retrospect had the ring of finality to it.

All the tickets for the four shows were scooped up in under an hour. Despite this lack of available tickets, stars such as Paul McCartney, Jimmy Page, Roger Waters, Mick Taylor, Steve Winwood, Brian May, and Bill Wyman managed to be front and center.

Their final journey was to New York City's Madison Square Garden for a series of concerts October 24–26, 2005. The concerts were commercially successful and critically acclaimed, and extravagant offers poured in for a tour. Clapton closed the issue by announcing there would be no more tours, nor would any new studio album be forthcoming.

Rumors would continue to surface since 2006 about another reunion, but Baker and Clapton have been very clear that Cream's time is finished. Clapton continues to state that the music has gone as far as it can go, which may be his way of being polite. Baker has been harsher about his not wanting any relationship with Bruce. It seems that he has had enough as well, and advancing age has solidified that decision.

Even Jack Bruce has accepted Cream's final ending. He also demonstrated that the animosity between him and Baker runs both ways when in a *Rolling Stone* article he was quoted as saying: "It's a knife-edge thing between me and Ginger. Nowadays we happily are co-existing in different continents (Great Britain and South Africa) although I was thinking of asking him to move. He's still a bit too close."

In February 2006, Cream received a lifetime Grammy Award in recognition of their contributions to and influence on modern music.

The 2005 Royal Albert Hall London concerts were released in October 2005, with much fanfare and a good deal of critical success. Cream had finally entered the modern age as a 115:35 CD and a 167:00 DVD were issued chronicling the historic event. A rare vinyl set was also issued for purists. The CD reached #59 on the U.S. album charts, which was quite an accomplishment for a pricey set from a band that had been inactive for three and a half decades.

The releases were assembled from performances covering the final three concerts (and oddly nothing from the first), and all the formats have something to recommend them. The compact disc listing is as follows: 1) "I'm So Glad" (6:18); 2) "Spoonful" (11:28); 3) "Outside Woman Blues" (4:33); 4) "Pressed Rat and Warthog" (3:21); 5) "Sleepy Time Time" (6:08); 6) "N.S.U." (6:02); 7) "Badge" (4:28); 8) "Politician" (5:08); 9) "Sweet Wine" (6:28); 10) "Rollin' and Tumblin'" (5:02); 11) "Stormy Monday" (8:09); 12) "Deserted Cities of the Heart" (3:56); 13) "Born Under a Bad Sign" (5:31); 14) "We're Going Wrong" (8:26); 15) "Crossroads" (4:55); 16) "White Room" (6:18); 17) "Toad" (12:06); 18) "Sunshine of Your Love" (8:46); 19) "Sleepy Time Time" (alternate take) (6:07).

The Royal Albert and to a lesser extent the Madison Square Garden concerts brought Eric Clapton's career as a member of Cream to a satisfying conclusion at least for his fans and hopefully for him as well.

When comparing the sixties material and performances with those of the new millennium, we find a very different Cream. People age, times change, and songs mature. Clapton may not be the long-haired, incendiary musician of his youth, but he had become recognized as one of the best guitarists to ever pick up the instrument.

Cream's catalog of music has been released and in some cases regurgitated in many forms through the years. Some were worthy of a quick death, but others assembled the music in new ways that made it live on and find new commercial success.

Best of Cream was released in 1969 to cash in on the group's fame. It was a good commercial decision at it quickly rose to #3 in the United States. It would prove so popular that the label reissued it in 1977 and 1985 before moving it into a CD format in May 1989.

Best of Cream was patterned after greatest hits albums that thousands of artists have assembled containing their top forty hits. Cream was never and will never be considered a singles band despite the success of "Sunshine of Your Love" and "White Room."

What the Atco label did was assemble the best of their studio tracks. It was a good move as these short, precise, and well-produced songs were an excellent introduction to the group and pulled in a host of new fans. Old fans were attracted to the album as well, as it was an era before technology allowed people to move material around, so having the better studio material on one disc was an appealing prospect.

The first side of "Sunshine of Your Love," "Badge," "Crossroads," "White Room," and "SWALBR" was enough to hook any music fan and especially those who were not familiar with Cream's work. The flip side was almost as good as "Born Under a Bad Sign," the studio "Spoonful," Tales of Brave Ulysses," "Strange Brew, and "I Feel Free" introduced hundreds of thousands of music lovers to the "Clapton Is God" concept. I have always felt that if you had switched "I Feel Free" with "SWALBR," you would have had the perfect album side.

While the album has been rendered obsolete by many newer releases, I still pull it out when I want a taste of Cream (pun intended). It is a nice introductory course.

Live Cream followed and was a nice companion piece. It was just as commercially popular, reaching #4 in the United Kingdom and #15 in the United States.

Four of the five tracks are long, sprawling improvisational explorations that captured their live sound well. The only anomaly was the short (2:46) "Lawdy Mama," which was recorded during the *Disraeli Gears* sessions. This traditional blues piece was arranged by Clapton and features his lead vocal.

The live tracks were typical of the band but contained an interesting selection of material. "N.S.U." was a little pop oriented in its original studio form, but this ten-minute rendition transforms it into a psychedelic rock piece. "Sleepy Time Time," recorded at Winterland in March 1968, was a Jack Bruce creation, but it is Clapton who provides the fireworks. It would be a staple of their reunion concerts. "Sweet Wine" is the longest track at over fifteen minutes and was written by Ginger Baker and Janet Godfrey. Its extended length is a good representation of the band's ability to stretch out. The final track was the old Muddy Waters staple "Rollin' and Tumblin'" and has Eric Clapton written all over it. It was a good vehicle for Clapton to shine, but every once in a while he is frustrating as he holds back when he should have stepped forward and just wrung every sound available out of his guitar.

Best of Cream and Live Cream, released back to back, made the label some extra cash but intentionally or not provided a double dose of Cream that complemented each other well.

If you really want to explore the Cream legacy more deeply and bask in the glow, reach back to 1997 for the six-hour box set *Those Were the Days*. Its sixty-three tracks cover material from their studio albums, one-off singles, plus two discs of live material with a few songs being released for the first time.

Cream reunited during 2005 for the last time as old issues quickly emerged.   *Author's collection*

It does not explore much new ground, but it does cover the familiar very well. If you do not own much of their material, this is a good and complete indoctrination.

Eric Clapton had traveled a lot of miles and now was considered one of the premier living guitarists. He had also been a part of two bands that would have dates with the Rock and Roll Hall of Fame. Not bad for someone in his mid-twenties. It was early 1969, and E. C. was ready to move on again.

20

Vanish from This Place

Whatever Happened To

Felix Pappalardi

Not many rock stars and producers were classically trained and attended the University of Michigan, but so it was with Felix Pappalardi.

His early career included a stint in Max Morath's Original Rag Quartet. He played an acoustic Mexican bass called the guitarron. Morath was a pianist/singer in the Scott Joplin tradition. Other band members included Barry Kornfeld, who was a folk and jazz guitarist, and Jim Tyler, a banjo and mandolin player, rounded out the group.

Pappalardi quickly became a busy session guitarist throughout the sixties. He was in demand as a bassist and provided support for the likes of Fred Neil, Buffy Sainte-Marie, Ian and Sylvia, Bo Grumpus, and dozens of others.

His breakthrough came as a producer and not as a musician. In early 1967, he produced the Youngbloods' self-titled debut album, which brought him to the attention of Robert Stigwood, who had produced the first Cream album. He would produce *Disraeli Gears, Wheels of Fire,* and *Goodbye*. In addition to his producing duties, Pappalardi served as a fourth musician in the studio as he was proficient on the keyboards, various string instruments, and assorted brass, all of which allowed the group to expand beyond a basic power threesome, at least in the recording studio. His time with Cream would elevate him to the elite of rock producers.

Pappalardi continued to produce after Cream's demise. *Songs for a Taylor* by Jack Bruce, *Love on the Wing* by Jesse Colin Young, plus artists such as Hot Tuna and the Flock benefited from his skills in the studio.

His life completely changed when he produced Leslie West's solo release *Mountain*, which was a commercial success in the United States. Pappalardi and West decided to form a hard-rock group and name it after West's first album, and so Mountain was born. He would produce their albums and compose most of the songs.

Pappalardi's bass work was a key ingredient of the Mountain sound. He was able to walk a fine line between a modern electric and traditional upright bass. His early use of a fuzz sound was unique and innovative among bassists at the time. It is a technique that is difficult to conquer even with modern-day technology. He, West, drummer at the time Norman Smart, and keyboardist Steve Knight performed at Woodstock.

Their sledgehammer rock 'n' roll proved popular, as *Nantucket Sleighride, Flowers of Evil,* and *Mountain* all charted in the United States. They even managed a top forty single with "Mississippi Queen." The original group's run was relatively short, although there would be numerous reunions as West and drummer Corky Laing, who joined in 1970, continue to perform as Mountain today.

Pappalardi was enticed back to Mountain in late 1973 and again in 1981. Several albums of material were recorded and issued, but the commercial success had dried up. He continued to produce albums by other bands, but during this period of his life cut down on his live playing due to an increasing hearing loss; and if Mountain was one thing, it was loud.

On April 17, 1983, Felix Pappalardi was shot and killed by his wife in their east side Manhattan apartment under mysterious circumstances. She was tried for second-degree murder but was found guilty of negligent homicide and was sentenced to sixteen months in prison. She has maintained the shooting was an accident. He is buried next to his mother in a modest grave in the Wood Lawn Cemetery in the Bronx.

Peter Brown

Peter Brown will be primarily remembered as the lyricist for many of Cream's most popular releases. Songs such as "Sunshine of Your Love," "White Room," and "I Feel Free" continue to be popular radio fare forty years after their creation.

Brown began his career as a poet and was first published as a teenager. He formed one of the more unique groups in recent memory. The Real Poetry Band, in addition to himself, included guitarist John McLaughlin, bassist Binky McKenzie, drummer Laurie Allen, and percussionist Pete Bailey.

He originally agreed to write with Ginger Baker, but it quickly became apparent that he was a better writing partner for Jack Bruce. The Bruce-Brown relationship would extend beyond Cream.

He formed Pete Brown and His Battered Ornaments in 1968. The band also included guitarist Chris Spedding and sax player Dick Heckstall-Smith. Their first album, *A Meal You Can Shake Hands with in the Dark*, and their second, *Mantle-Piece*, both caught the attention of the Rolling Stones, who invited them to be their opening act at a Hyde Park Concert. One day before the concert Brown was unceremoniously kicked out of the band he founded. They also dropped his name from the marquee and rerecorded the album with Spedding as the new vocalist. Oddly, Spedding would be asked to contribute to Jack Bruce's first solo release.

Brown quickly moved on and formed Peter Brown and Piblokto. The group received little attention or success for any of its three albums. This may have been due to a revolving cast of characters.

He was a virtual musical gypsy for the next several years. He hooked up with Graham Bond for an album and soundtrack to the movie *Maltamour* before forming Brown and Friends and then on to the Flying Tigers. An album of poetry followed before he moved on yet again to Back to Front.

Brown finally formed a lasting professional relationship with Phil Ryan, who had been a short-time member of Piblokto. He formed his own label and established the British film production company Brown Waters.

He continues to be active in the film industry and the studio.

Graham Bond

Graham Bond is one of the musicians who provided a training ground for others who would go on to great fame and commercial success, both of which would ultimately elude him.

He was educated at the Royal Liberty School in Gidea Park and joined the Don Rendell Quintet as a jazz saxophonist. His big break came in 1962 when he replaced Cyril Davies in Alexis Korner's Blues Incorporated.

Within a couple of years he was fronting his own band as a keyboardist/vocalist. The other members were Jack Bruce, Ginger Baker, John McLaughlin, and Dick Heckstall-Smith. Bond is considered a pioneer in the use of the keyboard. He was one of the first to use a portable Hammond organ. He also helped develop the mellotron, which such groups as Deep Purple and particularly the Moody Blues would refine.

Bond would never find huge commercial success. He released a dozen studio albums plus compilations, but only one would chart in the United Kingdom.

As the seventies progressed, his health worsened and his addictions increased. His financial situation continued to deteriorate, which resulted in his hospitalization in January 1973, with what was diagnosed as a nervous breakdown. He increasingly became drawn to the occult and on May 8, 1984, was run over and killed by a train at the Finsbury Park Station. His death was ruled a suicide.

Ginger Baker

Ginger Baker's reputation as a drummer of the highest caliber is secure. It was cemented by his work in Cream and to a lesser extent Blind Faith.

His career extended back to 1958 with the Storyville Jazz Men and the Hugh Rainey All Stars. He is the drummer on their album *Storyville Revisited*. The Graham Bond Organization, Cream, Blind Faith, a long solo career, and a trip to the Rock and Roll Hall of Fame would follow.

At the age of thirty, with Cream and Blind Faith in his rear mirror, Baker was without a band despite being one of the most recognizable drummers in the world. What does a drummer without a band do? He starts a band.

Ginger Baker's Air Force took flight in early 1970, with the issue of their self-titled debut album. *Air Force* would just make the top forty is his home country (#37) and only do a little better in the United States (#33).

Baker surrounded himself with a stellar group of musicians including keyboardist and old friend Graham Bond, former Moody Blues and future Wings guitarist Denny Laine, Blind Faith bandmate Ric Grech, sax player Harold McNair, and percussionist Remi Kabaka.

With his new group in place, he decided to record their first album live at Royal Albert Hall on Jan. 15, 1970. Baker supplemented his band with a number of sidemen and women including Steve Winwood; vocalist Janette Jacobs; saxophonist and flutist Chris Woods; a second sax player, Bud Beadle; and another percussionist, Phil Seamen. Winwood's participation meant that three quarters of Blind Faith was onstage together.

It all added up to the creation of one of the underappreciated albums of the early seventies. It was rock meets jazz meets African rhythms. It was eclectic, energetic, stunning, and holds up well four decades later.

Many of the songs are presented in an elongated form similar to Cream. Its double-album length encouraged the improvisational skills of the band, and while there was no Eric Clapton present, Ginger Baker has always been able to lay down a foundation, which encourages this type of format. Only eight songs are needed to fill both discs of the original vinyl release.

"Da Da Man" is short at 7:16 but introduces the cast of characters well. Jeannette Jacobs is a fine vocalist, and solos by Laine (guitar), Winwood (organ), and Bond (sax) quickly prove that Baker surrounded himself with a number of quality sidekicks.

Ginger remained in high demand after the breakup of
Cream. He participated in a number of bands as the years
passed.   *Author's collection*

Winwood's presence is the most critical and as he was a guest, would be
sorely missed in the future. In addition to his musicianship and stage presence, he also brought a clear male voice to the mix as opposed to Baker and
Bond. Winwood also provided a nice counterpoint to the drums because
with Baker, it always came back to the drums. Baker was always at his best
when he had a strong presence to play off of.

The old Cream track "Toad" is resurrected at over twelve minutes, and
it features drums, drums, and more drums. In fact, there are three drum
solos by Baker, Kabaka, and Seamen.

The most accessible of the longer tracks is the Winwood/Baker composition "Don't Care, with vocals by Winwood and Jacobs, who are a good match
for each other.

The album may be a bit long in places, but it is always interesting as
it explored a rock/jazz fusion centered on African rhythms, with Baker's
drumming located at the center of the mix.

Air Force 2 did not fare so well, as the move from the stage to the studio
and the loss of Winwood, and to a lesser extent Laine, sapped the band of

much of its energy and creativity. Air Force was one of those concepts that worked better onstage.

Their second album moved closer to jazz than the first, although it can still be considered a fusion work. Bond and Baker took over the vocal duties with limited success, as they were no match for the departed Winwood.

The material is solid but is presented without the fire and ultimately the constant surprises of their debut. Baker recognized this and folded the band in 1972, moving to Africa to build a recording studio and raise horses. He would constantly return to this home away from home between gigs and bands.

Late December 1974 found him part of the Baker Gurvitz Army. It was originally a power trio, with Adrian Gurvitz on lead guitar and his brother Paul on bass. They would later add a keyboardist and vocalist but seemed to work best as a basic trio,

Gurvitz has always been an underappreciated lead guitarist, and he was a fine fit for Baker. They produced three studio albums during their three-year career together, and they moved Baker back in a rock direction.

During the eighties and nineties, Baker constantly formed new and short-lived groups. Ginger Baker and Band, Ginger Baker's African Force, Ginger Baker and Friends, and the Ginger Baker Trio would quickly come and go, leaving behind at least eight albums.

He continues to play when the whim moves him but seems very content in South Africa. He is not open to another Cream reunion.

Jack Bruce

Since leaving Cream, Bruce's career has been as varied as that of his former bandmates. He first joined old colleague John McLaughlin in a jazz-fusion project, which resulted in an acoustic album.

His first solo album would be his biggest commercial success and remains one of the best creations of his long career. *Songs for a Tailor* was a deserved worldwide success, reaching the top ten in England and the top forty in the United States. The album was named and dedicated to Cream's deceased wardrobe designer Jeannie Franklyn, who was killed in a auto accident while touring with Fairport Convention. Bruce received a letter from her the day after her death.

The album is eclectic in nature as jazz, rock, and even chamber music share space, plus the lyrics are courtesy of old collaborator Pete Brown. Bruce's thumping bass would serve as the foundation for the project.

He wisely turned to old friend Felix Pappalardi as his producer. Pappalardi smoothed it all out and gave it a sheen that allowed the well-crafted and constructed songs to shine through. It has lost a little something over the years but is still very listenable today.

Bruce, like Clapton, had escaped from the confines of Cream and was exploring a number of new musical directions. He would never really settle down into one style, but what makes this album so interesting is his journey of exploration while providing some excellent music in the process.

If Jack Bruce could have produced a number of songs as accessible as "Theme for an Imaginary Western," he would have received the consistent commercial success that always eluded him. The song had a slick production and overdubbing on the keyboards. Its potential may have eluded him at the time but not producer Pappalardi, who was also a bass player and would remember the song when he moved to Mountain. Mountain would turn it into a memorable hard-rock anthem.

Also of note were the songs "Weird of Hermiston" and "The Clearout," which had been written for *Disraeli Gears* but were rejected by the label as not being commercial enough. Early demo versions were included on the Cream box set *Those Were the Days*. The other interesting fact was the guitar work of George Harrison on "Never Tell Your Mother She's Out of Time," which was credited to L' Angelo Misterioso.

Bruce would come to recognize the value of *Songs for a Tailor* as every track except for one would be recycled on other albums over the years.

One of the more interesting stops during his career was Bruce's participation in the hard-rock trio West, Bruce, and Laing. They would release three albums together (1972–1974), with moderate commercial success. Guitarist West and drummer Laing were former and future members of Mountain at the time. They would incorporate Mountain and Cream songs into their live act.

West and Laing continue to perform as Mountain but in 2009 began touring as West, Bruce Jr., and Laing. The junior is Jack Bruce's son Malcolm.

Jack Bruce has put together literally a dozen or so bands to support himself as the years have passed. In 1981, he became a member of another power trio, BLT, with guitarist Robin Trower and drummer Bill Lorden. In 1994, he joined BBM, with guitarist Gary Moore and Ginger Baker. I can't say or write this enough times, but whatever made Bruce and Baker form another group together is beyond me, although maybe hope does spring eternal. One can only imagine the thoughts of Eric Clapton when he first heard about this new band. Possibly his most unusual release was a single, both 7″ and 12″, of "I Feel Free." The love-hate relationship with Baker would continue when they united together onstage for Bruce's fiftieth birthday concert.

At the turn of the millennium, Bruce's health began to deteriorate, and he was diagnosed with liver cancer. He received a liver transplant in 2003, and his recovery was a slow process.

As the decade passed, he became more active again. He was well enough to be a part of the Cream reunions in 2005 and also participated with Gary Moore and drummer Gary Husband at the Dick Heckstall-Smith memorial concert in London. In 2008, he released another album title *Seven Moons* with Robin Trower.

Bruce celebrated his sixty-fifth birthday in 2008 by releasing two box sets, which spanned his career. *Spirit* is an interesting three-disc accumulation of his recordings for the BBC made in the seventies. These are valuable as they examine and present material from one of the best periods of his long career. *Can You Follow* is a massive six-disc anthology that spans his entire career, 1963–2003. If you have the cash, this is the set to get as it presents just about every important track of his career.

When Ginger Baker was given a lifetime achievement award, Bruce joined him onstage one more time, which gives credence to another old saying, "If at first you don't succeed, try try again."

Bruce issued his official biography in 2009, and some of his recollections of Cream do not match Clapton's or Baker's, which should not come as a shock. He continues to tour with members of John Entwistle's band.

21

I Know I Don't Have Much to Give

Not Enough Faith

T here is an old saying about jumping from the frying pan into the fire. Eric Clapton, in a sense, jumped from the fire back into the frying pan when it came to Blind Faith.

I have always been a little amazed that Clapton became involved in another group so quickly after the demise of Cream, given his level of dissatisfaction with that group. He had become tired of being the mediator between Bruce and Baker. Also, as with the Yardbirds, he was always uncomfortable with the pop/rock side of the blues, which had pushed Cream to its immense commercial success. If you examine the Cream catalog, you will find many traditional blues songs that bear the Clapton stamp, yet there is a lot of material that strayed from the pure blues sound that always attracted the guitarist.

Enter old Powerhouse cohort Stevie Winwood, who was in the same place. He had left the Spencer Davis Group to form the critically acclaimed psychedelic rock group Traffic. That band also featured guitarist Dave Mason, drummer Jim Capaldi, and flutist/sax player Chris Wood, who would all go on to solo careers of varying success. Their 1967 release *Mr. Fantasy* is a nice reminder of the era. Wood's sax and flute work, when combined with Winwood's keyboards, created a unique sound and pushed it all in a jazz direction.

When Traffic split up, Winwood had some time to kill and started to jam on a regular basis with old friend Clapton in his basement.

Clapton was initially wary of forming

JIM SALZER PRESENTS
IN SANTA BARBARA
AT EARL WARREN SHOWGROUNDS
Saturday Eve., August 16, 1969

AUGUST
16
1969

BLIND FAITH
FESTIVAL
AT GATE $5.00 ADVANCE $4.50
NO REFUND

No. 000285 ADMIT ONE GOOD ONLY SAT. AUG. 16 GLOBE TICKET CO. 495

Blind Faith was a great live band. Their only problem was a lack of original material. *Courtesy of Robert Rodriguez*

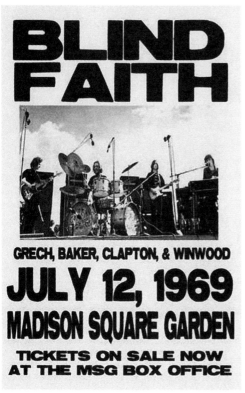

BLIND FAITH

GRECH, BAKER, CLAPTON, & WINWOOD

JULY 12, 1969

MADISON SQUARE GARDEN

TICKETS ON SALE NOW AT THE MSG BOX OFFICE

Blind Faith may not have lasted long as a band, but they were constantly on the road.
Author's collection

a new band. Ginger Baker dropped by one day and sat in with the duo. Clapton had even more reservations with Baker present. Less than three months after Cream's demise, two-thirds of the band was playing together again, and he was concerned about Jack Bruce's reaction. He was also leery of the hype that would surround the formation of another supergroup.

It was Winwood who pushed Baker and the band concept. In retrospect, Baker was a perfect drummer for Winwood as they both had always had jazz leanings in their music while Clapton was rooted in the blues.

By late spring of 1969, the band had been formed. Clapton had mentioned it was a leap of faith on his part, and so the name Blind Faith was conceived. He approached bass player Ric Grech, who he had known since his Bluesbreakers days. Grech was playing with Family at the time but quit in the middle of a tour, which did not endear him to the other band members.

Clapton's concerns about advance hype were right on, as anticipation was high when word leaked out about the band. They had not played a note but were being advertised as the second coming of Cream.

Not many bands make their debut on the same bill as the Rolling Stones, but so it was on June 7, 1969, in Hyde Park. It was also the only time Blind Faith would perform in their native country.

They went into the studio in early 1969, but the recording process became a drawn-out affair interrupted by tours of Scandinavia and the United States.

Touring before officially releasing an album caused problems, as there was not enough original Blind Faith material for a full concert. They filled in the blanks by performing old Cream and Traffic material, which pleased their fans but left Clapton unfulfilled. One of their opening acts was the white soul band Delaney and Bonnie. Clapton admired their group concept and the closeness of the members and began spending more time with them than Blind Faith. Unintentionally or not, this initiated a withdrawal from Blind Faith.

The one and only Blind Faith studio album was finally issued in June 1969. It rose to the top of the charts in both the United States and the United Kingdom and became a worldwide smash.

The original album cover proved to be extremely controversial and problematic even during the liberal atmosphere of the era. The picture of a topless young girl was unacceptable in many countries, including the United States. A new cover, which pictured the band, was quickly substituted in the United States. That their record company could initially think it would not be a problem sheds a lot of light on the mind-set of the late sixties.

This poster shows Blind Faith sharing the bill with Delaney & Bonnie, who would have a short but influential effect upon Clapton's career. *Courtesy of Robert Rodriguez*

Their self-titled album had some good points and some average ones. I have always thought that *Blind Faith* sounds better today than it did forty years ago. One of its initial problems was the comparison to Cream material, which was still being repackaged and released on a regular basis. Now it can stand on its own, and while it is not consistently excellent, there are some very good individual parts. The worst that can be said is that it remains a nice slice of late sixties rock.

The album was actually well done for a hastily assembled affair. Clapton's "Presence of the Lord" would be a part of his live act for decades. It's always interesting to compare his later vocals with Winwood's soulful style here. It's a song that lulls you until the Clapton solo in the middle jumps out and grabs your attention.

Winwood wrote three of the tracks. "Sea of Joy" contains one of his better vocal performances plus some nice acoustic guitar from E. C. "Had to Cry Today" is a rocker with several guitar bursts from Clapton.

The final tracks are a little problematic in places. "Well All Right" is an old Buddy Holly tune and never quite coalesces. "Do What You Like" is a

Tickets for the concert were $2.50–$4.50.   *Courtesy of Robert Rodriguez*

fifteen-minute Ginger Baker creation, but with "Toad" still fresh, it was a case of been there, heard that. While the drumming is still some of the best you will ever hear, it may have been used to fill out the album due to its length rather than its creativity.

The deluxe edition, in addition to the original six tracks, contained some unreleased material plus a series of extended jams, each twelve to fourteen minutes in length. The jams proved that Blind Faith did work, at least on an informal basis, and that the musicians enjoyed playing with one another, again, in an

Blind Faith did not record much material, but what was released was very commercially successful.

Author's collection

informal and unstructured environment.

If you want to examine the original concept of the band and its heart and soul, then "Slow Jam 1," "Slow Jam 2," and "Very Long and Good Jam" are good places to start. They present a laid-back and relaxed Clapton far from the expectations of the adoring crowds.

Oddly, as Blind Faith topped the U.S. charts, *Best of Cream* rose to #3, making it virtually impossible for Clapton to escape his past. The fervor for Eric Clapton and Blind Faith continued to rise.

In the middle of all this, and as Blind Faith topped the charts, Clapton joined John Lennon, Yoko Ono, Ringo Starr, and Klaus Voormann in the studio to record the single "Cold Turkey." Two months later, he joined them at a UNICEF Peace for Christmas Concert at London's Lyceum Ballroom.

The end of 1969 found Blind Faith virtually out of business. While a few tracks have surfaced over the years, including some live ones Stevie Winwood had stored away, a second album was never seriously considered, and it was a one-album-and-done career.

Clapton's feelings about Blind Faith have mellowed. "Presence of the Lord" and to a lesser extent "Can't Find My Way Home" have been an off-and-on part of his live show for years.

At the Crossroads Guitar Festival II in Bridgeview, Illinois, Winwood and Clapton reunited and performed several Blind Faith songs for the first time in nearly forty years. This led to them taking the stage for three shows in Madison Square Garden in February 2008, where Blind Faith material formed a major portion of their sets. In 2009, they toured the United States and then Europe together.

22

What'll You Do When You Get Lonely

A Little Help from His Friends

A s Blind Faith was falling apart, Eric Clapton traveled to Toronto, Canada, at the behest of John Lennon. Lennon had agreed to be an emcee at the Toronto Rock and Roll Revival Show, but at the very last minute he decided to perform.

The Plastic Ono Band took the stage September 13, 1969, with lead guitarist Eric Clapton, bassist Klaus Voormann, drummer Alan White, rhythm guitarist/vocalist John Lennon, and supporting vocalist Yoko Ono. The problem was that they did not have enough material for a set and had never played together as a unit. Nevertheless it was a historic performance.

The album, *Live Peace in Toronto 1969*, was released on December 12, 1969, and demonstrated the band made out just fine. It became a hit in the United States.

It is the disorganized nature of the first live side that gives the album its appeal. The group solved their material problem by reaching back into rock 'n' roll history. "Blue Suede Shoes," "Money (That's What I Want)," and the old Larry Williams classic "Dizzy Miss Lizzy," which had appeared on the Beatles' *Help* album, are raw, energetic, and pleasing. Eric Clapton could play material like this with one hand tied behind his back, and the album remains a charming performance for both him and Lennon.

The band moved on to the Beatles' "Yer Blues," which Lennon and Clapton had played together on the Rolling Stones' *Rock and Roll Circus*. What the attraction was to this song I'll never know, given the wealth of material at their fingertips. Lennon would play his hits of the day, "Cold Turkey" and "Give Peace a Chance," although he had to make up the lyrics on the second of the two verses as it went along, which gives another hint at his preparation. Your feelings about Yoko Ono will determine whether you stop at this point, as two of her compositions take up the entire second side of the original vinyl release.

The concert proved to be a nice stop in the careers of both Lennon and Clapton. However, Clapton was ready to move on again and was eying an association out of the limelight.

One can only imagine what Delaney and Bonnie thought when they were hired to open for Blind Faith, one of the most famous and hyped groups in the world. They probably thought that after several years of touring and producing good music, they had finally hit the big time. More surprises would quickly come for the duo.

Delaney and Bonnie had met at a bowling alley in 1967 and decided to form a band together as well as get married within a couple of weeks. They released their first album, *The Original Delaney and Bonnie—Accept No Substitutes,* in 1967, and it just snuck onto the American charts at #175.

Blind Faith was in its death throes, and Clapton was happily jamming with Delaney and Bonnie. They were everything Cream and Blind Faith was not: a hardworking band, far from the limelight, with a feel-good vibe. It was a unique experience for Clapton. In January 1970, he made the decision to join their backing band.

Delaney and Bonnie, not to mention their label, were savvy enough to name their next album *Delaney & Bonnie on Tour with Eric Clapton.* It would be the most successful of their career, reaching #39 in the United States and #29 in the United Kingdom.

It is one of my eternal musical regrets that I never saw this band live. In addition to Delaney, Bonnie, and Clapton, the tour included George Harrison, Dave Mason, bassist Carl Radle, keyboardists Leon Russell and Bobby Whitlock, drummer Jim Gordon, vocalist Rita Coolidge, and sax players Bobby Keys & Jim Price.

Clapton would step forward and take a classic solo now and then but was mostly happy to just stay in the background and blend into the mix.

Clapton has stated that Delaney Bramlett was a huge influence on his developing vocal style. He had a soulful voice that could bring tears to your eyes, while Bonnie was basically an emotional wailer. When you add in the fact that Delaney also taught George Harrison the rudiments of the slide guitar, you have a couple of accomplishments that would reverberate through music history.

On Tour contains two tracks where the old Clapton shines greatly. He cowrote "Comin' Home," and his pure guitar lines are very apparent. "I Don't Want to Discuss It" contains another one of his signature solos.

The album is still worth exploring both for its own sake and for Clapton's participation. If you want some rock 'n' roll at its best, check out "The Little Richard Medley" that closes the album. Also of note is "Poor Elijah/Tribute to Johnson Medley," where a number of guitars weave together as the vocals pay homage to the old blues master. A performance of Bessie Griffin's gospel tune "That's What My Man Is For" presents Delaney at his vocal best.

While Delaney and Bonnie post-Clapton were not as commercially successful as they were with him, they nevertheless continued to produce excellent work. *Accept No Substitute* (1969), *To Delaney from Bonnie* (1970), and *Motel Shot* (1971) remain excellent and worthwhile documents of their style.

Eric Clapton's time with Delaney and Bonnie would be short as his engines were recharged and he was ready to move on again. He left behind a positive experience of a group that worked well together.

23

When You Finally Get Back on Your Feet Again

A Lot of Help for His Friends

E ric Clapton was ready to establish his own group again but with a difference. He would be completely in charge and no more supergroups.

When he left Delaney and Bonnie, he did not go alone, as he took Jim Gordon, Carl Radle, and Bobby Whitlock with him. Guitarist Dave Mason also agreed to join him but left after one performance.

They decided to work out the kinks by touring small clubs in the United Kingdom in the summer of 1970. They took some time off to help George Harrison record his *All Things Must Pass* album, although Clapton's contributions would be uncredited. He also assisted former Delaney and Bonnie mate Leon Russell and Doris Troy on their albums. Late August found him back in the United States with his newly named Derek and the Dominos as they entered a recording studio in Miami.

There have been many unsubstantiated theories as to the origin of the Derek and the Dominos' name. Clapton was called Derek when he was with Delaney and Bonnie, and it carried over to his new band as a sort of joke. Another story was that Tony Ashton introduced Eric and His Dominos as Derek and His Dominos. A third possibility was that Clapton did not want his name on the marquee. Whatever the origin of the band name, Derek and the Dominos would go down in music history.

It was producer Tom Dowd who would become an important figure in the sound of their album and creation of the music. He was doing double duty at the time by producing *Idlewild South* for the Allman Brothers. Dowd allowed Duane Allman to sneak into the studio to watch Clapton record.

When Clapton realized Allman was in the studio, he made him retrieve his guitar, and over twelve hours of jamming began. Dowd just turned on the tape and let it run. These jams would finally see the light of day two decades later, and god bless Tom Dowd. Allman stuck around and became a fifth member of Derek and the Dominos in the studio, which gave the band and the resulting music two of the best guitarists in rock history.

If there was ever a guitarist who could match Clapton lick for lick and improvisation for improvisation, it was Duane Allman. While Cream and the Allman Brothers produced music that was worlds apart in style and sound, both of their respective guitarists fueled improvisational bands in concert. Allman was sensitive enough not to interfere or displace Clapton yet proficient enough to carve out his own territory.

Duane Allman does not appear on every track. He had some early September shows scheduled with the Allman Brothers and was away for several days while Clapton, Radle, Gordon, and Whitlock carried on alone. "I Looked Away," "Bell Bottom Blues," and "Keep on Growing" were recorded in his absence. The whole recording process took less than a month, which was very fast for a double album.

The central core of the album, and in many ways the heart and soul of Eric Clapton at the time, was the title song "Layla." He was addicted to heroin at the time and was in love with George Harrison's wife, which was not a good combination. It is a personal and tortuous love song featuring Clapton's emotional vocal. Allman's guitar introduction morphs into him and Clapton playing off each other. It was considered one of rock's greatest performances but its history and legacy did not end there. Twenty years later, it would return in a far different form when Clapton performed it on the *MTV Unplugged* concert series. It now featured an acoustic arrangement and an understated, philosophical vocal, which earned Clapton the Grammy Award for Best Rock Song of 1992. It also became a hit single in the United States.

The double album contains fourteen songs. Clapton wrote one himself and cowrote six more, five with Whitlock and one with Gordon. Whitlock also contributed two solo compositions. It all added up to more of a group effort than is often remembered.

"Tell the Truth," "Bell Bottom Blues," and Why Does Love Have to Be So Sad" are all lasting memorials to the excellence of the album. "Tell the Truth" was the standout and was brilliantly constructed as Clapton and Whitlock alternate vocals by verse and Allman contributes some signature slide guitar.

Cover songs are always interesting on any Eric Clapton album. "Key to the Highway" would become a Clapton staple. It was first recorded in the early forties. Big Bill Broonzy recorded his first version in 1941 and because he changed the lyrics received cowriting credit for the song. It was Broonzy's version that was inducted into the Blues Hall of Fame in 2010. Clapton extended it to over nine minutes and used it as a jumping-off place for him and Allman to jam together. The song was an accident as Sam Samudio of Sam the Sham and the Pharaohs was in an adjoining studio and Clapton literally stole the song upon hearing and recognizing it. Clapton began to play before Dowd was ready, which gives the track its odd beginning. Poor Sam Samudio's version was regulated to the B-side of an obscure single.

"Nobody Knows You When You're Down and Out" is an old blues song written by Jimmy Cox in 1923. It had been covered by dozens of artists before Clapton got ahold of it. Bessie Smith introduced the song to the world in 1923. Sidney Bechet and Count Basie took it in a jazz direction in the thirties and forties. LaVern Baker, Nina Simone, and Odetta all recorded it with memorable vocals. Sam Cooke and Otis Redding gave it a soul workout, while the Spencer Davis Group and the Blues Magoos rocked out on it. Liza Minnelli pushed it in a pop direction, and Tim Hardin pulled it in a folk direction. These were all setups for Clapton's precise, controlled blues interpretation. Many of these artists may have recorded the song, but Clapton brought it to life.

He just attacks "Little Wing." This song by Jimi Hendrix first appeared on his *Axis: Bold as Love* album in 1967, and *Rolling Stone* ranked it as one of the 500 Greatest Songs of All Time. Clapton is one of the few artists who can cover Hendrix and not be embarrassed.

Layla and Other Assorted Love Songs would initially only find moderate commercial success, which when combined with the state of Clapton's mind and life at the time left him depressed. It reached #16 in the United States but was almost ignored in the United Kingdom.

The album continued to sell and sell as the years passed. It recharted in the United States in 1974 and again in 1977. Today, it is recognized as a shining achievement.

After completing the album, the group embarked on a U.S. tour. Duane Allman was busy with other projects and only joined them for a couple of shows. While commercially successful, the tour was filled with drug use. Not all was lost, however, as it formed the foundation for an excellent live album.

The band convened in London to work on their second album but dissolved before it could come close to being completed. History would not be kind to the band's members as drugs, madness, estrangements, and death would plague every member of the band.

The years have seen the release of more material from Derek and the Dominos.

The first album to see the light of day was *In Concert*, which was issued in January 1973. It was a live double album recorded at the Fillmore East in

October 1970. Derek and the Dominos would finally chart in their home country, where it reached #36. Their popularity continued to be greater in the United States, where it checked in at #20.

Their live album was similar to Cream's in that they focused on extended, improvisational versions of their material and other selected songs. Nine tracks appeared on the original two-record vinyl release. Clapton has stated over the years that the original version of "Layla" was a complicated song and an extremely difficult one to play live and virtually impossible with only the basic four members who comprised the band at the time.

Less than half of the material was from their studio album, which was a good way to put the album together as it added extra appeal for their fans. One track that had appeared on *Layla* was "Have You Ever Loved a Woman," which would go on to appear on nine Clapton live albums if I have the count right.

Clapton reached back to his Delaney and Bonnie days for "Bottle of Red Wine" and a seventeen-minute version of "Let It Rain." The best tracks are the Blind Faith tune "Presence of the Lord" at a manageable six minutes and "Blues Power," which was cowritten with Leon Russell and at ten minutes contains some powerful guitar.

In Concert only features the four core musicians, so it allows Clapton's guitar playing to shine. The album makes one realize what a fine vehicle Derek and the Dominos was for Eric Clapton and how regrettable that it did not last very long.

It would be seventeen years before another Derek and the Dominos album would be released. The occasion was *The Layla Sessions: 20th Anniversary Edition*. It was released in September 1990, at a time when the original album was held in very high esteem.

It was well worth the wait as it clocked in at 218 minutes. The highlight of the three-disc set was the five Clapton/Allman jams, which take up the entire second disc. They remain a good look into the minds and skills of two supreme guitarists who were relaxed and just enjoying one another in a casual setting. They did not realize at the time that these jams together would ever be released commercially, which is part of the charm. They can be a little exhausting but ultimately leave you wanting more.

The third disc contains alternate and unreleased material. The most interesting is "Mean Old World," which first appears at a rehearsal, then with a full band, and finally as a duet. It is an enlightening look into the evolution of a song under Clapton's direction. The first disc covers the band's well-known studio material. If you have not explored this part of Clapton's career or want to delve a little deeper, this is the set for you.

The final Derek and the Dominos release came in 1994. *Live at the Fillmore* is another double album that was taken from their performances at the Fillmore East in October 1970. Some of the material had been released on their first live album, but included here are some different performances.

There is not much new here, but some of the old is covered well. The final four tracks—"Presence of the Lord" (6:16); "Little Wing" (7:00); "Let It Rain" (19:46); and the venerable "Crossroads" (8:29)—are a nice way to spend forty minutes and appreciate the essence of the band.

The album effectively closed the career of Derek and the Dominos, and given the history of its members, there is no hope for a reunion.

24

I Tried to Give You Some Consolation

Whatever Happened To

Steve Winwood

S teve Winwood's career has followed a similar path to that of Eric Clapton. He has participated in several successful bands but in the long run has flourished as a solo artist.

He may not have been as grounded in the blues as Clapton as he received his early training as a member of the Spencer Davis Group.

Davis formed the group in 1963 with himself on guitar, drummer Pete York, bassist Muff Winwood, and his fifteen-year-old brother Stevie as the keyboardist/vocalist/guitarist.

They quickly produced a series of hit singles in their home country. "Keep on Running" (#1), "Somebody Help Me," (#1), "Gimme Some Lovin'" (#2), and "I'm a Man" (#9) all helped to make them one of the more popular bands in the United Kingdom. They were not as popular in the United States, but "I'm a Man" and "Gimme Some Lovin'" both went top ten in 1966, and 1967. It all added up to Winwood being a star before the age of twenty, and in the spring of 1967, he left the band in search of further adventures.

He would find himself as a part of one of the most creative bands of the late sixties and early seventies. Guitarists Dave Mason, flutist/sax player Chris Wood, and drummer Jim Capaldi joined with Winwood to form Traffic.

Traffic was an English psychedelic rock band that caught the fancy of the American record-buying public. Albums such as *John Barleycorn Must Die, The Low Spark of High Heeled Boys,* and *When the Eagle Flies* all reached the American top ten, and they had four more enter the top thirty between 1968 and 1974, interrupted only by Winwood's short stint in Blind Faith. He

STEREO
ATCO 33 326

DELANEY & BONNIE
& FRIENDS
ON TOUR
WITH ERIC CLAPTON

Clapton's time as a part of Delaney & Bonnie's band made him one of the most well known sidemen in music history.   *Author's collection*

and Capaldi reunited in the early '90s and released the well-received and commercially successful *Far from Home* in 1994.

Winwood's self-titled solo album became a hit on both sides of the Atlantic, but it was only a taste of the popularity that would be his during the decade to come. The 1980s pushed him in a pop/rock direction and to huge commercial success. In late 1979, he began to record *Arc of a Diver*. He ended up playing every instrument himself in addition to supplying the vocals.

It took over two years to put together, but the wait was worth it as it would become his breakthrough album, especially in the United States, where it would top out at #3 and produce the top ten single "While You See a Chance." He continued his strategy of playing every instrument and reached the top ten in the United Kingdom.

In 1983, Winwood participated in a charity concert at London's Royal Albert Hall for the benefit of Faces member Ronnie Lane, who was suffering from multiple sclerosis. He joined the former Yardbirds trio of guitarists Eric Clapton, Jimmy Page, and Jeff Beck onstage and accompanied them on a very short tour of the United States.

He released *Back in the High Life* in 1986. It was a smooth piece of pop/rock and won the Grammy Award for Record of the Year and Best Pop Vocal Performance. The single "Higher Love" topped the American singles charts in August 1986.

By the end of 1987, Winwood was firmly entrenched on top of the pop/rock world and signed a new recording contract worth over $12 million, and this was before ever playing a note. The money was well spent by his record label as his next album *Roll with It* topped the *Billboard* album top 200 album charts, and the title song topped the singles charts as well.

He has continued to record through the nineties and into the new millennium. Like his former bandmate Eric Clapton, he has been a constant guest on many albums and in concerts for friends and acquaintances.

He and Clapton appeared together in the film *Blues Brothers 2000* as the Louisiana Gator Band. In July 2007, he guested at Clapton's Crossroads Guitar Festival, which renewed their relationship. They went on to play three sold-out concerts together at Madison Square Garden in February 2009 and then to tour during the summer of that year.

Now in his early sixties, Winwood is the most successful of Clapton's old bandmates. The best retrospective of his career is *The Finer Things*, which includes most of his import milestones from his days with the Spencer Davis Group through 1995.

Ric Grech

Ric Grech was doing fine as the bass player for the group Family until Eric Clapton and Steve Winwood came a-knocking. He had jammed with both back in the early sixties and had made a lasting impression, and so when they needed a bass player in their new band, he was the man.

While Family had released several albums that received positive reviews, their mainline commercial success was moderate at best. Grech jumped at the opportunity to join one of the biggest bands in the world and quit Family right in the middle of a tour, which antagonized the other members. He thus became the lesser light in the supergroup Blind Faith. Who was the fourth member of Blind Faith is a good rock trivia question today.

Grech's time in the limelight was brief as Blind Faith quickly fell apart, which initiated Grech's musical odyssey. He followed Ginger Baker into

Another of the over 100 singles that Clapton was a part of during his career.   *Author's collection*

Air Force as their bass player, and then it was on to the reformed Traffic. He played on their *Welcome to the Canteen* and *The Low Spark of High Heeled Boys* albums. His time with the band came to an abrupt end when he was fired for drug use and alcoholism.

Grech moved into session work with time out in 1973 to play at Eric Clapton's Rainbow Concert, which Pete Townshend had organized to help Clapton with his drug problems. The irony seemed lost on Grech.

His final chance at stardom came as a member of KGM with another guitarist deluxe, Mike Bloomfield, plus keyboardist Barry Goldberg, drummer Carmen Appice, and vocalist Ray Kennedy. Bloomfield, whose addictions were legendary, quit after one album, and Grech quickly followed.

He retired from the music industry in 1977. He died in 1990 at the age of forty-three of kidney and liver failure as a result of years of alcohol abuse.

Delaney Bramlett

My favorite fact about Delaney Bramlett is that he was a member of the Shindogs, the house band on the television show *Shindig*. He was in good company, as Glen Campbell, Billy Preston, James Burton, Larry Knetchel, and Leon Russell were also members at one time or another.

Bramlett's union both professionally and personally with Bonnie Bramlett began in a bowling alley where the Shindogs were performing. Bonnie was present, and a band and marriage quickly followed. They fronted a hardworking band that included many members who would go on to distinguished careers. Delaney and Bonnie always produced excellent albums, but it was their association with Eric Clapton that increased their popularity to heights they could not have imagined even a few months before Clapton's inclusion.

It was a good ride while it lasted, but by 1973, Eric Clapton was long gone, and so were Bonnie and the band. Delaney's popularity faded, but he could always attract top musicians to contribute to his solo albums. His 1977 release, *Class Reunion*, featured Eric Clapton, George Harrison, Leon Russell, Billy Preston, and Ringo Starr.

One of his last performances was a duet with Jerry Lee Lewis on his 2006 release, *Last Man Standing*. He issued his last studio album, *A New Kind of Blues,* in 2008 before passing away December 27 of that year. His final resting place is Forest Lawn Memorial Cemetery in Los Angeles.

Delaney & Bonnie were a hardworking band with middling commercial success. That all changed when Clapton joined and brought along a friend or two.
Courtesy of Robert Rodriguez

Bonnie Bramlett

An interesting fact about Bonnie Bramlett is that she was the first white female to be a member of the Ikettes, Ike and Tina Turner's backing vocal group.

After splitting with Delaney, she continued on with a solo career, releasing eight albums between 1973 and 2005. She also began acting in films and television. She has appeared in such films as *Vanishing Point, The Doors,* and *Wild Hogs* in addition to being a semiregular on the *Roseanne* television show from 1991 to 1992. Now in her mid-sixties, she continues to be active as a session vocalist.

Bobby Whitlock

Bobby Whitlock was born in one of the centers of rhythm and blues country, Memphis, Tennessee. At a young age, he formed associations with some of the artists signed to the Stax label. By the age of twenty-one, he was playing keyboards for Delaney and Bonnie.

He was introduced to Eric Clapton on their famous tour together and upon its conclusion immediately joined Derek and the Dominos. He accompanied Clapton into the studio with George Harrison and played

Derek and the Dominos are a sometimes-underrated stop in the career of Eric Clapton.   *Author's collection*

uncredited on the legendary *All Things Must Pass* album.

Whitlock was a major contributor to the group's only studio album, writing or cowriting half a dozen tracks in addition to supplying the keyboards. He probably took the Dominos' split the hardest and had little contact professionally or personally with Clapton for decades.

His first self-titled album was released in April 1972 and includes all the members of Derek and the Dominos (except Duane Allman), plus such luminaries as George Harrison, Klaus Voormann, Bobby Keys, and Chris

The singles just kept on coming for Eric Clapton and company. *Author's collection*

Wood. There have been conflicting reports as to when this album was actually recorded, but given his lingering animosity toward Clapton, it was probably prior to the group's breakup. Also given the Harrison/Voormann involvement, I am guessing it was recorded around the time of their *All Things Must Pass* participation.

Whitlock released a second solo album, *Raw Velvet,* with little fanfare or commercial success. He finally settled in Ireland, where this transplanted American southerner had his own television program for a spell. Two more studio albums followed, but reaching the end of his commercial viability, he moved back to the United States, lived on a farm in Mississippi, and become an in-demand session player for years.

He released his first new solo album in decades in 1999 with *It's About Time.* He continued to be active during the last decade, releasing *Love Songs, Live from Whitney Chapel* (with CoCo Carmel), *Lovers, Vintage, My Time,* and *Metamorphosis.*

Whitlock finally made an appearance with Eric Clapton on the BBC's *Jools Holland Show* in 2000. His autobiography is due in 2010, and Eric Clapton wrote the foreword. He continues to tour with his wife CoCo Carmel.

Carl Radle

Carl Radle made an inauspicious music debut as a part of Gary Lewis and the Playboys, who had a number of popular but lightweight pop hits during the 1960s.

His association with Eric Clapton began as a part of Delaney and Bonnie, continued with the formation of Derek and the Dominos, and as a member of his own band until 1979. He is even listed as a producer for the *No Reason to Cry* album. He also joined Clapton and George Harrison onstage for *The Concert for Bangladesh.*

Radle's career and association with Eric Clapton was cut short when he died of a kidney infection on May 30, 1980.

Jim Gordon

Jim Gordon was one of the legendary session drummers in rock history and one of its most tragic figures.

At the age of seventeen, he was on tour with the Everly Brothers. He has appeared on dozens and dozens of albums by the elite of rock 'n' roll including the Beach Boys, the Byrds, the Beau Brummels, George Harrison, Gene Clark, Nilsson, and Frank Zappa. By the end of the decade, he was

DEREK AND THE DOMINOS   ATCO RECORDS

Eric Clapton   Bobby Whitlock   Jim Gordon   Carl Radle

The story of Jim Gordon is one of the most tragic in music history.

Courtesy of Robert Rodriguez

"Layla" would make the charts twice in very different versions.
Author's collection

touring with Delaney and Bonnie. He was not Clapton's first choice as the drummer for his new group, but with Jim Keltner unavailable, he was the final choice. During his short tenure with the Dominos, he cowrote "Layla" with Clapton.

Other notable appearances by Gordon included Joe Cocker's *Mad Dogs and Englishmen* tour with former Delaney and Bonnie bandmates Leon Russell and Rita Coolidge, Frank Zappa's *Grand Wazoo Big Band* tour, and a stint with Steely Dan on their *Pretzel Logic* tour. From 1973 to 1975, he was the drummer for the Souther-Hillman-Furay Band.

During the seventies, he began hearing voices, which was attributed to alcoholism. It turned out he was an undiagnosed and unmedicated schizophrenic. This condition resulted in the killing of his mother with a hammer on June 3, 1983. Convicted of second-degree murder, he was sentenced to sixteen years to life in prison in 1984. All pleas for parole have been denied.

In 1992 "Layla" won the Grammy for Best Rock Song. *Rolling Stone* ranked it at #27 on their list of the 500 Greatest Songs of All Time. Gordon continues to collect royalties from it and his other work.

Duane Allman

Duane and his brother Gregg went through a number of musical incarnations before the Allman Brothers were formed. The Kings, the House

Rockers, the Schufflers, the Allman Joys, and Hour Glass, who issued albums for the Liberty label, all came and went during the early part of their careers. Hour Glass even supported Eric Burdon and the Animals at the Fillmore West.

The newly named Allman Brothers signed a contact with Capricorn Records in 1969. Their debut album slipped onto the American charts in February 1970, at #188.

Duane Allman also became a noted session guitarist. One of the better examples of his work can be found on *Games People Play* by King Curtis, which won the Grammy for Best Rhythm & Blues Instrumental Performance.

Allman's prowess as a guitarist grew quickly, which brought him to the attention of Eric Clapton and the invite to participate in his Derek and the Dominos project.

The Allman Brothers quickly climbed the ladder of rock's elite. The combination of the dual lead guitars of Allman and Dickey Betts, mixed with the dual drumming of Jaimoe Johanson and Butch Trucks, made the band unique and powerful and the finest example of what became known as Southern Rock. *Idlewild South* and *At the Fillmore East* were commercial breakthroughs for the band.

The Allman Brothers and Duane Allman were known for their legendary live jams. Just when you thought a song was coming to a conclusion, Duane would take off in a new direction. He was one of the few guitarists who could match Eric Clapton in the studio and onstage.

He became one of the great what-ifs in rock history when he was killed in a motorcycle accident on October 29, 1971. *Eat a Peach*, with the final three studio performances of his career, reached #4 in the United States.

Howard Duane Allman has been resting in Reese Hill Cemetery, Macon, Georgia, for the past forty-two years.

25

I Swear It Was Self Defense

Surviving the Seventies

Sometimes the gods smile on people. Eric Clapton's addictions were no worse and no better than many of his contemporaries who would die young. Today, his health seems to be fine and his skills undiminished. The thought of his ever reaching retirement age in the seventies was a long shot at best.

He and others have extensively chronicled Clapton's heroin addiction. The talk began to surface with Cream, and by the time Derek and the Dominos disbanded had become full blown. Their tours were awash in drugs, and when combined with his depression over the death of Jimi Hendrix, his yearnings for George Harrison's wife, and his dissatisfactions with the band, it all added up to a potentially lethal situation.

The difference between immortality and becoming a footnote in history many times is survival, and survive Clapton did. He would emerge from the seventies with new respect, greater fame, and an enlarged body of work.

Clapton had been a constant on the music scene for nearly a decade, first with the Yardbirds, then John Mayall's Bluesbreakers, Cream, Blind Faith, Delaney and Bonnie, and finally Derek and the Dominos. He now became less visible and at times virtually disappeared.

One fact that is often overlooked is that he was still only twenty-seven years old. He had been a recognized superstar since he was in his early twenties, with money, fame, and adulation but little supervision and control. In the sports and entertainment world, those situations have been recipes for disaster.

Eric Clapton (Solo Album)

In the midst of all this, his first solo album was released in August 1970, four years before his second. It was for the most part Clapton fronting the

Whether he was in a band or solo, Eric Clapton has always
toured extensively.   *Author's collection*

Delaney and Bonnie Band, with the Bramletts also lending their writing
skills.

Delaney Bramlett produced the album, and present bandmates Leon
Russell, Jim Price, Bobby Keys, and Rita Coolidge joined future bandmates
Carl Radle, Jim Gordon, and Bobby Whitlock.

Clapton would increasingly attract quality guest musicians to his solo
projects and likewise would appear on innumerable side projects himself.
Stephen Stills is credited here, as are Crickets Sonny Curtis and Jerry
Allison.

Clapton's self-titled debut remains not only an excellent outing but an
interesting one as well, as it catches him at one of the crossroads of his
career.

The album was recorded from November 1969, when he was still an
active member of Delaney and Bonnie, through January 1970. There is now
little doubt who was in charge. He may have disappeared while playing with
them in concert, but now he steps forward. The Bramletts cowrote seven of
the eleven tracks, but two of my three favorites are ones they did not write.

J. J. Cale's "After Midnight" remains one of Clapton's signature songs
and is representative of a lot of what would follow later in his career. The

bluesy vocal and the laid-back approach would serve him well for decades. "Blues Power," which was coauthored with Leon Russell, is wonderfully constructed, and Clapton gives a powerful performance using his backing band as support. "Let It Rain" is a short guitar clinic. The solos are precise and are a demonstration that short can indeed be good.

There were some other fine performances. "Easy Now" is a nice acoustic ballad and is the best of the rest. "Bottle of Red Wine" is a rocker, which in this case has an all-too-brief guitar solo. The rest is not bad, just different, as some of the Delaney and Bonnie compositions take him out of his comfort zone.

In its original form, it remains an interesting if sometimes forgotten album in Clapton's long career and extensive catalog. It served the purpose of preparing him for a solo career and proved he could assemble a credible solo release.

If you really want to explore this early solo album, track down the deluxe edition.

This was an album that was extensively bootlegged back in the day. It seems there were three different mixes, and the Eric Clapton mix was the preferred bootleg copy.

The first disc of the deluxe edition is the Tom Dowd mix and includes the original album plus extra tracks such as "Teasin'" with King Curtis plus "She Rides," which uses the "Let It Rain" backing track with different vocals.

Disc two is titled the "Delaney Bramlett mix," and his presentation of the original album pales next to Dowd's. Bonus tracks here are unreleased versions of "Don't Know Why" and "I've Told You for the Last Time." The final two tracks were the A- and B-sides of their December 1969 single "Comin' Home"/"Groupie (Superstar)." Bonnie Bramlett and Leon Russell wrote the B-side, and when hearing it, one would assume it would quietly disappear into music history. The Carpenters of all people would hear something they liked in it, renamed it "Superstar," issued it as a single, and took it to the #2 position in the United States in 1971.

It would have been interesting to hear Clapton's own mix beside the other two, but it was left to the bootleggers at the time.

All Things Must Pass

Clapton may not have been well, but he supported friend George Harrison in the recording studio May–September 1970. The result was Harrison's post-Beatles coming-out party. *All Things Must Pass* is one of the grand achievements in rock history, selling six million copies in the United States alone, which was extraordinary for a triple album. It topped the U.S. charts for seven weeks and the U.K. for eight. It reached the #1 position in such countries as Australia, Italy, Norway, and Canada.

George Harrison was a premier guitarist himself, but when he added Eric Clapton to the mix, it took the musicianship to the next level. Clapton would go uncredited on the U.K. release, but his name does appear on the U.S. issue.

The songs on the first four sides such as "My Sweet Lord," "Wah-Wah," "Isn't It a Pity," "What Is Life," and "All Things Must Pass" have gone down in music history, sides five and six of the original release are often overlooked and underplayed. They are comprised of a series of jams that Eric Clapton was so good at initiating. As good as Clapton is, it is these informal and relaxed settings that seem to have brought out the best in him.

"Out of the Blue" (11:14), "Plug Me In" (3:18), "I Remember Jeep" (8:07), which was named after Clapton's missing dog, and "Thanks for the Pepperoni (5:31) are all Clapton driven.

"Thanks for the Pepperoni" remains my favorite and features the original Dominos with Dave Mason plus Harrison. "I Remember Jeep" features Harrison's sidekicks Klaus Voormann and Billy Preston plus two-thirds of Cream, as Ginger Baker was in the house. "Out of the Blues" included some horns, which get in the way at times. "Plug Me In" is the shortest and most structured of the lot, with just the Dominos and Harrison again.

The Concert for Bangladesh

He would do one more favor for George before withdrawing from the music scene for over a year and a half. He would join him onstage August 1, 1971, at Madison Square Garden for what has become known as the *Concert for Bangladesh.*

It was Clapton's first live performance in four months. His heroin addiction had gotten so bad that he was unable to attend any of the rehearsals except for a final sound check.

Harrison's band consisted of drummers Jim Keltner and Ringo Starr, keyboardists Bobby Whitlock and Billy Preston, guitarists Eric Clapton and Jesse Ed Davis, bassist Carl Radle, the Apple label-recording group Badfinger, a horn section, and an array of backing singers.

The concert and resulting album have long been a part of the musical landscape, but at the time it was an event of the highest order. Harrison was an ex-Beatle who had been the least known of the four until the release of *All Things Must Pass,* which had been a revelation. This combined with his enticing Bob Dylan to appear made it an anticipated and much-hyped event.

Clapton's performance was for the most part anticlimactic. A number of musicians stepped forward for solos, but he was mainly content to be a part of the band. He did play the lead on "While My Guitar Gently Weeps." It would add to his legend as many fans did not realize he had played the solo on the original.

A lost Clapton performance surfaced on the 2005 deluxe edition as a DVD extra. The old Robert Johnson tune "Come On in My Kitchen" featured Harrison's lead to Clapton's rhythm part with a Leon Russell vocal.

Following the concert, he returned to the road with Derek and the Dominos and in his spare time entered the studio with Dr. John and Harrison to assist on their new albums. He also joined blues legend Howlin' Wolf for his *London Sessions*. He finished 1971 by joining Leon Russell onstage at the Royal Albert Hall in London.

People today remember records and cassettes, but 8-tracks are largely forgotten.   *Author's collection*

The next found him among the missing. His addictions had worsened, and he withdrew from the music world.

The History of Eric Clapton

He may have been out of sight, but he was not out of mind. That was doubly true of his label, as they began releasing just about any Clapton material they could get their hands on.

The History of Eric Clapton was issued in March 1972 and presented a short overview of his career 1964–1970. This double album served the dual purpose of making money for all concerned and keeping Clapton in the public's consciousness. It was a commercial success, reaching #6 in the United Kingdom and #20 in the United States.

The album finally made one of his most famous songs a hit. "Layla" was initially released in late 1970 but only reached #51 in the United States and did not even chart in Great Britain. It now reached the top ten on both sides of the Atlantic.

While most of the tracks were familiar, there were some interesting inclusions. "I Ain't Got You" by the Yardbirds was an odd choice but worked well as it was a nice introduction to the early Eric Clapton. "I Want to Know" by the Powerhouse was a rare find back in 1972.

There are two versions of "Tell the Truth," which were presented back to back on side four. The first is the up-tempo single that was released in July 1970. The second was a previously unreleased nine-minute jam. It was a slow and smoldering rendition. I would have liked to have seen the third version included as well. The version contained on *Layla and Other Assorted Love Songs* was a combination of the two.

I also appreciated the four-song section of Cream's "Sunshine of Your Love," "Crossroads," the sixteen-minute "Spoonful," and "Badge." If you are a Clapton fan, it doesn't get much better than that.

The jacket featured Clapton playing "While My Guitar Gently Weeps" at *The Concert for Bangladesh* on his Gibson Byrdland guitar.

Eric Clapton at His Best

Not content with just one compilation album, Polydor issued the four-sided *Eric Clapton at His Best* in September 1972. This album was less satisfying and less commercially successful than its predecessor. However, just reaching #87 in the United States proved there were fans who would buy just about anything issued under the Clapton banner.

The album did not contain any Cream tracks, as *Heavy Cream* had been released at the same time. Instead, it focused on Clapton's work with Blind Faith, Delaney and Bonnie, Derek and the Dominos, and his solo album. The material was just too new and readily available to give the album a broad appeal.

Eric Clapton's Rainbow Concert

There are interventions, and then there are interventions. Pete Townshend of the Who organized one of the grandest, most elaborate interventions of all time. He enticed Clapton to join him and some selected friends onstage January 13, 1973, at London's Rainbow Theatre. It would mark the start, and let me emphasize start, of Clapton's professional comeback.

Guitarist Ronnie Wood, bassist Ric Grech, keyboardist Steve Winwood, and drummers Jim Capaldi and Rebop Kwaku Baah joined Clapton and Townshend. The resulting album, *Eric Clapton's Rainbow Concert,* was released September 10, 1973, and reached the top ten in the United States and the United Kingdom.

This is another album I played to death when it was released, but in retrospect it was a modest affair and only scratched the surface of what had taken place onstage. At the time, however, ignorance was bliss.

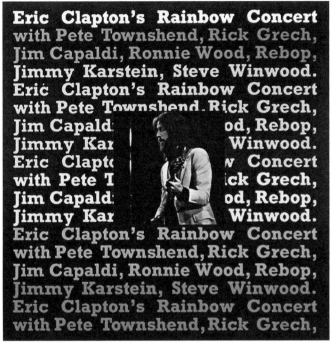

Clapton's friends staged a concert to help him with his addictions.   *Author's collection*

Six tracks were released on the original vinyl album and ranged in length from 3:32 to 7:00. They are a good listen but were picked somewhat at random and do not present continuous concert feel or experience.

"Badge" is the shortest and most controlled track at three and a half minutes but only gives a taste of the band's talents. It is not until the Clapton/Whitlock composition "Roll It Over" and his own "Presence of the Lord" that Clapton, Townshend, and Wood begin to heat up. The Traffic song from their self-titled 1968 album, "Pearly Gates," is more a Winwood piece. The last two tracks, "After Midnight" and "Little Wing," get to the heart of the matter as far as Mr. Clapton is concerned as he steps more into the limelight.

The 1995 remastered edition is a much better release. It has a complete concert feel and contains fourteen tracks: 1) "Layla" (6:25); 2) "Badge" (3:18); 3) "Blues Power" (6:03); 4) "Roll It Over" (4:38); 5) "Little Wing" (4:36); 6) "Bottle of Red Wine" (3:51); 7) "After Midnight" (4:25); 8) "Bell Bottom Blues" (6:25); 9) "Presence of the Lord" (5:18); 10) "Tell the Truth" (6:04); 11) "Pretty Queen" (4:55); 12) "Key to the Highway" (5:46); 13) "Let It Rain" (7:46); 14) "Crossroads" (4:19). And that, my friends, is a concert.

Townshend's motives were pure, and while he did induce Clapton to emerge from hiding and back onstage, Clapton quickly disappeared again. It was not until November 1973 that he participated in a supervised program to kick his heroin addiction, and it was not until April 1974 that he felt well enough to become active again.

He began his real comeback by putting together a new backing band of drummer Jamie Oldaker, keyboardist Dick Sims, guitarist George Terry, old friend Carl Radle on bass, plus singers Yvonne Elliman and Marcy Levy. These musicians would be his basic band until the end of the decade. They would also be representative of how he would record and tour the rest of his career. He was a part of his own band and the unquestioned leader.

461 Ocean Boulevard

461 Ocean Boulevard represented the first fruits of his comeback and was released in July 1974. The album was produced by Clapton and Tom Dowd, who had worked together successfully in the past. The album was ranked #409 on *Rolling Stone*'s list of the 500 Greatest Albums of All Time.

It is an album that has grown on me over the years. When it was released, it was immediately compared to his past work and found not living up to his legacy. It was not a Cream regurgitation, as it was far removed from their sound. I, and a lot of music fans, considered it too mellow.

I now consider it one of Clapton's stronger solo albums. It is still a laid-back affair with little of the jamming that had made him famous, yet his signature guitar sound is recognizable throughout. Clapton seems relaxed and in control. The vocals show a confidence that would sustain him through dozens of albums. It turned out to be one of his more successful albums and is one of only two solo releases to reach the #1 position in the United States.

Its most famous song, and one of the most enduring of his career, was his cover of Bob Marley's "I Shot the Sheriff." It received massive airplay during the summer of 1974 and ascended to the top of the single charts in the United States.

I was living in Rhode Island at the time, and there was a local Sunday morning radio personality who began his show each week with this song. Complaints poured in week after week to no avail. The song was the perfect combination of rock and reggae, which coalesced into a feast of sound.

There were a number of other strong performances. The 1958 Johnny Otis dance hit "Willie and the Hand Jive" is given a fun-filled workout that was close to the spirit of the original. If you want to see the hand jive performed, check out the movie *Grease*. "Mainline Florida" contains

This "Layla" picture sleeve from Japan demonstrates Clapton's ongoing international appeal.   *Author's collection*

layers of guitars and keyboards. "Let It Grow" demonstrated Clapton's growth as a songwriter and is notable for the fine vocal work by Yvonne Elliman. You can't have a Clapton album without some traditional blues. Robert Johnson's "Steady Rollin' Man" and Elmore James's "I Can' Hold Out" are given respectable workouts.

461 Ocean Boulevard has held up well over the years as it catches a still young Eric Clapton establishing himself as a solo artist. It is still worth seeking out.

He would solidify his comeback with a live performance at the Hammersmith Odeon in London before leaving for a tour of Japan.

There's One in Every Crowd

All was not well, however, as a growing alcohol problem was rearing its ugly head. It was with this handicap that Clapton headed to Jamaica to record his follow-up to *461 Ocean Boulevard*. *There's One in Every Crowd* was issued in March 1975, eight months after his last release.

It would be an extension of his previous album without the huge hit song and ultimately without the overwhelming commercial success. It reached #21 in the United States and #15 in the United Kingdom. The traditional "Swing Low Sweet Chariot" was the lead single, and while it had some success in his home country at #19, it did not chart in the United States. Without any single reaching the chart, the album had a difficult commercial road to travel in the States.

There's One in Every Crowd is one of the more mundane solo efforts of his career. Sometimes I think I remember the dog on the cover better than I remember the music. It is never a good sign when my old vinyl copy looks like it was never played.

There's nothing truly bad about the album but nothing truly memorable either. It is an eclectic group of songs ranging from blues to gospel to reggae to rock, but all of it falls into the mellow category. Many of the songs just don't stay with you. "We've Been Told (Jesus Is Coming)" and "Swing Low, Sweet Chariot" are both smooth and have a gospel feeling. The best track is probably the Elmore James blues song "The Sky Is Crying," on which Clapton provides a few short bursts of his guitar proficiency. He wrote the final four songs, and while none stand out, at least "Pretty Blues Eyes" has some gentle acoustic playing.

There's One in Every Crowd pales when compared to a lot of his solo work. If you are going to explore his music, this is probably not the place to start.

I still like the dog, however!

E. C. Was Here

Clapton would live with his alcohol problems during this period of his life with constant touring and recording.

The first of his live albums appeared in August 1975, having been recorded July 19–20, at the Long Beach Arena in California; December 4, 1975, at the Hammersmith Odeon; and June 25, 1975, at the Providence Civic Center in Rhode Island. This piecemeal approach meant that while it would be a live album, it would not be a concert album.

E. C. Was Here was another average release and quickly became obsolete. Its importance today is as a document for the band that served him so well during the late seventies. Especially of note are supporting vocalists Marcy Levy and Yvonne Elliman, who both had the talent to also have successful solo careers. They added a unique dimension to his sound that would be missed after their departure.

I have two major complaints about this release. The first is while Clapton is listed as the lead guitarist and George Terry as the rhythm guitarist, all too often they switch places. Terry is more than a competent guitar player, but when I purchase a Clapton album, especially a live one, I do not want George Terry to take the lead.

The second problem was the choice of material. There was nothing really unusual or challenging. Interestingly, there was only composition by Clapton.

"Have You Ever Loved a Woman" (7:49) and "Presence of the Lord" (6:46) had been overdone at the time. "Can't Find My Way Home" (5:18) is a Steve Winwood composition. The best three tracks were "Drifting Blues" (11:30), "Ramblin' on My Mind" (7:38), and "Further on up the Road" (7:30), but even on these where their length should have been to his benefit, Clapton hangs back.

The album's real positive was its commercial success as it reached #14 and #20 in the United Kingdom and United States respectively, again proving that his fan base was insatiable.

No Reason to Cry

Clapton continued his prolific output with his release of *No Reason to Cry* in August 1976. It was a competent album bordering on very good but decades later slips under the radar. In hindsight, it also suffers from the fact that it preceded one of the stronger releases of his career.

Clapton always enjoyed working with other artists. Here he partners with several members of the Band and Mr. Bob Dylan himself, and while the results did not break any new ground, at least they retain your attention.

The Band tracks pushed him away from his British blues roots. "Beautiful Thing," written by Richard Manuel and Rick Danko, is American music (by way of Canada) at its best and contains some strong vocal work by Marcy Levy. "All Our Past Times" finds him duetting with Danko. While the track is enjoyable, a live performance would appear later that was superior to this studio version.

Bob Dylan's "Sigh Language" was unreleased at the time it appeared on this album. While it may now be relegated to the pile of average Dylan tunes today, this duet remains earnest and charming.

Clapton is on more solid ground when he is on his own. "Country Jail Blues" has some nice slide guitar straight out of the Delta and leaves you wanting more. "Double Trouble" is another return to his blues roots. "Hello Old Friend" is probably the overall best track as it fused rock and blues. It was wisely chosen as the lead single and became a top thirty hit in the United States.

No Reason to Cry is a quick and quiet album that was a fun project for Clapton, but its lasting impact is negligible.

The Last Waltz

Clapton continued to be a road warrior in 1976 and on Thanksgiving night performed at one of the legendary concerts in rock history. *The Last Waltz* was the Band's farewell live show, and they were joined by an array of friends. The accompanying film by Martin Scorsese would receive critical acclaim as well. Clapton shared the stage with Paul Butterfield, Neil Diamond, Emmylou Harris, Muddy Waters, Neil Young, Van Morrison, Bob Dylan, and others.

He performed "Further on up the Road," which had been a hit for Bobby "Blue" Bland in 1957. It is a basic 12-bar blues piece that Clapton could play in his sleep. Clapton tended to speed up the tempo on this song, which was first heard on *E. C. Was Here*. It would become a staple of his live show and reappear on *Just One Night* and again on *The Secret Policeman's Other Ball* with Jeff Beck.

Slowhand

By 1977, Clapton was running close to the edge of exhaustion and alcoholism. At an April 30th performance at the Rainbow Theatre, he took a ten-minute break in the middle of the show because he was unable to continue. He made it to the end of the tour, but his battle with the bottle continued.

Problems may have been present, but they did not prevent him from entering the studio to create a truly wonderful album. *Slowhand* was released in November 1977 to critical acclaim and huge commercial success. *Rolling Stone* ranked it as one of the 500 Greatest Albums of All Time. It spent five weeks in the #2 position in the United States. The soundtrack to the film *Saturday Night Fever* kept it and a lot of albums from the top spot during its twenty-four weeks at #1. Even *Saturday Night Fever's* run would pale next to Fleetwood Mac's thirty-one weeks at the top in 1977.

The decision to have Glyn Johns produce the album was an inspired one. He was a veteran of the producing wars and would continue to be so for decades after *Slowhand*. He would not be intimidated, and the album reflected his skills. He had worked with dozens of rock music's superstars including Bob Dylan, the Rolling Stones, the Who, Led Zeppelin, Eagles, Fairport Convention, and the list goes on and on.

Slowhand was a breath of fresh air after the two laid-back and somewhat lackluster efforts that preceded it. If I had to pick my ten favorite

One of Clapton's biggest hits and one of his signature solo performances.   *Author's collection*

Clapton songs of his solo career, the first three tracks of this album would make the list.

Clapton finally stepped forward again and put his guitar front and center. Whether this was a decision by Glyn Johns or Clapton does not really matter, as fans breathed a sigh of relief and welcomed him back.

The song "Cocaine" begins the album on a ringing note. Great chords and riffs by Clapton on this antidrug song (at least according to Clapton). J. J. Cale wrote the song in 1976, and some of the original lyrics sound very drug related. The antidrug message is found more in the ominous sound, which when combined with Clapton's personal history is chilling. He would later insert the word "dirty" before "cocaine" in order to make the message clearer. It remains one of rock's great performances.

"Wonderful Tonight" takes the listener in a different direction. This gentle ballad was written for the love of his life, Pattie Boyd. More about Pattie later. The vocal is sincere, and it remains a very personal performance.

"Lay Down Sally" was a #3 singles hit in the United States. It is about as country as Clapton gets, with a shuffle or staccato guitar beat. Marcy Levy cowrote the song and provides some memorable vocals.

The delights extend beyond the first three tracks. "The Core," also written with Marcy Levy, checks in at close to nine minutes. Longer Clapton studio tracks are always interesting in that they have a jam feel but more often are well thought out. It also has the benefit of being a Clapton/Levy duet. Arthur Crudup's "Mean Old Frisco" is a blues tune that allows Clapton to demonstrate some effective slide guitar techniques. "We're All the Way," penned by Don Williams, is another foray into country music.

Slowhand was a masterpiece when it was released and remains one today. For anyone interested in the solo work of Eric Clapton, it all flows through this album.

If you want to the rarest copy of this album, try tracking down a gold copy presented to the members of the soccer/football teams West Bromwich Albion and Galatasaray from Turkey in a match sponsored by Clapton.

Backless

He returned to the studio in mid-1978 with producer Glyn Johns. Yvonne Elliman was missing as she had left to resume her solo career, but the rest of his seventies band was in place for the last time in the studio. The resulting *Backless* was released in November 1978. Another success, it reached the top ten in the United States and the top twenty in Great Britain. It may not have had the consistent excellence of *Slowhand*, but it was still very good.

The cover photo says a lot about what is inside. It pictures a relaxed Clapton casually strumming his guitar. The music fit the picture, in that while it was a collection of various styles and traditions, they were on the mellow side. "Tulsa Time" was another country-based song that is moved over to rock and is one of the album's best tracks. It was released as a single in the United States and deserved better than just cracking the top thirty. "Watch Out for Lucy" is another rock outing and has a more primitive sound, or as primitive as any Glyn Johns production gets.

"Promises," which did become a hit in the United States, is a subtle song with subdued vocals and understated slide guitar. The vocal has a country feel as the lyrics explore relationships.

The blues are represented with the traditional "Early in the Morning." It is a slow blues tune, and while it runs over eight minutes, it is still too short. There are two guitar solos and some tempo changes, which make it interesting throughout. A contribution by Bob Dylan, "Walk out in the Rain," is another bluesy, mid-tempo track with fine vocal work.

One surprising failure was the J. J. Cale penned "I'll Make Love to You Anytime." After the brilliance of "Cocaine" and "After Midnight," this one was just a little too mild.

Backless is just a step below Clapton's best work but has stood the test of time well and remains a fine effort.

Late 1978 found Clapton off on another tour, but this time he went back to basics. He toured Europe with only bassist Carl Radle, drummer Jamie Oldaker, and keyboardist Dick Sims. The fact that he did not take second guitarists forced him to shine on the guitar leads.

One other piece of business remained before the decade ended. He and Pattie Boyd Harrison were quietly married on March 27, 1979, but the party thrown several months later at their home in Surrey on May 19 was very high profile indeed. George Harrison was in attendance and played an impromptu set with Paul McCartney and Ringo Starr. Where was John Lennon when you needed him? Also in attendance were the likes of Mick Jagger, Elton John, David Bowie, and even old skiffle artist Lonnie Donegan.

It is not known what George Harrison's feelings were that day, but they may have been relief, as his relationship with Clapton would last much longer than Boyd's.

26

How Many Bridges Have I Crossed

Cruising the Eighties

T he seventies drew to a close with Clapton retiring/firing his long-time band. The ones I personally missed were Yvonne Elliman and Marcy Levy. Their strong voices gave his live shows a verve, uniqueness, and strength that would be hard to replace.

His new band consisted of guitar player Albert Lee, keyboardist Chris Stainton, bassist Dave Markee, and drummer Henry Spinetti. Keyboardist Gary Brooker would be added early in 1980. I have always wondered if he would have retained old friend and bassist Carl Radle, who had stood by Clapton through thick and thin. Radle's health precluded his continuing, and he passed away May 30, 1980, from the cumulative effects of alcohol and drugs.

The real coup of the new band was Lee. He was a guitarist very close to Clapton in talent, and his ego made him a perfect support character who could push Clapton without overwhelming him or getting in the way.

Just One Night

Clapton's new band would get a quick workout with the recording of a concert at the Budokan Theatre in Tokyo, Japan, in December 1979.

Clapton's first album of the decade was the live *Just One Night* issued in April 1980. This two-disc release was taken from the Budokan show.

This remains my favorite Clapton live album. While his guitar playing had often been muted and laid-back on much of his solo work, here he steps forward and demonstrates why Clapton still was god when it came to the guitar. Also, continued blessings on Albert Lee for bringing out the best in E. C. Songs such as "Tulsa Time," "Cocaine," and "Blues Power" were all excellent studio creations, but live they travel in different directions and exhibit new textures.

The eight songs that comprised disc one have a number of high points. Clapton gives a rollicking version of "Tulsa Tine," and he reproduces the staccato beat of "Lay Down Sally" just right. The traditional blues number "Early in the Morning" is a great vehicle for Clapton. "Wonderful Tonight" and "After Midnight" are also given fine interpretations.

As good as the first disc is, it is only a warm-up for the second. It contains one of the finest stretches of live material ever recorded, which is saying something. The crashing chords of "Cocaine" and

A mellow effort that moved in a country direction.
Author's collection

the raw energy of "Blues Power" are spectacular and memorable. The Robert Johnson blues masterpiece "Rambling on My Mind" is close to nine minutes of Clapton twisting chords and improvising. Despite all this, the album's best track is Otis Rush's "Double Trouble." The phrasing plus the clarity of Clapton's playing is some of the best you will ever hear.

Just One Night remains a timeless live album. It was a huge commercial success, reaching #2 on the American charts and three in the United Kingdom. There is a lot of live material out there, but if you are a fan of Clapton and the guitar, this is an album for you.

Another Ticket

Clapton went about two and a half years without releasing a new studio album. The interim was filled with live and compilation releases. He had been recording in 1980 between tour performances, and finally *Another Ticket* appeared on February 14, 1981.

I am always somewhat suspicious of albums released to fulfill contracts. This was the case with *Another Ticket*, as it was the final release owed Robert Stigwood and the RSO label. Artists in situations like this fill the record with bottom-of-the-barrel material. Happily, Clapton took the high road and produced a somewhat mellow but consistent album. It continued his commercial success, going top ten in the United States and top twenty in the United Kingdom.

Another Ticket undeservedly slips beneath the radar when it comes to Clapton's vast catalog.

The first notable thing that strikes me is the production of Tom Dowd. Each instrument, even on my old vinyl copy, is crystal clear. The parts then meld together into a whole. If Dowd could do this with the equipment of the early eighties, there is no excuse for shoddy production today.

There is a lot of good material here, and while it may not force you out of your chair, it will relax and intrigue you.

Clapton wrote five of the nine tracks himself and cowrote a sixth with Gary Brooker. His "I Can't Stand It" and "Rita Mae" are basic rock songs. The first became a #10 singles hit in the United States but topped *Billboard*'s Mainstream Rock chart. "Rita Mae," "Blow Wind Blow," and "Catch Me if You Can" also reached the top twenty-five on the Mainstream Rock chart, giving the album massive airplay publicity.

Billboard instituted the Mainstream Rock chart during the week of March 21, 1981. It was created because of the increasing play of album cuts by radio stations. The days of singles dominating the airwaves were on the wane. The chart tracked which album songs received the most airplay, whether they had been released as singles or not. The name of the chart changed several times throughout the years, but the intent basically remained the same. Clapton had reached the point in his career where he was idolized by millions, and you can't get more mainstream than that. "I Can't Stand It" went down in history as the first song to top this new, and what would become important, chart.

There are several other tracks that consistently draw me back to this album. The Clapton-penned "Hold Me Lord" has a gospel feel and, given his addictive nature, comes across as a personal plea. His cover of Muddy Waters's "Blow Wind Blow" finds Clapton presenting a new vocal style that would come to fruition on *From the Cradle*. The best track is "Floating Bridge," written by Sleepy John Estes. Clapton patterned his cover after that of Elmore James, and at six and a half minutes, it has the Delta blues written all over it as it quietly meanders along and ultimately lulls you and draws you in. There is mellow, and then there is the brilliant mellow of this performance.

Another Ticket is an album I return to every so often. It helps me center myself musically, and I can't help but think it represents a lifestyle, real or imagined, that was just beyond Clapton's reach at the time.

After the release of *Another Ticket,* he would run into some physical problems again that impacted his career, at least in the short run. In mid-March, he was hospitalized in Minnesota with a bleeding ulcer. It was a slow recovery, and it forced him to cancel sixty dates on his latest U.S. tour. No sooner was he on the road to recovery from this setback than he ended up back in the hospital from injuries sustained in a car accident.

In the middle of all this, he embarked on one of the most important business ventures of his life when he formed his own label in September 1981 and signed a deal with WEA for their Reprise label to distribute his material.

Time Pieces: The Best of Eric Clapton

Clapton may have created his own label, but his old one, RSO, owned the rights to much of his material and on May 14, 1982, issued *Time Pieces: The Best of Eric Clapton*. It was as close to a traditional greatest hits album as he would have. At first glance, one would think this release had only moderate chart success, reaching #20 in the United States. But it kept on selling until it finally passed the seven million mark in the United States alone, making it one of his biggest sellers.

The album basically contained the shorter versions of his well-known songs, and for fans that wanted just those and had not purchased his studio albums, this was an extremely appealing release. This was the top forty Eric Clapton, and in the United States of the early eighties, top forty was still an important music form.

"I Shot the Sheriff," "After Midnight," "Knockin' on Heaven's Door," "Wonderful Tonight," "Layla," "Cocaine," "Lay Down Sally," "Willie and the Hand Jive," "Promises," "Swing Low Sweet Chariot," and "Let It Grow" may not be bluesy to a great degree, and they are not improvisational, but they are the popular Clapton at his best.

Money and Cigarettes

Clapton began work on his next studio album in late 1982 by dismissing all of his bandmates except Albert Lee. He added a third first-class guitarist in Ry Cooder, plus well-known bassist Donald "Duck" Dunn was also on hand. Drummer Roger Hawkins completed the band.

Money and Cigarettes was a creative yet ultimately depressing title. It pictured a melted guitar on the front. Clapton had stated that all he had left now was money and cigarettes.

This is a sort of middling album in the Clapton catalog, and in some ways it seems as if he put the recording process on cruise control. The guitar

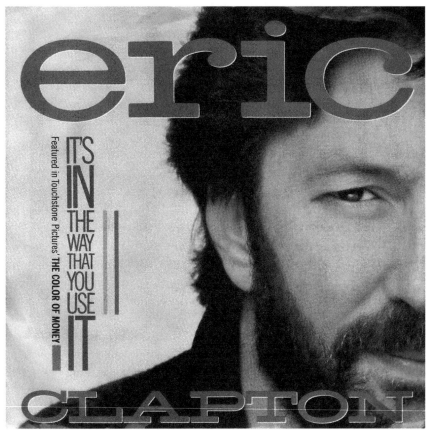

Clapton's career showed little sign of slowing down during the 1980s, as the releases and hits just kept on coming.   *Author's collection*

licks are still present, but they come mostly in short bursts. It proved to be one of the least commercial releases of his career.

The most memorable song was "I've Got a Rock 'n' Roll Heart," which became a hit single in the United States but was largely ignored in his home country. It is a rocking celebration of the music he loves.

There are several other tracks worth finding. "The Shape I'm In" features some fine guitar interplay between Lee and Clapton. "Ain't Going Down" is a nice return to his Derek and the Dominos days. His previous cover of Johnny Otis's "Willie and the Hand Jive" had produced one of the more fun tracks of his career. He now channeled Otis again for a joyful "Crazy Country Hop." The best track may be "Pretty Girl," which included one of the most unique solos of his career, which should be sampled rather than read about.

There is some very good music here, but in the final analysis, Clapton seems to put more effort into some of the tracks than others. It can be pleasurable but is not essential.

Clapton spent the rest of 1983, and most of 1984, as a road warrior, including doing a lot of philanthropic work. He participated in three different concerts for Action for Research into Multiple Sclerosis (ARMS).

ARMS grew out of concern for Small Faces/Faces guitarist Ronnie Lane, who had been diagnosed with the disease. He had formed the Small Faces in 1965, with Steve Marriott and Kenney Jones who were soon joined by Ian McLagan. Lane would cowrite their biggest hit "Itchycoo Park." McLagan, Jones, and Lane would go on to form Faces with Rod Stewart and Ronnie Wood, with great commercial success.

Lane's diagnosis prompted his girlfriend to contact producer Glyn Johns about organizing a benefit concert to support ARMS. Johns was in the middle of arranging Clapton's command performance for Prince Charles at Royal Albert Hall. They booked the theatre for another couple of nights and held the concert on March 17th. Jimmy Page, Jeff Beck, Carmine Appice, Bill Wyman, Kenney Jones, Charlie Watts, and Andy Fairweather-Low answered the call. They held a second concert in September and a third at Madison Square Garden on December 8.

Lane tried to remain active as his condition worsened but finally passed away on June 4, 1997. Jimmy Page, Ronnie Wood, and Rod Stewart took care of his medical bills when his royalties stopped.

Two things happened during his latest studio hiatus. First, he put together a new, or more correctly, an old studio band. Bassist Donald "Duck" Dunn was retained, and returning drummer Jamie Oldaker, vocalist Marcy Levy, and keyboardist Chris Stainton joined him. The new face was guitarist Tim Renwick.

While Clapton may not have had any new material, the old just kept being rereleased.

Time Pieces II: Live in the Seventies

His old label, which had released *Time Pieces: The Best of Eric Clapton* to massive sales, decided to go to the well once again in 1983. *Time Pieces II: Live in the Seventies* gathered eight live tracks together. Notice the word "best" was not in the title. It was a rare Clapton album that did not chart on either side of the Atlantic.

Five of the eight tracks were recorded at the Budokan concert in late 1979, one was from his old Fillmore East concert with Derek and the Dominos, and the other two were from 1974. While the first *Time Pieces* album featured memorable and appealing tracks, the second contained neither. "Tulsa Time" and "Knockin' on Heaven's Door" were too recent, and "Presence of the Lord" and "Blues Power" were too old and familiar. It remains an album for the Clapton fan who must have everything.

Backtrackin'

Another compilation album was released in March 1984. *Backtrackin'* reached #29 in the United Kingdom. I'm not sure if it was released in the United States, but if it was, it received no chart action. The label was Starblend Records, which sounds like one of those labels that lease material, similar to the old K-Tel and Pickwick labels, or the type of material that is sold via television. In England, albums of this type would continually chart.

Backtrackin' contained twenty-five tracks spread across two discs. It was a real hodgepodge with no rhyme or reason. On the positive side, a selection of Clapton's best studio work was present. Anytime you assemble the likes of "I Shot the Sheriff," "Lay Down Sally," "Wonderful Tonight," "Sunshine of Your Love," "Cocaine," "Strange Brew," and "Crossroads" in one place is never bad. The only issue was at this point in Clapton's career, this album was not needed.

Behind the Sun

Clapton finally released his next, long-awaited studio album March 11, 1985. He was under some pressure to produce a big seller after the somewhat disappointing performance of *Money and Cigarettes. Behind the Sun* fit the bill and was considered a comeback album. It was an album of the eighties featuring synthesizers and some programmed drums but also contained his best overall studio guitar work in years.

His band of the day was present, but he also added an array of backing musicians and guests such as drummer Jeff Porcaro, keyboardist Greg Phillinganes, and guitarist Lindsey Buckingham. He also used three producers, Phil Collins, Lenny Waronker, and Ted Templeman, in addition to himself. Despite this fractured approach, the album held together well.

Behind the Sun ushered Clapton into the modern age as it was issued on the usual vinyl and cassette formats but for the first time on CD as well. The video for "Forever Man" received heavy MTV play. The song topped *Billboard*'s Mainstream Rock chart with "She's Waiting" (#11) and "See What Love Can Do" (#20), which also received heavy airplay.

Clapton had been looking for some commercial material, and Texas songwriter Jerry Lynn Williams came to his attention. He recorded three of Williams's songs, all produced by Ted Templeman. "Forever Man," "Something's Happening," and "See What You Can Do" all had commercial appeal while providing a foundation for Clapton's guitar playing. Templeman's production provided a nice counterpoint to the slick work of Collins.

"She's Waiting" was the album's lead track and was emblematic on the Clapton/Collins relationship. The drums, keyboards, and production are straight eighties, but the guitar playing is classic Clapton.

The album does have some average to it. "Same Old Blues" and "Never Make You Cry" are just too long at eight and six minutes respectively. They are ultimately saved from the scrap pile by Clapton's virtuosity.

The only real downer was the title track, which also closed the affair. Clapton wrote the song after separating from his wife and features just his guitar, keyboard, and an emotional vocal.

Behind the Sun's place in Clapton history is that of a transition album. It does have a few flaws but has a number of high points as well, and I can't emphasize enough how good his guitar playing is here.

It was back on the road for the rest of 1985, but playing was not the only thing on Clapton's mind. He hooked up with model and would-be actor Lori Del Santo, who he met at a party in Italy. The party's ultimate party favor was his son Conor.

Clapton's studio work took a new turn as the decade reached its halfway point. He had never been active in scoring films. His "Heaven Is One Step Away" had appeared in the popular film *Back to the Future*, but his effort was minimal.

The Edge of Darkness

Clapton agreed to write the music for the British television series *The Edge of Darkness*. Realizing he was a little over his head, he asked Michael Kamen for assistance, thereby establishing a long-term relationship.

Kamen was a solid choice as he had written pop songs as well as the soundtracks for dozens of movies. His success included, but was not limited to, the three *Die Hard* movies, *Robin Hood: Prince of Thieves, Mr. Holland's Opus, The Iron Giant*, the *Lethal Weapon* series, plus *From the Earth to the Moon* and *Band of Brothers* for HBO. Kamen was nominated for two Oscars and won three Grammys and two Golden Globe Awards.

The Edge of Darkness soundtrack was a modest effort, with six songs clocking in at around eighteen minutes. Despite it brevity, it was well received and earned the duo a British Academy Television Award for Best Original Television Music.

The soundtrack was released in November 1985, but finding it today is a difficult task. It was originally a vinyl and cassette release and finally a CD three years later. The title song reached #65 as a single in the United Kingdom. It was not released in the United States. A live performance surfaced on the live *24 Nights* in 1991.

A highlight of 1986 was Clapton's participation in Chuck Berry's sixtieth birthday party concert in St. Louis, which was organized by Keith Richards of the Rolling Stones. The concert took place October 16th and later became famous for Richards's unhappiness with Berry.

August

August was released November 24, 1986. It reached #3 in England but continued Clapton's recent trend of not charting high in the United States (#37) but selling well over a long period of time, eventually receiving a Platinum sales award. Clapton, Phil Collins, and Tom Dowd share producing credits.

He was now firmly entrenched on *Billboard*'s Mainstream Rock chart as "It's the Way That You Use It" (#1), "Tearing Us Apart" (#5), "Miss You" (#9), and "Run" (#21) all received extensive airplay.

Two things immediately stand out on this release. The first was that Clapton did not write any of the songs by himself but was content to cowrite six of the eleven tracks. Secondly, there was again a long list of supporting musicians with new names appearing for the first time. Phil Collins provided most of the drum work himself. The two constants throughout the project were Nathan East and keyboardist Greg Phillinganes.

August was another album of the eighties and as such was heavy on the synthesizers. It was also very slick and polished in many places due to Collins's influence. The Brecker Brothers headed up a jazz section, which filled in the sound on a number of tracks.

The songs just roll smoothly along. "It's the Way That You Use It," cowritten with Robbie Robertson of the Band, features a gritty vocal and fine guitar solo. "Tearing Us Apart" contains an excellent vocal performance by Tina Turner. "Taking a Chance" finds Clapton's guitar floating above Phillinganes's keyboards.

My two favorite tracks a quarter of a century later are "Run" and "Hung Up on Your Love," which were both written by Motown songwriter deluxe Lamont Dozier. Both receive a horn-laden treatment in support of Clapton's guitar playing, which moves away from the eighties in style.

In the final analysis, *August* is a product of the eighties, but it is good eighties. It remains a very solid effort in the vast Clapton repertoire.

In January 1987, he performed six concerts at his favorite arena, the Royal Albert Hall in London. He returned to this venue again and again before the end of the decade, including nine times in 1988, and twelve in 1989.

Lethal Weapon

Clapton next joined Michael Kamen and David Sanborn in another soundtrack project. This time the film was titled *Lethal Weapon*, and it would be the first in a series of four films, which would gross hundreds of millions of dollars worldwide and make an international star of Mel Gibson. The original soundtrack was released in 1987. While not a huge seller, it was a competent soundtrack, which enhanced this action film well.

His soundtrack work is often overlooked as it is far different from his rock/blues material, but it did give him a fresh and relaxed way to express himself far from the fame of the rock world.

The Cream of Eric Clapton

Meanwhile, back at his old label, RSO/Polydor assembled still another compilation album. *The Cream of Eric Clapton,* which did not contain just Cream tracks, was released in Great Britain, Australia, and Germany and became another hit and moneymaker. It patterned itself after the first *Timeless* album in that it assembled short, singles-type material onto one album.

The only Derek and the Dominos track was "Layla." It is joined by six Cream tracks, including "Sunshine of Your Love," "Badge," "White Room," "I Feel Free," "Crossroads," and "Strange Brew." The last ten tracks contain the best of Clapton's solo material, but the album had me from the Cream material. It may not be an essential release as it contains material that had been released many times previously, but it is still very appealing.

Homeboy

One of the more difficult Clapton releases to locate is his soundtrack to the film *Homeboy,* starring Mickey Rourke, which was issued in 1988. While he partners again with Kamen, it bears more of his imprint than his previous soundtrack work. It may still be background music, but his signature guitar sound is more prominent in places. He gives it a moody and bluesy feel, and it is worth the search for any Clapton fan.

Nineteen eighty-eight marked his twenty-fifth year as a recording artist, and he was honored the evening of June 7th at the Savoy in London. George Harrison was the main speaker.

Crossroads

The real celebration of his twenty-fifth anniversary was the *Crossroads* box set. It was a massive four-CD, seventy-three-track, digitally remastered set that spanned the entirety of his career. It clocked in seven minutes short of five hours.

Crossroads was another moderate-charting album in the United States at #34 but would eventually sell in the neighborhood of three million copies. It remains the definitive release of the first half of his career. The tracks break down as follows: the Yardbirds (9), John Mayall and the Bluesbreakers (6), Cream (12), Blind Faith (3), Delaney and Bonnie (1), Derek and the Dominos (11), and solo material (31). They are presented in chronological order, and every musician who played on each track is listed.

The enclosed booklet, written and compiled by Anthony DeCurtis, won a Grammy itself. *Crossroads* may have been a little cheerleaderish in places, but it was extensive and exhaustive plus contained a number of rare photos.

This is a rare box set that gets everything right and receives a grade of A+. If I had to give up every Clapton release but one, this may be the one I'd keep. It is a solid taste of the first half of his career.

I have always been amazed at the energy Clapton has exhibited throughout most of his career. World tours, combined with one-off performances, plus trips to the recording studio for himself and friends, would have completed sapped the energy reserves of most human beings.

Journeyman

Clapton returned to the recording studio twice and completed one important piece of business before the eighties ended.

The first time was to contribute to the soundtrack of *Lethal Weapon 2*. Michael Kamen and David Sanborn again joined him. The music was not the focus of the films in this series but rather provided support and enhancement. The songs did give his evolving soundtrack skill a great deal of exposure as a massive audience viewed the films.

Journeyman was released on November 7, 1989. It included a large and eclectic group of musicians. Drummer Phil Collins, saxophone player David Sanborn, guitarists Robert Cray and George Harrison, bassist Nathan East, vibraphone player Hank Crawford, drummers Steve Ferrone and Jim Keltner, keyboardists Greg Phillinganes and Richard Tee, and a virtual choir of background singers all joined him in the recording studio. The album reached #16 on the U.S. charts but eventually sold over a million copies. It reached #3 in England.

The hit singles just kept on coming for E.C.
Author's collection

Clapton returned to Jerry Lynn Williams for material, and he responded by writing four of the ten tracks and cowriting a fifth. Williams's "Pretending" reached #1 on *Billboard*'s Mainstream Rock charts, and his "No Alibis" was close behind at #4. The Clapton-penned "Bad Love" also reached #1, and the old blues song "Before You Accuse Me" joined them at #9. The George Harrison tune "Run So Far" edged into the top forty at #40, giving the album five breakout tracks.

Journeyman is the last Clapton album I have on vinyl, so somewhere between the late eighties and early nineties I departed from the true faith and switched to CDs.

As I travel through the Clapton catalog, every once in a while an album will continually surprise me, and *Journeyman* falls into that category. I don't pay it enough attention, as it is one of his better solo efforts.

It contained more hard rock and blues than many of his recent solo releases at the time. Phil Collins was back as a drummer and supporting vocalist but not as a producer. Clapton took what he had learned from Collins in regard to slick pop music, toned it down a bit, and produced a modern-sounding album that was true to his roots.

The first and last tracks were as good as any solo material he had produced. "Pretending" is a modernization of Clapton's blues sound and technique, which also includes a stunning vocal. The album concludes with Do Diddley's "Before You Accuse Me." Diddley straddles the rock and blues line, and Clapton brings this 1958 creation into the modern age complete with a stinging guitar solo.

There are a number of other treats to be sampled. "Bad Love," with Foreigner guitarist Mick Jones, includes another memorable solo. I just wish they had ditched the synthesizers here as they are a bit much. Clapton's take of "Hound Dog" is different, as it had to be since the song is an Elvis Presley signature. "Breaking Point," at over five and a half minutes, contains some nice guitar work. "No Alibis" is notable for fine vocal accompaniment by Daryl Hall and Chaka Khan.

Journeyman allowed him to finish his eighties musical journey in style and set the tone for the decade ahead.

The last piece of eighties business was not in the recording studio but rather in the courtroom, as Clapton's divorce from Pattie Boyd was finalized. I think I know what George Harrison was thinking this time.

27

The Healing Rain Which Restores the Soul

Redemption in the Nineties

T he nineties had dawned, and the middle-aged (forty-five) Clapton was recognized as one of rock's enduring superstars. Despite this massive appeal, he would emerge from the decade even more popular than ever.

He began the decade with an auspicious series of concerts at the Royal Albert Hall, playing eighteen nights at the venerated venue. He basically presented three different programs with different bands. They can best be labeled as the Robert Cray Band, the Buddy Guy Band, plus he performed with a full orchestra. The concert series concluded in mid-February, and then it was on to a tour of the United States. At the beginning of his tour, he stopped off at the set of *Saturday Night Live* as their musical guest.

A few side projects, some time off, and taking care of some business along the way interrupted his six-month tour of the United States. One piece of business was paying a traffic violation for driving in excess of one hundred miles per hour in late December of the previous year.

Clapton had reached the point in his career when awards and honors had started coming his way. On June 6, he was honored as the Living Legend of the Year at the Second International Rock Awards in New York City. After the presentation, he performed with Billy Joel and Steven Tyler of Aerosmith.

Later in the month he traveled back to England for a benefit performance at Knebworth Park. The cream of British rock joined him to help raise funding for the Nordorff-Robbins Therapy Centre. Cliff Richard, Paul McCartney, Genesis, Pink Floyd, the Shadows, Elton John, Mark Knopfler, Status Quo, and Tears for Fears joined him onstage. He and Knopfler began to cement a relationship that would bear fruit in the future.

Clapton's touring band at the time was drummer Steve Ferrone, guitarist Phil Palmer, keyboardists Alan Clark and Greg Phillinganes, percussionist Ray Cooper, and backup singers Tessa Niles and Katie Kissoon.

The tour was near its completion when tragedy struck on August 27. Clapton had just finished a concert at the Alpine Valley Music Theatre in West Troy, Wisconsin, before a crowd of roughly thirty thousand. The final number was a jam with Stevie and Jimmie Vaughan, Robert Cray, and Buddy Guy. A helicopter crash shortly after the concert's conclusion killed Stevie Ray Vaughan, Clapton's business manager, bodyguard Nigel Browne, and agent Bobby Brooks. Clapton and Guy traveled to Dallas, Texas, four days later for Vaughan's funeral service.

He began 1991 in the usual fashion with a series of concerts at the Royal Albert Hall. The series was his most ambitious yet. Beginning in early February, he played twenty-four separate dates with five different bands. His supporting groups were as follows: 1) bassist Nathan East, keyboardist Phillinganes, and drummer Phil Collins; 2) the same as the first except with Steve Ferrone replacing Collins; 3) his nine-piece concert band; 4) a blues band with Albert Collins, Buddy Guy, Jimmie Vaughan, and Robert Cray, who were backed by his nine-piece band; 5) a complete orchestra conducted by soundtrack friend Michael Kamen.

The greatest personal tragedy of his life struck on March 20, 1991, when Clapton's four-year-old son Conor fell out of a fifty-third-floor window of the Manhattan apartment where he was staying with the boy's mother, Lori Del Santo. Conor's death was instantaneous. He was buried in the St. Mary Magdalen Churchyard, Ripley, Surrey, England.

Two weeks later, Clapton began a U.S. tour at the Meadowlands in New Jersey. It was probably the safest place for him to deal with his grief at the time.

24 Nights

The new decade finally yielded a Clapton album when *24 Nights* was released on October 8, 1991. It was a reasonable success, reaching #7 in the United States while receiving a gold record for sales. It had more modest success in the United Kingdom, where it reached #38.

The album's title was taken from his twenty-four-night string of performances at the Royal Albert Hall. The title was a little misleading, as the album was comprised of performances from both 1990 and 1991, which actually added up to forty-two different shows. Compounding the confusion was the fact that songs from only seven nights were used.

To clarify the situation, the following performances were used: 1) January 1970, with a four-piece band: "Running on Faith" (6:49), "White Room" (6:10), and "Sunshine of Your Love" (9:11); 2) February 5, 1990, with his blues band: "Worried Life Blues" (5:28), "Watch Yourself" (5:39), and "Have You Ever Loved a Woman"; 3) February 9, 1990, with a full orchestra: "Bell Bottom Blues" (6:39) and "Hard Times" (3:45); 4) February 10, 1991, with his basic four-piece ensemble: "Badge" (6:51); 5) February 18, 1991, with his full nine-piece backing band: "Pretending" (7:08), Bad Love" (6:25), "Old Love" (13:08), and "Wonderful Tonight" (9:11); 6) February 28, 1991, with his blues band: "Hoodoo Man" (5:41); 7) March 8, 1991, with Michael Kamen and orchestra: "Edge of Darkness." (6:30).

Clapton's performance of "Worried Life Blues" is almost worth the price of admission alone. It was one of the first songs inducted into the Blues Hall of Fame in 1983. Major "Big Maceo" Merriwether is the credited writer, as he issued a Decca single in 1941. He probably borrowed a lot of it from Sleepy John Estes's "Someday Baby Blues." This borrowing was so common then that many times it is impossible to know who actually wrote some of the songs. "Worried Life Blues" was one of the most popular of the early blues songs and was covered by a bevy of artists including Sonny Boy Williamson, Lightnin' Hopkins, John Lee Hooker, Muddy Waters, Big Bill Broonzy, Mississippi Fred McDowell, Freddie King, plus modern artists the Animals, Blues Magoos, and Canned Heat.

Clapton welcomed the song into the modern age with his blues band. It is a tighter performance than many of his traditional blues forays but is no less brilliant and enjoyable. It's all in the guitar work, and here that work is exemplary. It's interesting to compare it to the longer version issued on *Just One Night*.

"The Edge of Darkness," from the television soundtrack of the same name, finally saw the light of day live. Clapton had an orchestra at his disposal and made use of it by performing a song that was virtually impossible to play with his usual cast of characters.

There is not a lot of new here, but the old is presented in unique ways at times. The variations in his backing groups are always intriguing. My favorite tends to be the small four-man bands as they force him, as the only guitarist, to step forward and take charge. A close second is the blues band and its accompanying guitarists who push him a little.

24 Nights is a worthy addition to his live legacy and was welcomed by his fans at the dawn of the nineties, but there is thirty-five nights were of material still out there, and who knows what treasures they contain.

Clapton began 1992 by participating in *MTV Unplugged* series. I used to enjoy this concept as artists of the day performed acoustic sets before small and intimate audiences.

Clapton was joined by guitarists Andy Fairweather-Low, percussionist Ray Cooper, bassist Nathan East, drummer Steve Ferrone, keyboardist Chuck Leavell, and backing vocalists Katie Kissoon and Tessa Niles.

It was one of the memorable performances of his career. This January 16 performance was broadcast March 11 in the United States and on the 27th in Europe. It was a show that would not fade from memory, as it would be released as an album.

Rush

Clapton continued to be busy in the soundtrack world. *Rush* is probably his most recognized film work and the most commercially successful as well. The original January 14 release was comprised of ten tracks, but this time two contained vocals. Buddy Guy sang the old Willie Dixon tune "Don't Know Which Way to Go," which clocked in at 10:46. The second vocal performance was Clapton's "Tears in Heaven," which he coauthored with Will Jennings and dealt with the loss of his son Conor.

The song became one of his big hits, reaching #2 on the American singles charts for four weeks. It was kept from the top spot by Vanessa Williams's "Save the Best for Last," which held the #1 position for five weeks, proving that at times there is indeed no justice in the world. It would reach #5 in the United Kingdom. For the record, the soundtrack was released two days before Clapton's performance on *MTV Unplugged*. The song won three Grammys in 1993.

He had another soundtrack waiting in the wings. He, Michael Kamen, and David Sanborn reunited for the third *Lethal Weapon* film. The movie was another blockbuster, but the soundtrack veered from the approach of the first two in that it contained two Clapton duets. Both were top forty hits in the United Kingdom but saw no chart action in the United States. "Runaway Train" with Elton John and "It's Probably Me" with Sting propelled the album to some notice beyond just the usual movie buffs. John and Clapton would team up for a series of U.S. concerts later in the year.

Unplugged

I don't know what Eric Clapton was thinking when he entered the MTV studio that mid-January day for his *Unplugged* performance, but it is doubtful he could have imagined he was about to record one of the biggest-selling albums of his career.

The acoustic *Unplugged* was released August 25, 1992, and was an immediate smash. It topped the U.S. album charts for three weeks and ultimately sold seven million copies. It debuted at #2 in Clapton's home country.

The all-acoustic release combined old and new material. While his "Tears in Heaven" and a reworking of "Layla" remain the centerpieces of the album, it was the old blues tunes that bring me back to this album over and over again.

"Before You Accuse Me" (Bo Diddley), "Hey Hey" (Big Bill Broonzy), "Nobody Knows You When You're Down and Out" (Jimmy Cox), "Walkin' Blues" (Robert Johnson), "Malted Milk" (Robert Johnson), and "Rollin' and Tumblin'" (Muddy Waters) form the heart and soul of Clapton's music. The format of the concert meant there were no extended improvisational tracks. The longest performance is just over four minutes. This made him stay close to the original intent of the material, as the old blues artists were limited by the technology of the day, which kept things short. When you add in the acoustic nature of the performance, they are performed as they were meant to be. The added bonus was that many people who bought the album for the pop material were introduced to these old blues classics at the same time.

The gentle performance of "Layla" joined "Tears in Heaven" on *the Billboard* Hot 100 at #12. Both songs also appeared on the Adult Contemporary chart with "Tears in Heaven" (#1), "Layla," (#8), plus "Running on Faith" (#28).

The other song of note was the folk tune "San Francisco Bay Blues," written by Jesse Fuller in the mid-fifties. It was so un-Clapton-like that it was a brilliant addition.

Unplugged remains a different and signature performance by Eric Clapton.

By the end of the year, he was an official member of the Rock and Roll Hall of Fame. The Yardbirds' induction included Clapton, Beck, Page, Chris Dreja, Jim McCarty, Keith Relf, and Paul Samwell-Smith.

The year 1993 began in the usual fashion with a series of concerts at Clapton's favorite hall. He limited himself to twelve performances this time around.

The year would ultimately be one of his least cluttered. It was partially filled with some one-stop performances and awards.

One of the highlights of the year was Cream's induction into the Rock and Roll Hall of Fame for the second time. This prompted the long-hoped-for reunion of the group at the induction ceremony that led to a series of further concerts together.

In 1994, he returned to the Hall to induct the Band. He also partici-pated in the traditional all-star jam at the conclusion of the ceremony.

February found him back at the Royal Albert Hall, and for anyone keep-ing track, it included his one-hundredth performance at the hall.

From the Cradle

What his fans were really anticipating was a new album, as he was back in the studio for the first time in the nineties. His vision for the album precluded the long list of musicians that had inhabited his recent studio releases. Andy Fairweather-Low was on hand as the second guitarist, and bassist Dave Bronze, drummer Jim Keltner, harpist Jerry Portnoy, keyboard-ist Chris Stainton, and a horn section of Roddy Lorimer, Simon Clarke, and Tim Sanders completed the lineup.

Clapton decided to release an entire album of blues covers. It would be the first of a number of blues projects that would follow. I don't know if the acoustic blues performances of *Unplugged* had anything to do with the album, but it was a tremendous idea that was embraced by the music-buying public as it reached #1 in both the United States and Great Britain.

From the Cradle was a true blues album in that it was recorded live in the studio. Very few musicians would have had the confidence and talent to take classic compositions by Elmore James, Muddy Waters, Lowell Fulsom, and others and just have at it. Clapton was more than up to the task as his gritty vocals and always superb guitar playing modernize many of the songs while paying homage to their origins at the same time.

There is a lot of outstanding material from which to choose. The Willie Dixon/Eddie Boyd composition "Third Degree" is the type of slow blues song that fit Clapton's style and temperament so well. "Blues Before Sunrise" is a vehicle for his well-defined slide technique. A personal favorite is the Muddy Water classic "Hoochie Coochie Man," which features an emotional vocal. "Groaning the Blues," at over six minutes, contains some creative improvisational excursions.

From the Cradle was ambitious, innovative in an old-school way, and most importantly authentic. Clapton let it be known that he was still a musician of note and power within the context of the blues. It remains one of his essential modern-day releases.

It was announced on January 1 that Clapton would be awarded the Most Excellent Order of the British Empire (OBE). Prince Charles presented it at Buckingham Palace on November 7. A ceremony far removed from the OBE was the Silver Clef Award presented by Cher at their annual dinner in London's Park Lane Hotel.

The Cream of Eric Clapton

His old label RSO/Polydor returned to the vaults and released another compilation album with a recycled name. *The Cream of Eric Clapton* (not to be confused with the 1987 European release) was released in the United Sates. Oddly, both releases reached #3 on their country's respective charts.

Ten of the tracks were repeats from the European release. The best thing about this album, unlike the 1987 issue, was that the tracks were presented in chronological order. The biggest omission was the deletion of "Layla."

While popular, it was basically another rehash of his sixties and seventies material, which had been reissued ad infinitum by this point. It did prove that there was still an insatiable desire for anything Clapton, and a new generation of fans had come along that made his older material commercially viable again.

The year 1996 marked his tenth anniversary of concerts at the Royal Albert Hall.

While he did not score the John Travolta film *Phenomenon,* he did provide one memorable contribution. The writing team of Tommy Sims, Gordon Kennedy, and Wayne Kirkpatrick presented him with "Change the World." It was included on the soundtrack and released as a single, which reached the #5 position on *Billboard*'s pop charts. The Adult Contemporary chart would be its home as it spent thirteen weeks in the #1 position.

Retail Therapy

Clapton's most adventurous musical journey was his collaboration on TDF's *Retail Therapy.* It was an album of electric music and quite a stretch for him at the time. He had not explored this musical form, not even in his soundtrack work.

There are some interesting tracks here. "Angelica" is a beautiful acoustic performance, which is a welcome addition to any Clapton collection. His guitar also shines on "Sno-god." The same can be said for "Seven."

Clapton is listed as X-Sample in the credits. This fake name probably caused the album to receive little notice when it was released.

His partner for the project was Simon Climie, who would work with Clapton in the future. Climie's influence is all through the album as it is layered, techno, and basically electronic, so any Clapton fan will have to approach it with an open mind. TDF was short for Totally Dysfunctional Family.

While I'm sure his 1996 relationship with Climie was interesting, I'm convinced the relationship with Sheryl Crow was even more interesting for

Clapton in that it went beyond the music. They performed together at her Central Park Concert with a version of "White Room," which I have always considered to be a somewhat odd choice. She returned the favor at his 2007 Crossroads Guitar festival. The relationship did not last but was a mature stop on his journey through life.

Crossroads 2: Live in the Seventies

In 1996, on April 2, a new live compilation album, *Crossroads 2: Live in the Seventies,* was issued. The first *Crossroads* set remains his signature studio compilation. This second volume was less comprehensive. It did not claim to be the best of anything but basically confines itself to the seventies and only part of the decade at that (1974–1978).

It is a massive four-disc, close to four-and-a-half-hour set. There is interesting material here, but my main complaint is that it is too focused on one period and could have been a lot better and a lot more comprehensive.

A big plus is the sound. It is crystal clear throughout, which shows that some real effort was put into the production.

The first disc is highlighted by the eleven-minute-plus performance of "Willie and the Hand Jive"/"Get Ready" and "Drifting Blues"/"Rambling on My Mind" from a July 20th show at the Long Beach Arena.

Disc two contains a ten-minute performance of "Badge," which was usually presented as a short, tightly structured song. It starts out just that way, but then Clapton takes off and rocks out for close to seven minutes. "I Shot the Sheriff" is nearly the same length, and Clapton ultimately twists it all out of shape. He keeps "Layla" short, but his guitar strips it and rock 'n' roll to the bare essentials.

If you want some extended Clapton with Santana in tow, "Eyesight to the Blind"/"Why Does Love Have to Be So Bad" at twenty-four minutes is bound to please. There may be a few repetitive stretches, but surprises do lurk around the corners. Santana and Clapton push each other as they alternate solos.

Disc three contains a live performance of "Cocaine," and I don't think he has ever given a bad performance of the song. I can even get into the thirteen-minute performance of the old standard "Stormy Monday."

The fourth CD is mundane. Tracks such as "Worried Life Blues," "Tulsa Time," "Wonderful Tonight," and "Crossroads" were overdone by this point in his career.

It is by no means a bad set and does contain a number of high points. If you do not have any or much of his live material, it is worth the investment. It you are a Clapton collector, it will provide some nice treats. In the final analysis, however, I return to my original complaint: it could have been much better.

Pilgrim

The highlight of the late nineties was Clapton's release of *Pilgrim* on March 20, 1998. Given that *From the Cradle* was a blues cover album, this was his first release of new material in almost a decade.

The album was a modest and modern affair. It sold very well at the time, but in retrospect, tucked in between *From the Cradle* and his collaboration with B. B. King, it has been underappreciated, quite.

The modern feel, which did not always serve Clapton well, was probably due to Simon Climie's presence. There are drums, strings, and synthesizers, and sometimes they push the guitar sound a little too far into the background. When I listen to this album, I can't help but think I would like to see it rerecorded with just a basic guitar, bass, and drums.

"My Father's Eyes" is the album's best-known track. It winds through Clapton's modern-day catalog, and I'm always touched by the emotional vocal and poignant lyrics about a father and son. It won a Grammy for Best Male Pop Vocal.

If you take the time to sift through the fourteen tracks, you will find some keepers. "Sick & Tired" is about the blues. "She's Gone" is one of those instances when he lets his guitar sound just flow. "Going Down Slow" is an old blues song written by Jimmy Oden and popularized by Howlin' Wolf. The lyrics tell the story of a dying man looking back at his life. These songs return Clapton to his comfort zone, and it shows.

Pilgrim is one of those albums that sounded better at the time of his release. Today, it is an album I rarely reach for when I want to hear some Clapton.

Lethal Weapon 4/The Story of Us

There was still some soundtrack business to be finished before the end of the decade. The music to *Lethal Weapon 4* has some controversy to it. Clapton, Kamen, and Sanborn all returned to score the fourth and last film (to date) in the popular series.

The original release contains the music of the film. Recent releases describe the tracks as "Pilgrim" (original by Eric Clapton), "Cheer Down" (original by George Harrison), "Fire in the Hole" (original by Van Halen), and so it went through the entire album. And if you are not paying attention, what you expect is not what you will get.

Clapton's last soundtrack of the decade appeared in 1999. *The Story of Us* is mostly an album of musical snippets written by Clapton. He wrote twenty-one of the twenty-four tracks, and thirteen of them are under a minute in length, which fit the action of the film well. They may be beautiful but are a difficult listen when they have to stand on their own.

One of the non-Clapton tracks was "Classical Gas" by Mason Williams. This was another of those songs that convinced me I would never be a guitarist. It is a guitar player's song, and Williams took it to the #2 position on the U.S. singles charts in 1968. I salivate at the thought of Clapton grabbing his acoustic guitar and giving this old chestnut a workout.

Clapton Chronicles: The Best of Eric Clapton

Two more compilation albums appeared in the last half of 1999.

Blues was another release from his old RSO label, a two-disc set divided between studio and live tracks. It was commercially successful, reaching #52 in both the United States and the United Kingdom.

While RSO had released just about every combination of his music thought possible, *Blues* does have some appeal. Most of the material is familiar, but it is nice to have it in one place. There are a few unreleased tracks, the best of which are Willie Dixon's "Meet Me at the Bottom," which was an outtake from *461 Ocean Boulevard*, and an acoustic outtake of "Before You Accuse Me" from the *Backless* sessions.

The rarity of the set was a third bonus disc, which was only issued with very early copies. "Blues in A" (10:25) from his self titled debut album, "Eric After Hours Blues" (4:20) from *461 Ocean Boulevard*, "B Minor Jam" (7:10) also from *461 Ocean Boulevard*, and "Blues" (2:59) from *No Reason to Cry* were all written by Clapton. If you can find this third disc, it makes the set very worthwhile.

Clapton Chronicles: The Best of Eric Clapton closed the decade. Clapton and his new label decided to join the compilation parade. The release sold over a million copies in the United States and United Kingdom, reaching #21 and #6 on their respective charts.

After the constant repackaging of his sixties and seventies material, this album focused on his '80s and '90s material, which made it different from all the compilation albums that preceded it. It was a nice overview of his latest studio work.

Clapton Chronicles focused on his pop/rock releases, but millions of fans embraced that side of his music, and songs such as "Change the World," "My Father's Eyes," "Tears in Heaven," "Pretending," and "Forever Man" are among his most popular. It was meant to be a commercial release and in that succeeded. If you are only a fan of his blues material, you should look elsewhere.

The nineties ended with Eric Clapton in his mid-fifties. There was a time when his generation of musicians could not have imagined making rock 'n' roll at such an advanced age, and some of his contemporaries did not make it. Jimi Hendrix, Janis Joplin, Carl Radle, Jim Morrison, Duane Allman, and dozens more had passed away before coming close to their mid-fifties. Clapton and a number of other stars would quickly prove that age was no barrier to good music.

28

You Give 'Em a Smile and They Melt

Enduring Superstar

The new decade dawned with another journey to the Rock and Roll Hall of Fame. Clapton was inducted as a solo artist, making him the only person to date to be inducted on three separate occasions. His fellow inductees that March 6th evening were Earth, Wind and Fire, the Lovin' Spoonful, the Moonglows, Bonnie Raitt, and James Taylor.

Riding with the King

The other highlight of the year was his collaboration with B. B. King. *Riding with the King* was released on June 13, 2000, and won a Grammy for Best Traditional Blues Album. It reached #15 in the United States and climbed to #3 in the United Kingdom.

I doubt that Eric Clapton and B. B. King could have created a bad or even average album had they tried. In this case they put together a brilliant one.

Clapton had been a guest on countless albums through the years, but here he formed a partnership with one of the giants of the blues world. They made an interesting and effective combination, as King's Delta heritage style meshed well with Clapton's blues/rock foundation.

A nice, tight band was assembled to provide support in the studio. Andy Fairweather-Low and Doyle Bramhall II are superb musicians, but here they were relegated to a rhythm guitar role, and they laid down a fine foundation that fills in the sound for the two soloists. In many ways, the musical key is pianist Joe Sample, who pushes the music along, allowing the two principals to take off on their solo excursions. Bassist Nathan East and drummer Steve Gadd formed the rhythm section.

Both King and Clapton have always been able to create a crystal-clear sound and put the focus on each individual note. They are also able to take a song and transform it so that it travels in new and unexpected directions.

Three of King's early compositions were resurrected for this album. "Three O'Clock Blues" (1951), "When My Heart Beats Like a Hammer" (1954), and "Ten Long Years" (1955) are vehicles for them to trade solo licks.

Other highlights include a wonderful acoustic version of Big Bill Broonzy's "Key to the Highway" and a blues rendition of Sam and Dave's soul hit "Hold On, I'm Comin'" that included some of the best guitar lines on the album, which is saying a lot.

Clapton's material has been issued over and over again, as this early Master Recording demonstrates.

Author's collection

Riding with the King was one of those ideas that sounded great on paper and worked better in execution. It was the second of a trio of all-blues albums Clapton would produce and matches well with 1994's *From the Cradle* and the then unissued *Me and Mr. Johnson*. Fans of B. B. King, Eric Clapton, the blues, and just good music should be pleased with this release. It is a journey down a highway not traveled very often.

Reptile

Clapton had gone years between studio albums in the eighties and nineties but this time surprised everyone by issuing another one nine months after his last.

Reptile was released on March 13, 2001, and clocked in at just over an hour. It featured five of his own compositions plus two more he cowrote among the fourteen tracks. Beginning with 1989's *Journeyman* and continuing through 2005's *Back Home*, Clapton would rotate albums consisting of blues covers with albums containing blue/rock fusions that boasted many original compositions.

Reptile returned producer Simon Climie and many of his band members from the *Pilgrim* project, and the results were very different and ultimately superior. Clapton managed to keep Climie's inclination to program instruments under control. The drum machines were turned down and the synthesizers used more judiciously. The final result was an intimate and very good album.

Andy Fairweather-Low and Doyle Bramhall II returned as the second guitarists, while Joe Sample and Billy Preston handled the keyboards. Other main musicians were drummer Steve Gadd, bassist Nathan East, and percussionist Paulinho Da Costa. The real inspiration was the inclusion of the legendary soul group the Impressions as the backing vocalists.

As with many of his nonblues studio albums, sometimes Clapton's guitar playing disappears into the background, and many of the solos are too short. Still, what is present is representative of his talent.

Two instrumentals bookend the album. The title song has a smooth, almost jazz feel to it, while "Son & Sylvia" contains some nice acoustic work.

The Ray Charles tune "Come Back Baby" is given a superior treatment. Billy Preston's joyful organ playing drives the song along as he blends well with Clapton's bluesy guitar runs, while Clapton's near gospel vocal performance floats above the mix. "I Ain't Gonna Stand for It" is a rare successful cover of a Stevie Wonder composition. "Superman Inside" and "Travelin' Light" find Clapton in rock mode, while his own "Believe in Life" is a quiet love song.

Reptile presents the modern studio Clapton at his near best, and while it may not contain the guitar pyrotechnics that I would have liked at the time, it is still a very satisfying album.

The Concert for George

Clapton experienced another personal loss in late 2001, when his longtime friend George Harrison passed away November 29 at the age of fifty-eight. Harrison had been fighting cancer since 1997 and had undergone continuing treatment until his death. He was cremated, and his ashes scattered in the Ganges River.

Clapton organized a memorial concert for his old buddy at the Royal Albert Hall on November 29, 2002, to commemorate the anniversary of his death.

When Clapton calls, people respond. Jeff Lynne, Gary Brooker, Joe Brown, Tom Petty, Billy Preston, Ringo Starr, and Paul McCartney all performed and shared vocal duties. In addition, Harrison's son Dhani, guitarist Albert Lee, bassist Klaus Voormann, and drummer Jim Keltner were on hand to provide support.

The Concert for George was released a year later, November 17, 2003, on the second anniversary of his death. A film of the concert was released on October 10, 2003, and would win a Grammy for Best Long Form Music Video.

The CD set begins with three pieces of Indian music composed by Ravi Shankar, which were performed and conducted by his daughter Anoushka. She was in her early twenties at the time, yet was already a virtuoso of the sitar. The twenty-three-minute "Arpan" is a production, and whether the track is enjoyed or passed over will be determined by the listener's affinity for this type of music. Nevertheless, the music was an appropriate addition to his tribute as it was an important part of his life. The fourth track was an interesting cover of the Beatles tune "The Inner Light," performed by Anoushka and Jeff Lynne.

The second disc gets to the heart of the concert. Jeff Lynne kicks it off with the vocal on "I Want to Tell You" from the Beatles' *Revolver*, and from that point on it is a concert to remember.

Some of the songs work better than others. Ringo Starr's two-song set is one of the highlights of the concert. He cowrote his #1 hit "Photograph" with Harrison, and here he gives a performance that provides an emotional center for the album and the concert. This was followed by his rendition of "Honey Don't" with fine guitar work from Albert Lee.

Another highlight are the vocal performances by Joe Brown. He was a somewhat famous early rock–era British performer and personality but was little known outside his home country. His vocal on "Here Comes the Sun" is perfection. His choice of performing the obscure "That's the Way It Goes" from *Gone Troppo* is brilliant.

Billy Preston's exuberant performance of "My Sweet Lord" was the result of the song being a part of his own live act for decades. Paul McCartney's take on "Something" proves that many times, simple is best. He also shines on "All Things Must Pass," which is a tad ironic and amusing, as it was a one-time Beatles reject. On the other hand, the Tom Petty tracks are somewhat average, and Jeff Lynne's voice is not in its best form.

Eric Clapton presented the lead guitar and vocals on four tracks; "If I Needed Someone," "Beware of Darkness," "Isn't It a Pity," and "While My Guitar Gently Weeps," where he reproduced his famous solo. His greatest importance was his presence onstage and his ability to hold everything together.

The evening drew to a close with Joe Brown performing the classic "I'll See You in My Dreams."

Concert for George was the best and most fitting gift Eric Clapton and friends could have given George Harrison. This is a rare tribute album that works.

One More Car, One More Rider

One More Car, One More Rider was released on November 5, 2002. It was a live album recorded August 18–19, 2001, at the Staples Center in Los Angeles. Many of his recent cast of characters were present, including Nathan East, Billy Preston, Steve Gadd, Andy Fairweather-Low, plus keyboardist David Sancious. Clapton had announced that this would be his last world tour, and while I'm sure some fans took him seriously at the time, nine years later the tours have continued to flow with regularity.

The first six songs are acoustic. "Key to the Highway," "Reptile," "Got You on My Mind," "Tears in Heaven," "Bell Bottom Blues," and "Change the World" reinforce his talent and diversity as an acoustic artist. As with many of his acoustic performances, the songs are more compact, ranging from 3:41 to 6:16. They have a warm and intimate feel and are all very appealing.

Just as you are relaxed and content, the electric Clapton takes over and snaps you awake. The band is smooth and polished, and maybe just a little too much so on the blues numbers, but it is a minor point. There is not much interaction between the band members and the audience, which takes away from the concert experience. The focus is kept directly on the music. The electric set finds Clapton in good form. Sometimes people have become too accustomed to him, so it's difficult for him to surprise us very often. That is especially true on a live album. The surprise, of course, has been his continuing live excellence.

Yes there are times when he steps back and lets the keyboards take over, but that has been a recurrent issue throughout his career.

The album also came with an accompanying DVD, and if there's anything better than hearing Eric Clapton play the guitar, it's seeing him play the guitar.

"Badge" is the song that finally kicked the album into gear, and "(I'm Your) Hoochie Coochie Man," "Cocaine," "Layla," and "Sunshine of Your Love" keep it going.

The album closer was a little perplexing. Judy Garland's signature song, "Over the Rainbow," is presented acoustically. Maybe Clapton was feeling his mortality closing in on him, but given his recent history, he seems to have gotten past this issue, if it ever existed.

One More Car, One More Rider is a good modern live album, and he makes it all look so easy. It was a middling success, reaching #69 and #43 on the U.S. and British charts respectively.

The first half of the decade proved to be a very prolific period for Clapton. In addition to his heavy touring schedule, he was cranking out the albums with regularity.

Me and Mr. Johnson

Me and Mr. Johnson was released on March 23, 2004, and completed his blues trilogy begun with *From the Cradle* and continued with *Riding with the King.*

In retrospect, it's surprising that it took so long for him to release an album of Robert Johnson covers. If Eric Clapton has ever had a consistent idol, this is the man. Johnson's compositions were spread throughout Clapton's recording and concert career. If there is one album that can be labeled his returning to his roots, this is the one.

Clapton's face has appeared on all sorts of items and collectables.

Author's collection

The project actually began by accident. He had a recording session booked but had no new material to record. Rather than just go home, he suggested they record some Robert Johnson songs. Somewhere along the line a light went on in Clapton's mind, and it became a full-blown Robert Johnson blues album. The fourteen tracks were recorded in 2003–2004.

My main criticism with the release is the slickness in places, which could have been due to Simon Climie's presence as coproducer. Johnson was passionate, intense, ominous, and a great technician, but he was definitely not slick. The CD cover pictures a stark Clapton, seated in front of a picture of Johnson, holding an acoustic guitar. If he had taken the cover to heart, he probably would have been better off in the long run. Johnson recorded mostly with just a twelve-string guitar, while Clapton

One can only wonder if people who hold lighers up at the end of his concerts are using ones like this.

Author's collection

had his band in tow. It all led him to veer away from the original style and intent of the music. I wish he had tackled the songs with just his guitar and let the chips fall where they may.

There is no doubt that Clapton loves the music and truly tries to be faithful to his idol. "Traveling Riverside Blues" is played as a traditional blues piece. "They're Red Hot" was an unusual Johnson piece as he did not use a twelve-string guitar, and it fits Clapton's style well. "Hellhound on My Trail" is one of the most revered blues songs of all time, and he interprets it well with a vocal that presents the intense imagery of the lyrics.

"Love in Vain" is representative of the album's problems as the performance is rather bland. The version pales next to the one done by the Rolling Stones on their *Let It Bleed* album.

I have appreciated many of Clapton's Johnson interpretations that were sporadically recorded throughout his career. Maybe it was the technical proficiency of fourteen of them taken together that was just overwhelming. If you want to hear the music of Mr. Johnson interpreted just right, check out Peter Green's *Me and the Devil* and *The Robert Johnson Songbook*. Of course, there is always the man himself and his *Complete Recordings* box set issued in 1990.

Sessions for Robert J

Clapton did not stop with *Me and Mr. Johnson*. He followed it on December 4, 2004, with *Sessions for Robert J*. It was a CD/DVD combo, and the project worked better as a visual presence.

I always enjoy watching Clapton play, and here he presents himself as the technician he is. Also, some of the smoothness of the audio is not as apparent on the video while the passion and intensity take over.

The most interesting part of the release are Clapton's comments about Johnson's legacy to music and himself. Another treat are the acoustic performances by Clapton and Doyle Bramhall II. The final jewel is Clapton performing in the same hotel room in Dallas that Johnson used as a make-shift recording studio.

The CD part of the package is a little different from the original release as four new songs make an appearance. If you have a choice, my advice it to buy this bigger set and pass on the CD-only release.

The Crossroads Guitar Festival

Clapton had made almost too many charity appearances to count. In 2004, he organized the Crossroads Guitar Festival to benefit the Crossroad Center in Antigua, which is a drug treatment facility. The festival was held on June 4–6, 2004, at the Cotton Bowl in Dallas, Texas. It is nice to know that he was thinking big right from the beginning. A two-DVD compilation of the three-day festival was released on November 9, 2004. It featured close to four hours of music, which only scratched the surface. Special features included artist interviews, a photo gallery, and a really cool alternate angle feature.

Guitar players young, old, famous, and not so famous flocked to Clapton's invite. B. B. King, Jeff Beck, Bo Diddley, Robert Cray, Buddy Guy, Eric Johnson, Pat Metheny, Carlos Santana, Steve Vai, and Joe Walsh were just the tip of the iceberg.

The DVD contains thirty-four performances and should satisfy the fan of the guitar or Clapton. It makes me wish it had come with a third and even fourth disc, but this snapshot will have to do. What was released contained a number of highlights.

Disc one begins with Eric Clapton doing what he does best, and this time it is on his eternal favorite "Cocaine." The energy is immediately apparent as the artists come and go in quick succession. Sometimes a longer set by some of the artists would have been appreciated, but that was beyond the scope and intent of the release.

There is a set of four songs—"Killing Floor," "Sweet Home Chicago," "Six Strings Down," and "Rock Me Baby"—that features a stage full of musicians such as Robert Cray, Hubert Sumlin, Jimmie Vaughan, Buddy Guy, Robert Randolph, B. B. King, and E. C. himself, which is a lot of guitar talent in one place. It's amazing that they do not get in each other's way, and while not everyone can take a solo, everything works out fine.

The Clapton/J. J. Cale duo on "After Midnight" and "Call Me the Breeze" works well and may have got Clapton thinking about their future together. Doyle Bramhall II steps out of Clapton's backing band shadow with "Green Light Girl," which shows what an accomplished guitarist he is in his own right.

I was pleasantly surprised by Vince Gill's performance with Jerry Douglas on "Oklahoma Borderline" and "What Cowgirls Do." At first, I thought him to be an odd inclusion, but Gill does not embarrass himself to say the least. James Taylor gets a little lost in the proceedings, although Joe Walsh helps a bit on his performance of "Steamroller." John Mayer's performance of "City Love" pales compared to what is going on around him.

As good as disc one was, it is only the warm-up for the second. It includes three more performances by Clapton. "If I Had Possession over Judgement Day," "Have You Ever Loved a Woman," and "I Shot the Sheriff" are all as good as or better than what was swirling about him.

Eric Johnson has always been a somewhat underrated guitarist but has produced a fine catalog of instrumental albums during the course of his career. His "Desert Rose" finds him at his best. Joe Walsh follows and escapes his Eagles confines with "Funk 49" and "Rocky Mountain Way."

John McLaughlin on "Tones for Elvin Jones" and Larry Carlton's "Josie" take the proceedings in a different direction, as their jazz and funky sounds serve as a nice break from the blues/rock attack. I wish Jeff Beck could have been included right behind these performances, but he regrettably does not make an appearance on the DVD. The same with Pat Metheny, who would have been a welcome addition to the release. Likewise, the sets by B. B. King and Buddy Guy could have filled an album by themselves.

I would not have closed the concert and album with ZZ Top, but they were deep in the heart of Texas. I would also have liked to have seen the

Neil Schon and Randy Jackson performance of "The Star Spangled Banner" rather than just have had it played over the closing credits.

Crossroads: Eric Clapton's Guitar Festival 2007

His first guitar festival was such a success that he brought it back a second time. It was probably a wise decision to wait three years, as it built up the anticipation. The tickets for the July 28, 2007, show at Toyota Park in Bridgeview, Illinois, sold out in less than a half hour.

I found *Crossroads: Eric Clapton's Guitar Festival* to be a superior release to the first set. It was another big three-hour, two-disc, thirty-nine-song extravaganza. From Bill Murray's rendition of "Gloria" to Buddy Guy leading an all-star ensemble through a rousing "Sweet Home Chicago," this is a guitar aficionado's delight. The set can be exhaustive due to its size and can also be somewhat disjointed due to the constant coming and going of the various artists, but these are small handicaps as the album contains a lot of unforgettable music.

Sonny Landreth kicks off the first disc with his high-energy "Umbresso." He is a good opening act as he sets the bar high for all who will follow. Landreth has a fascinating slide style of playing that is better viewed than just heard. Clapton joins him for "Hell at Home" and about halfway through the performances just takes off with an extended solo. That performance and several others—"Tell the Truth," "Little Queen of Spades," and "Isn't It a Pity"—are the Clapton I want to see.

John McLaughlin returned to the festival for the second year in a row. Here he does "Maharina," which is a typical performance. His jazz/rock guitar fusions run counter to the melody set by the keyboards, bass, and drums. McLaughlin has always traveled his own musical journey, and, appreciate him or not, there is no denying his talent.

I didn't know at the time how many performances B. B. King had left in him. It turned out to be quite a few. He had to remain seated, but his voice sounded strong, and his playing had lost none of its energy or technique. His two numbers, "Pay the Cost to Be the Boss" and "Rock Me Baby," set a standard that artists twenty or fifty years younger can only hope to emulate.

There is a nice run of performances by Doyle Bramhall and the Derek Trucks Band. Both were in Clapton's backing band at the time, but here they step forward to star. "Rosie" and "Outside Woman Blues" show Bramhall's polished technique. Trucks is one of the finer young guitarist working today. He is particularly effective when his wife Susan Tedeschi joins him.

Clapton, Jeff Beck, Steve Winwood, and Buddy Guy dominate the second disc.

Beck performed briefly at the first Crossroads festival but did not appear on the official release. He looks relaxed as he performs "Cause We Ended Up as Lovers" and "Big Block." He remains one of the few guitarists who can match Clapton note for note. He was accompanied by one of the finest young bassists on the planet in Tal Wilkenfeld. Her solos are some of the best I have seen and heard.

Clapton and Winwood join for a series of performances. They go back a long way and immediately settle in together with "Presence of the Lord," "Can't Find My Way Home," and a powerful "Crossroads." Winwood also steps from behind the keyboards to pick up a guitar for a solo version of "Mr. Fantasy." Their time together helped to reacquaint them with each other, which would bear fruit in the near future.

Clapton's old paramour Sheryl Crow more than holds her own against the big boys. Vince Gill proves that his performance at the first festival was not a fluke as he takes his country sound in a more rock direction that is helped a great deal by having Albert Lee as the second guitarist.

A few artists did struggle, as is the norm for a concert of this nature. Willie Nelson, an ill-looking Johnny Winter, and another performance by John Mayer are all lost in the festivities and are relegated to connector roles.

The second Crossroads Festival was another success, and its proceeds were donated to the drug rehabilitation center of the same name.

Back Roads

In addition to his Cream reunions, 2005 saw the release of his latest studio album, *Back Roads,* on August 29. Clapton wrote five of the tracks with Simon Climie in addition to composing one himself. The album peaked at #19 in the United States and received a gold record award for sales, while reaching #13 in the United Kingdom.

Clapton's latest studio band included keyboardists Steve Winwood and Billy Preston, bassists Nathan East and Paul Palladino, drummers Steve Gadd and Abe Laboriel, and guitarists Vince Gill and John Mayer, who obviously impressed Clapton more at his first Crossroads Festival than he did me. He also added violinist Gavyn Wright to the mix.

The album was released during a very happy and content period of Clapton's life. He had remarried and now was a family man. His career was still befitting that of a superstar, but now there were other priorities as well and a home to return to. The question is, should a blues artist be content? The answer is yes personally, but professionally it will make a difference. But life does move on.

"So Tired" is a catchy and humorous examination of family life. "One Day" has some nice, compact solos. "Run Home to Me" is probably the album's best track as Clapton delivers a poignant and moving performance. He does not forget old pal George Harrison as he includes his "Love Comes to Everyone."

Expectations for any Clapton release are always high, and the fact that he was in the midst of his latest Cream projects only increased the anticipation. The music was far from the sound of Cream and caught some critical flack at the time for being too light or too easy listening.

Back Roads is an album that needs to be accepted on its own terms. Clapton's life was moving on, and he produced a heartfelt, versatile, and comfortable release. People do change, and as his personal life went in new and for him better directions, he took his music along with him.

There was also a dual-disc version of the album, for the technologically advanced, which presented the whole affair in surround sound. Even with a mellow album such as this, the listening experience was spectacular and makes it clear why Alan Douglas and Mick Guzauski won the Grammy for Best Engineered Album (Non-Classical). There was also an interview with Clapton plus five songs played in the studio. It even came with five guitar picks, making it an appealing packing for his fans.

For a guy who retired from the road several years ago, Clapton maintained a heavy schedule. He embarked on a series of ambitious tours during 2006–2007, which included Europe, the United States, Japan, Australia, and New Zealand. He was accompanied by one of his strongest bands as it included both Doyle Bramhall and Derek Trucks on guitar. Trucks was doing triple duty at the time as he was fronting his own band plus was the lead guitarist for the Allman Brothers. Jim Carmon, Chris Stainton, Willie Weeks, and Steve Jordan were on hand as the keyboardists, bassist, and drummer respectively.

In 2008, he was on the road again minus Trucks but added Robert Rudolph to fill in on slide guitar for the North American leg of his world tour. The drummers were now Ian Thomas (North America) and Abe Laboriel (Europe), plus bass player Pino Palladino (North America). These were some of the musicians who went into the studio with him in August 2005 for another collaboration project.

The Road to Escondido

Clapton had recorded a number of J. J. Cale compositions through the years, including two of his signature songs, "After Midnight" and "Cocaine." The original intent had been for Cale to produce an album for Clapton, which quickly evolved into a dual project. It took a while, but *The Road to Escondido* was finally released on November 7, 2006. It reached #50 in the United States and #23 in England, receiving sales awards in both countries. It won the Grammy for Best Contemporary Blues Album.

Cale and Clapton were brothers of the blues, although their approaches were different. Cale was always understated, while Clapton would travel from mellow to pyrotechnic.

The album contained superb guitar playing as Bramhall, Trucks, John Mayer, and Albert Lee all assisted the duo at various points.

"When the War Is Over" has a honky-tonk feel with some shuffle guitar thrown in for good measure. It was a nice melding of both of their styles. "Missing Person" has Cale and Clapton trading verses vocally before joining together on the chorus. If you want a guitar solo, check out "Who Am I Telling You." "Don't Cry Sister" contains some nice harmonizing by the pair.

Some other highlights to look for are Taj Mahal's harmonica playing on "Sporting Life Blues," a bluegrass sound on "Dead End Road," and the catchy rhythms of "Danger."

Cale wrote eleven of the fourteen tracks, and the album reflects his overall influence. "Clapton's "Three Little Girls" sounds more like a Cale composition than his own.

The Road to Escondido is not groundbreaking or earth-shattering. It is comfortable, restrained, and ultimately enjoyable. While the sound is closer to Cale's, it is nevertheless a welcome addition to the Clapton catalog. It is a reminder of just how adaptable Clapton could be as this bluesy/folk type collaboration remains an outstanding album for both of the participants.

Complete Clapton

The year 2007 saw the release of another Clapton compilation album. *Complete Clapton* was a two-disc, thirty-one-track set that clocked in at just over two and a half hours. It was released to coincide with his new autobiography and was comprised of tracks from both his former and current label, although the first disc was suspiciously similar to *The Cream of Clapton*. It was another successful commercial enterprise, reaching #2 in the United States and #14 in England.

Despite the title, it is not complete but does contain most of his well-known and popular material. It should be approached as a modern-day greatest hits album.

I have few complaints about the release as it was intended to be a commercial overview of his musical journey, and in that it succeeds well. While the material is available elsewhere and in different forms, it should be accepted for what it was intended to be.

The liner notes were well done, with information about each song, a list of musicians, and some photos.

Most fans could probably guess at least half the tracks on the album without ever seeing the song list. I use the album as part of my car inventory, and I have found it to be a perfect driving companion for traveling down the road of life while enjoying Clapton's journey.

Live from Madison Square Garden

The years 2008–2010 were busy ones for Clapton. He was approaching the retirement age of sixty-five with no signs of slowing down. Life tends to rush by as people age, and it seems as if he wanted to pack as much as possible into the years that remain, which hopefully are a lot.

His 2009 touring band of Japan, New Zealand, and Australia included Bramhall, Stainton, Weeks, Laboriel, plus backup singers Sharon White and Michelle John. The Ireland/U.K. leg added Andy Fairweather-Low plus Steve Gadd replacing Laboriel. Tim Carmen was added as a second keyboardist.

Clapton's relationship with old bandmate Steve Winwood continued to develop. They had remained friends since the dissolution of Blind Faith but had rarely performed together.

They decided to play a series of concerts together at Madison Square Garden on February 25–28, 2008. Over a year later, a two-CD/two-DVD set was released chronicling the event. Their time onstage together was so enjoyable they toured the States in June 2009. The album may have only reached #40 in the United States but sold two million copies.

Live from Madison Square Garden is an essential listen and a modernized trip back to another era. The music travels in a wide arc, including four Traffic songs, to the first side of the only Blind Faith release, to solo material, to such tracks as Jimi Hendrix's "Voodoo Child" and Buddy Miles's "Them Changes." Each performed one solo song: Clapton with an acoustic performance of "Rambling on My Mind" and Winwood at the organ for a moving "Georgia on My Mind." There were also some nice switches such as Winwood's vocal on "Forever Man" and Clapton's guitar solo on "Glad."

They wisely used a basic backing band. Keyboardist Chris Stainton, bassist Willie Weeks, and drummer Abe Laboriel Jr. were the only other instrumentalists. The focus was kept on the two stars, where it should have been.

The overall feel of the concert was happiness and comfort. They seemed to be enjoying themselves and were able to transmit that feeling to the audience, both live and through this release.

The sixty-five-year-old Clapton continued to tour heavily. Stainton, Weeks, and Gadd remain his basic band. He toured Europe with Winwood from May 18 to June 13.

Eric Clapton Guitar Festival 2010

Clapton held his third Crossroads Guitar Festival on June 26, 2010, back at Toyota Park in Bridgeview, Illinois. He was joined by the usual array of guitar star power. The Robert Cray Band, Jimmie Vaughan, ZZ Top, Doyle Bramhall, Vince Gill, Earl Klugh, Buddy Guy, Derek Trucks, Johnny

One of the more memorable concert posters of Eric Clapton's career. *Courtesy of Robert Rodriguez*

Winter, Jeff Beck, B. B. King, and the ever-present John Mayer all joined him for another day of guitar-based music.

Eric Clapton Guitar Festival 2010 was released November 9, 2010, and is another two-DVD extravaganza featuring an eclectic group of musicians that come together in a number of fine performances.

Bill Murray is back as emcee and introduces the individual acts.

Disc one blasts out of the starting gate with Clapton and Sonny Landreth performing "Promised Land." Gypsy Blood," and "In My Time of Dying" by Bramhall keep the momentum flowing. The combination of Sheryl Crow with Derek Trucks, Susan Tedeschi, and Gary Clark join Bramhall on "Long Road Home," and then Clapton joins in as well on "Our Love Is Fading."

Sometimes, a good idea is really a good idea. His *Unplugged* project was one of the most successful of his career.   *Author's collection*

Vince Gill's stature, at least with me, has continued to grow with each Crossroads appearance. "Mystery Train," "Lay Down Sally," and "One More Last Chance" with an assortment of musicians including the great James Burton, Earl Klugh, Albert Lee, and Keb Mo help propel him to another stellar performance.

Earl Klugh is always welcome, and his jazz guitar on "Angelina" and "Vonetta" is a welcome counterpoint to the sounds that are swirling around him.

Husband and wife Derek Trucks and Susan Tedeschi are a highlight with "Midnight in Harlem," "Comin' Home," and "Space Captain." Other high points are Buddy Guy with Johnny Lang and Ronnie Wood on "Five Long Years" and "Miss You" plus Jeff Beck's "Hammerhead" and "Nessun Dorma."

Clapton is represented by a seven-song set. "Hands of the Saints," a twelve-minute "I Shot the Sheriff," "Shake Your Moneymaker" with Jeff Beck, and "Had to Cry," "Voodoo Child," and "Dear Mr. Fantasy" with Steve Winwood are enough to whet the appetite of any Clapton fan. The set and concert come to a close with an all-star lineup featuring B. B. King, Clapton, and Robert Cray.

Clapton's Crossroad Festivals and resulting albums have become an interesting collection of guitarists and music that rarely happens. It is a testimony to his stature that he is able to continually attract such talent to give their time to such a worthy cause.

Clapton

Eric Clapton released his nineteenth studio album on September 27, 2010, just in time for entry into this book. Proving that sixty-five is not too old, he reached the top ten in the United States, Great Britain, Austria, Belgium, Canada, Denmark, the Netherlands, France, Germany, Czechoslovakia, Hungary, Italy, Norway, Spain, Poland, and Switzerland. The personnel included Bramhall (who also coproduced), J. J. Cale, Derek Trucks, Jim Keltner, Willie Weeks, Walt Richmond, and Steve Winwood, among others.

Clapton is a polished affair. He only cowrote one of the tracks but chose the other thirteen wisely. There is a mixture of blues, rock, a little jazz, and even some R&B thrown in for good measure.

The core of the album is made up of pop standards. "Autumn Leaves," "How Deep Is the Ocean," "Crazy About You Baby," and "When Somebody Thinks You're Wonderful" are good vehicles for his vocals and are interpreted effectively and uniquely.

He does rock a little as well. "Travelin' Alone," "Judgement Day," "Everything Will Be Alright," and "Run Back to Your Side" will all keep your attention.

"My Very Good Friend the Milkman" has a New Orleans jazz flavor courtesy of Allen Toussaint and Wynton Marsalis.

Now in his mid-sixties, Clapton can still play in the style of Cream and Derek and the Dominos but has reached a point in his life when he has decided to travel a different path, at least in the studio.

Clapton is a vibrant exploration of styles. It may be a little too easy on the ears for some, but it is representative of the Clapton of 2010.

29

All Around My Home Town, They're Trying to Track Me Down

Whatever Happened To

Tom Dowd

V ery few record producers could boast that they worked on the Manhattan Project during World War II as a nuclear physicist.

What does a discharged soldier, who served in the U.S. Army as a scientist do for a living? In Tom Dowd's case, he became one of the most noted engineers and producers in music history.

His career extended back to the era of the 78-rpm record and very primitive recording equipment. His first project that would produce a hit record was with traditional pop singer Eileen Barton. Her recording of "If I Knew You Were Coming, I'd Have Baked a Cake" reached #1 on the *Billboard* singles chart April 15–27, 1950.

His first steady job was for the Atlantic label, working with such artists as Ray Charles, the Drifters, the Coasters, and Ruth Brown. He engineered one of the biggest hits of the fifties when Bobby Darin's "Mack the Knife" topped the American singles charts for nine weeks in 1959; it remains one of the best-selling singles of all time. The release won a Grammy for Record of the Year. *Rolling Stone* ranked it as one of the 500 Greatest of All Time.

Dowd made several important contributions to the improvement of engineering sound quality. He first used an 8-track recording system at Atlantic, which allowed their artists to be recorded using multiple tracks, which would then be combined. While stereo had been around for several decades, he was the first to refine it and use it to enhance the sound of records. He would also go on to revamp the entire sound system of the Stax label in Memphis.

During the sixties, he worked as a producer and sometimes an engineer with many of Atlantic's leading artists including Aretha Franklin, the Young Rascals, Herbie Mann, the Sweet Inspirations, the Drifters, King Curtis, Dusty Springfield, Wilson Pickett, Solomon Burke, and Sam and Dave.

These experiences led him to engineer an album by a group with a far different sound who were signed to Atlantic's subsidiary label, Atco.

Cream was recording what would become the classic *Disraeli Gears*, and Tom Dowd was hired as the engineer. This would begin a lifetime association with Eric Clapton.

He produced *Layla and Other Assorted Love Songs* by Derek and the Dominos and because of his relationship with the Allman Brothers Band would be the connector between Eric Clapton and Duane Allman.

Clapton would turn to Dowd a number of times during the course of his career. He produced *461 Ocean Boulevard, August, Another Ticket, E. C. Was Here,* and *Money and Cigarettes.* Many of Clapton's compilation albums bear Dowd's imprint, including both of his huge *Crossroads* box set hits.

Dowd would be an in-demand producer for over half a century. He received a Grammy for his lifetime achievements in February 2002. He passed away a little under nine months later at the age of seventy-seven from emphysema.

His role in the music of Eric Clapton should not be underestimated. He was able to steer the drug-laden Derek and the Dominos project not only to completion but to its status as one of rock's superior albums.

I am constantly amazed at how many singles and albums contain the Dowd name. Eric Clapton called him "the Ideal Recording Man," which is a legacy to be cherished. He was inducted into the Rock and Roll Hall of Fame on April 14, 2012.

Yvonne Elliman

Yvonne Elliman had a nice solo career before and after her professional relationship with Eric Clapton.

She was the product of Irish, Japanese, and Chinese ancestries that gave her an exotic and alluring look, which when combined with her singing talent brought her to the attention of Tim Rice and Andrew Lloyd Webber. They promptly recruited her to play the part of Mary Magdalene in their new rock opera, *Jesus Christ Superstar.* She toured with the cast for the next four years, singing on the #1 album of the same name, and reprising her role for the movie, which earned her a 1974 Golden Globe Nomination for Best Actress in a Musical or Comedy.

Her signature song from the production, "I Don't Know How to Love Him," became a top thirty single in the United States. While the song only reached #47 in the United Kingdom, it became a worldwide hit.

Nineteen seventy-four found her working on Broadway, where she met and married Bill Oakes, who worked with Robert Stigwood. After being introduced, Stigwood hired her as a backing vocalist for the "I Shot the Sheriff" single, which began a professional relationship with Clapton that would last for several years and albums.

She can he heard on *461 Ocean Boulevard, There's One in Every Crowd, No Reason to Cry, E. C. Was Here,* and *Slowhand* plus countless compilation albums. She was a member of his touring band from 1974 to 1977 and in tandem with Marcy Levy formed what is probably the strongest backing vocal duo of his career.

Elliman continued her association with Robert Stigwood by participating in his *Saturday Night Fever.* The Bee Gees originally wrote "How Deep Is Your Love" for Elliman, but Stigwood insisted they record it themselves. Elliman had to settle for "If I Can't Have You." It was a wise decision for everyone concerned as both singles topped *Billboard*'s Pop Singles chart during the height of the disco era. I truly hope she signed a good royalty deal, as the song was a part of the film soundtrack, which topped the U.S. album charts for twenty-four weeks and sold fifteen million copies.

This would be the highpoint of her career. Her Albums *Love Me* (1976) and *Night Fright* (1978) charted at #68 and #40 respectively. Her singles "Love Me" and "Hello Stranger" were both top twenty hits in the United States, but by the end of the eighties she was in semiretirement raising her children.

She released her first new album in a quarter of a century in 2004 with *Simple Needs.* She has since resumed touring and performing. I wonder if Clapton needs a backup singer?

Marcy Levy

Marcella Levy may have had the strongest and best rock voice of any of Eric Clapton's backup singers. She also impacted his career as a songwriter.

Levy was born on June 21, 1952, in Detroit, Michigan, and by the age of twenty was touring as a backup singer with Bob Seger. She moved on to Leon Russell's touring band, which brought her into the Eric Clapton orbit.

She became a member of his road and touring bands from 1974 to 1978, and again from 1984 to 1985. She sang on *E. C. Was Here, There's One in Every Crowd, No Reason to Cry, Slowhand, Backless,* and *Behind the Sun* in addition to her hundreds of concert appearances. She also contributed (cowrote) eight songs to Clapton's albums. "Innocent Times," "Lay Down Sally," "The Core," "Roll It," "Hungry," "Promises," "Walk Away," and "Tangled in Love" all bear her authorship stamp.

The only chart single in the United States to feature her own name was a duet with Robin Gibb. "Help Me," from the film *Times Square,* peaked at #50 during a ten-week run from 1980 to 1981.

Levy's greatest fame came as a member of Shakespears Sister with Siobhan Fahey, formally of Bananarama, 1988–1993. Their greatest success was in Great Britain, where their two albums *Sacred Heart* (#3) and *Hormonally Yours* (#3) were very commercially successful. Their most famous song was "Stay," which reached #1 in England and #4 in the United States. They issued six top forty singles in the United Kingdom. By the mid-nineties, the band was gone, and Levy, who had changed her name to Marcella Detroit, was on her own again.

Her greatest solo success also took place in England as her 1994 *Jewel* album reached #15 and produced such solo hits as "I Believe" (#11); "Ain't Nothing Like the Real Thing," which was a duet with Elton John (#24); and "I'm an Angel."

Levy has continued to release albums on various labels. *Feeler* (1976), *Dancing Madly Sideways* (2001), and *The Upside of Being Down* (2006) were all well produced and driven by her strong vocals but slid under the commercial radar. She has returned to her old name and continues to be active on the concert circuit.

Tessa Niles

Tessa Niles is a career backup singer who has worked with some of the elite of the music world. The Rolling Stones, Duran Duran, Annie Lennox, Paul McCartney, Tina Turner, George Harrison, David Bowie, the Police, and Cliff Richard have all used her powerful vocals.

She appeared on Clapton's *August, Journeyman, Unplugged,* and *24 Nights* albums plus was a part of his touring band 1988–1992, 1997, and his 1999 tour of Japan. She also appeared at the 1999 Crossroads Benefit and 2002's *Concert for George.*

Katie Kissoon

Katie and Mac Kissoon were siblings who had a top twenty single in the United States with "Chirpy Chirpy Cheap Cheap." They were originally from Trinidad but moved to England with their parents at a young age.

After the duo's career ended, Katie became primarily a backup singer and joined Eric Clapton's recording and touring bands in 1986. This began a long association for the two, which included *August, Journeyman, Unplugged, 24 Nights,* and *Pilgrim.*

Sharon White

Sharon White has been a part of every major Clapton tour, U.S. and world-wide, since 2006.

She was, and is, a member of the family country band the Whites, who are regular performers at the Grand Ole Opry. They have charted five albums and fifteen singles on the U.S. country charts from 1983 to 2007. She remains another of those artists who balances a career as a Clapton backup with one of her own.

Nathan East

Much of the attention regarding Eric Clapton's backing bands has always focused on his guitarists and with good reason, but his other supporting musicians are just as accomplished in their own right.

Nathan East was Philadelphia born but raised in Southern California since the age of four. He was a cello and bass player from an early age and obtained a bachelor of arts degree in music from the University of California.

Among his accomplishments are as cowriter of the huge hit "Easy Lover" for Phil Collins and Philip Bailey and performing at the *We Are the One: The Obama Inaugural Celebration* at the Lincoln Memorial. In addition, he has been a noted session musician for three decades, appearing with Elton John, Michael Jackson, Quincy Jones, Barbra Streisand, Sergio Mendes, Lionel Richie, and Phil Collins, among others.

East gained his greatest fame as an Eric Clapton sidekick. He has contributed to *Behind the Mask, August, Journeyman, Unplugged, 24 Nights, Riding with the King, Reptile, Me and Mr. Johnson, Sessions for Robert J, Back Home,* and *The Road to Escondido.*

He began touring with Clapton in 1984, and except for a small stretch during 1994–1995, he continues to do so to the present day, making him the longest tenured of any of Clapton's bandmates. He has assumed the position of musical director on a number of recent tours.

In his spare time, East is a member of the respected jazz group Four Play, with keyboardist Bob James; drummer Harvey Mason; and in order of their involvement, guitarists Lee Ritenour, Larry Carlton, and Chuck Loeb. They released their tenth studio album, *Let's Touch the Sky,* in 2010.

Jamie Oldaker

Jamie Oldaker was born on September 5, 1951, in Tulsa, Oklahoma, and in his early twenties began playing with Bob Seger's backing band alongside Marcy Levy. He moved on to Leon Russell, through whom he met Carl Radle, who invited him to the *461 Ocean Boulevard* sessions. Oldaker was a member of Clapton's backing band from 1983 to 1986. He also backed Clapton at the Royal Albert Hall 1990–1991. His drumming can be heard on *461 Ocean Boulevard*, *Backless*, *Slowhand*, *24 Nights*, and *Behind the Sun*.

After leaving Clapton, he joined Kiss guitarist Ace Frehley's band Frehley's Comet and contributed to the 1988 self-titled album. In the early nineties, he was a founding member of the alternative country band the Tractors.

Oldaker released a solo album, *Mad Dogs & Okies*, in 2005. Vince Gill, J. J. Cale, Willie Nelson, Bonnie Bramlett, and old boss Eric Clapton joined him. He continues to be active as a session drummer, music publisher, and artist manager.

George Terry

George Terry is one of those little engines who could—and did.

He was born in Philadelphia, Pennsylvania, in 1950. He became a session musician based out of Criteria Studios in Miami, Florida, where he worked with Simon and Garfunkel, Sonny and Cher, Neil Diamond, and Bill Wyman.

In 1974, he was playing in a studio near Eric Clapton and was invited to come over and jam. This chance meeting led to his playing on *461 Ocean Boulevard* after Dave Mason withdrew from the project. He stayed for *There's One in Every Crowd*, *E. C. Was Here*, *No Reason to Cry*, *Slowhand*, and *Backless*.

Terry was a member of Clapton's touring band in the mid-seventies, which was a troubled period in Clapton's life. Many times he assumed lead guitar duties as Clapton would withdraw from the spotlight onstage.

He also authored three songs recorded by Clapton: "Mainline Florida," "Don't Blame Me," and "Lay Down Sally" with Marcy Levy.

The end of the decade found him back in Florida working with the likes of Barbra Streisand, the Bee Gees, and Kenny Rogers. He also released his own studio album, *Guitar Drive*.

Greg Phillinganes

Greg Phillinganes was born in Detroit, Michigan, on May 12, 1956, and has been one of the most in-demand session musicians of the last three decades.

His big break came when he joined Stevie Wonder's Wonderlove Band 1976–1981. He played on Wonder's huge-selling album *Songs in the Key of Life*.

Phillinganes went on to play on a number of Michael Jackson albums including *Off the Wall* (1979), *Thriller* (1982), *Bad* (1987), and *Dangerous* (1991). He was also the keyboardist and musical director for Jackson's *Bad* and *Dangerous* tours.

He released two solo albums during that time. *Significant Gains* (1981) and *Pulse* (1984) were well-written and produced pop/rock affairs. *Pulse* featured the song "Behind the Mask," which had a great deal of success on the dance charts. Clapton later covered the song on his *August* album.

After working with two giants of the music industry, Phillinganes worked with a third when he joined Eric Clapton's touring band, 1986–1990, before rejoining in 1991. He played on *Behind the Sun, August, Journeyman,* and *24 Nights.*

He continues to be active, contributing to projects by Stevie Nicks, the Bee Gees, Aretha Franklin, Paul McCartney, Mick Jagger, Babyface, Mariah Carey, and Diana Ross. He was a member of Toto from 2005 to 2008 but is not a member of the band as of 2010.

Henry Spinetti

Henry George Spinetti is an English drummer who was born on March 31, 1951. He is one of those session musicians who float under the radar but whose name constantly appears in the album's credits of a large number of releases.

A partial list of his accomplishments includes Joan Armatrading (*Show Some Emotion* and *To the Limit*), Roger Daltrey (*Rock Horse*), Bob Dylan (*Down in the Groove*), George Harrison (*Gone Troppo*), Alexis Korner (*Just Easy*), Paul McCartney (his Russian album), plus Chris Spedding, Pete Townshend, and a host of others.

He was a member of Clapton's all-British band from 1979 to 1982. He appeared on *Just One Night, Another Ticket, August,* and his 1986 *Lethal Weapon* soundtrack. He continues to play occasional dates with Clapton.

Chris Stainton

Chris Stainton is a British keyboardist born March 22, 1944. At the age of twenty-two, he joined Joe Cocker's Grease Band and participated in the famous *Mad Dogs and Englishmen* tour of Canada and the United States. He remained with Cocker through the end of 1972. He supported a number of artists in the seventies in addition to fronting his own Chris Stainton Band from 1972 to 1976.

In 1980, he joined Clapton for his *Just One Night* tour and remained with his touring band for eight years. He then returned to Cocker's band. Stainton served a second stint with Clapton from 1993 to 1997 before rejoining Cocker for a third time. He continued his band-hopping by joining Clapton for the third time. He has participated in every major tour from 2006 to 2010.

Stainton's keyboards can be heard on *Just One Night, Another Ticket, Money and Cigarettes, Behind the Sun, From the Cradle,* and *Pilgrim.*

Will Jennings

Will Jennings may seem like an odd person to collaborate with Eric Clapton as his fame comes primarily from his film soundtrack contributions, yet he has worked with a number of artists including B. B. King, Linda Ronstadt, Aaron Neville, Roy Orbison, and Jimmy Buffett.

His most successful work were his compositions for Buffett's *Riddles in the Sand* (1984) and *Last Mango in Paris* (1985). He cowrote Dionne Warwick's Grammy-winning "I'll Never Love This Way Again," but it was his work with Steve Winwood that ultimately brought him to the attention of Eric Clapton.

He cowrote four of seven songs for Steve Winwood's 1980 *Arc of a Diver.* He then cowrote, with Winwood, all nine songs for the latter's *Talking Back to the Night* and then five of the eight tracks for *Back in the High Life* including the hit "Higher Love." His journey with Winwood continued with seven of eight tracks on *Roll with It* and seven of eight on *Refugees of the Heart.*

Despite his pop success with Winwood, his greatest fame came from several movie songs. He coauthored "Up Where We Belong," for the film *An Officer and a Gentlemen,* which won the 1983 Oscar and Golden Globe Award for Best Song.

That was just the warm-up for "My Heart Will Go On" from the film *Titanic.* It was the key song on the movie soundtrack, which sold thirty million copies worldwide. It became one of the biggest-selling singles of all time and won an Oscar, Golden Globe, and four Grammy awards. A number of polls rank it as the most played song in radio history.

Jennings crossed paths with Eric Clapton when he was asked to provide the lyrics for "Tears in Heaven." At first he was reluctant to write about such a personal subject but finally relented. His lyrics captured Clapton's grief just right. It remains one of his most popular and beloved songs, and Jennings shares the 1993 Grammy for it with Clapton.

Jerry Lynn Williams

Jerry Lynn Williams was an obscure Texas blues/country/rocker when he joined Eric Clapton in the studio. In reality, his career extended back to a stint in Little Richard's backing band with another guitarist named Jimmy James, who would become famous as Jimi Hendrix. By the mid-seventies, he had released two solo albums with little commercial success.

When Clapton went into the studio to record 1985's *Behind the Sun*, he was looking for commercial hit material. He was sent three songs by Williams and was so impressed he used all three. "See What Love Can Do," "Something's Happening," and the hit single "Forever Man" helped to put Williams in the public eye.

He contributed four more songs to 1989's *Journeyman*. "Pretending," "Anything for Your Love," "No Alibis," and "Breaking Point" served as the middle ground for the album. They were not hard-core blues but were not too pop either. They softened Clapton's hard-blues proclivities and moved the album in a more commercial direction.

When Clapton began his blues trilogy with *From the Cradle* and his association with Simon Climie, Williams's songs were no longer needed, but they had served their short-term purpose well.

Williams contributed songs to Bonnie Raitt and B. B. King. He moved to the island of St. Martin at the turn of the twenty-first century and passed away from kidney and liver failure on November 25, 2005.

J. J. Cale

J. J. Cale has only produced one top forty single during his long and illustrious career. "Crazy Mama" reached #22 in 1972. It was followed by "After Midnight," which peaked at #42 (1972). "Lies," at #42 (1972), and "Hey Baby," at #96 (1976), complete his list of chart singles.

Cale's career extends back as far as, if not further than, Clapton's. He released three singles between 1958 and 1961, first as Johnny Cale and then as the Johnny Cale Quintet. "Sock Hop"/"Sneaky" (1958), "Troubles"/"Purple Onion," and "Ain't That Lovin' You Baby"/"She's My Desire" all disappeared very quickly but remain a worthwhile challenge for collectors. His first album, *A Trip down the Sunset Strip*, was released in 1966, and his last to date was 2009's *Roll On*.

While Clapton's laid-back style has been frustrating for his fans at times, J. J. Cale's is considered charming. His songs are usually stripped to the basics, which puts the focus on his lyrics. His concerts range from solo performances to being backed by a full band, which allows for some improvisation. The best introductions to his music are 2001's *Live* and 1998's *The Very Best of J. J. Cale.*

Clapton's career became intertwined with Cale's early on, when he recorded "Cocaine" and "After Midnight." They remain an important part of Clapton's legacy, and his performances raised the profile of Cale. Both remain important parts of each live show. The two men finally collaborated on the dual project *The Road to Escondido* in 2006.

Their relationship has been beneficial to both. In some ways Clapton has found a soul mate who can write words and music that exemplify what he would like to create himself. The relationship seems to be a place where Clapton is comfortable, and that fact should not be underestimated.

Simon Climie

Climie Fisher, comprised of Simon Climie and Rob Fisher, had a #2 British hit in 1988 with "Love Changes (Everything)." It also reached #23 on the U.S. singles chart. Listening to that song at the time gave no hint whatsoever that you were being introduced to a person who would have an impact on the career of Eric Clapton almost a decade later.

It was the TDF project in 1997 that cemented their relationship, and yes, their *Retail Therapy* album attributed to TDF has to be the oddest of Clapton's long career. Climie has always been a pop techno guy at heart, but he is also an impeccable producer. Sometimes he may have been a little too polished for Clapton, but he could put together an album. Most importantly, Clapton respected him and returned to him as a producer a number of times.

Pilgrim, Riding with the *King, Reptile,* and *Me and Mr. Johnson* were all coproduced by Climie and for better or worse bear his imprint. He also cowrote five tracks on the *Back Home* album.

Climie continues to be active in the music industry. He has worked with Michael McDonald, which seems like a good fit, and produced the 2009 album by *American Idol* winner Taylor Hicks titled *The Distance.*

There will never be a Climie Fisher reunion as partner Rob Fisher passed away August 25, 1999, following surgery.

Andy Fairweather-Low

Andy Fairweather-Low's career has reached the forty-five-year mark, and while he has become a well-known session musician, particularly with Eric Clapton, he began his career as a pop idol in Great Britain.

He was the founder/leader of the pop group Amen Corner, who were very successful during the late sixties. They hit #1 on the singles charts with "(If Paradise Is) Half As Nice" plus "Bend Me, Shape Me" and "Gin House" reached the top ten. "Gin House" was performed on Clapton's 1999 tour of Japan.

In 1969, he formed Fair Weather with drummer Dennis Bryan and keyboardist Blue Weaver. They produced another hit single in the United Kingdom with "Natural Sinner" but by 1972 had dissolved.

Fairweather-Low released eight solo albums from 1974 to 2008. *Wide Eyed and Legless: The A&M Recordings* was a 2004 CD reissue that combined his first three solo albums, *Spider Jiving* (1974), *La Booga Rooga* (1975), and the excellent *Be Bop 'N' Holla* (1976), into one release. *Live in Concert* DVD, released in 2008, brings his career and music up to date.

Despite his popularity in England, Fairweather-Low never had a hit in the United States and would not become a household name.

During the late seventies, he became a session guitarist of note. He supported Roy Wood, Leo Sayer, Gerry Rafferty, and Richard and Linda Thompson. In 1978, he provided backing vocals on four tracks for *Who Are You*. He also played guitar on "It's Your Turn" from the Who's *It's Hard* album when Pete Townshend was not available. He joined Bill Wyman's group, Willie and the Poor Boys, for two albums during the '80s.

Fairweather-Low joined Clapton's band in 1992 and as of 2009 took part in the U.K. Ireland tour. His service as Clapton's second guitarist is the longest of E. C.'s long career. He played in the backing band for George Harrison's *Live in Japan* album and also played in 2002's *Concert for George* at the Royal Albert Hall. He can be heard on *Unplugged, From the Cradle, Pilgrim, Riding with the King*, and *Reptile*.

In addition to his work with Clapton, he has backed Roger Waters for a quarter of a century. He has played guitar on three major tours: *The Pro and Cons of Hitchhiking* tour of America in 1985, the three-year *In the Flesh* tour in 1999–2002, and *The Dark Side of the Moon* tour 2006. He also played on a number of Roger Waters albums, including *Kaos* (1987), *The Wall—Live in Berlin* (1990), *Amused to Death* (1992), *In the Flesh—Live* (2002), and *Flicker Flame: The Solo Years, Volume 1* (2002).

In 2005, Fairweather-Low played rhythm guitar on Joe Satriani's self-titled album along with Clapton bandmate Nathan East.

Buddy Guy

Eric Clapton has many times referred to Buddy Guy as his favorite blues guitarist.

Guy was born in the metropolis of Lettsworth, Louisiana, on July 30, 1936. By the time he was in his early twenties, he had relocated to Chicago and was playing with such legends as Muddy Waters, Howlin' Wolf, and Little Walter. He also was a Chess label session guitarist throughout most of the sixties.

Chess did not know what to do with this flamboyant blues rocker. It was not until 1967 that he released his first solo album for the label: *I Left My Blues in San Francisco.* A string of excellent releases for the Vanguard Label followed, but by decade's end his career was in decline.

For many years, he toured with harpist Junior Wells. Clapton remembers seeing Guy perform at the Marquee Club in 1965, with B. B. King and play the guitar with his teeth.

Guy formally entered Clapton's life onstage with Led Zeppelin, Jack Bruce, Stephen Stills, Buddy Miles, and, yes, Glen Campbell at the "Supershow" in Staines, England, in April 1969.

Clapton and Guy have shared the stage together many times through the years. Their performances at the famed Ronnie Scott's in London were filmed for the *South Bank Show.* He also joined Clapton for his yearly series of concerts at the Royal Albert Hall in 1990 and 1991 and appeared on the album *24 Nights.* Guy also provided a vocal track for the *Rush* soundtrack. They appeared together at the Concert for New York City on October 21, 2001. Guy has also played at Clapton's Crossroads Festivals.

While Guy was a Chicago-based blues guitarist, he was not a blues artist in the traditional sense of the word in that he bridged the gap between rock and blues, which when combined with his stage antics, not only influenced two generations of guitarists but expanded the limits of rock 'n' roll itself.

On March 14, 2005, Eric Clapton journeyed to the Rock and Roll Hall of Fame once again. This time it was to join with B. B. King to induct his old friend and fellow guitarist Buddy Guy.

If you are passing through Chicago, don't forget to stop at his blues club, Buddy Guy's Legends.

Albert Lee

Albert Lee was born on December 21, 1943, in Leominster, England, into a musical household. By the time he was sixteen, he had left school to play the guitar full time.

His first successful bands as the lead guitarist were Chris Farlowe and the Thunderbirds and Heads, Hands and Feet, who backed one of his idols, Jerry Lee Lewis, on *The Session,* which was recorded in London and released in 1973.

Lee went on to spend some time as a member of the Crickets, Buddy Holly's former backing band, with Sonny Curtis and Jerry Allison. If you would like to hear his style during this period, you will need to track down the Crickets' *Long Way from Lubbock*. In 1976, he joined Emmylou Harris's Hot Band.

It was his years, 1978–1983, with Eric Clapton that would bring Lee some fame. He played in Clapton's touring band plus recorded with him on *Just One Night, Another Ticket*, and *Money and Cigarettes*. He also joined him for the *Concert for George* plus appeared at his 2007 Crossroads Festival.

In recent years, he has again toured with Emmylou Harris as well as Bill Wyman's Rhythm Kings.

Doyle Bramhall II

Doyle Bramhall was a Texas drummer best known for playing with Jimmie and Stevie Ray Vaughan. He died on November 12, 2011. His son proved the old adage that the apple does not fall far from the tree, as he too would become a musician of note. The apple did roll a bit after hitting the ground as he grew up to be not a drummer but one of the leading guitarists of today.

The second Doyle Bramhall was born December 24, 1969, in Dallas, Texas. At the age of sixteen, he was the second guitarist for Jimmie Vaughan's Fabulous Thunderbirds.

In 1992, he formed the Arc Angels with Charlie Sexton, plus drummer Chris Layton and bassist Tommy Shannon. They split in 1993 due to Bramhall II's addiction problems. They have since reunited several times and in 2009 opened for Clapton on his European tour. They released *Living in a Dream* (CD + DVD) in 2009.

It was his 1999 solo album *Jellycream* that brought Bramhall to the attention of Eric Clapton. Clapton decided to use two of his compositions, "Marry You" and "I Wanna Be," for his *Riding with the King* project. Bramhall joined him for the recording session and has become a fixture with Clapton on tour and in the studio ever since.

He wrote "Superman Inside" for *Reptile* and joined Clapton for the recording sessions. Bramhall's band, Smokestack, opened for Clapton on his 2001 world tour. He took over as the second guitarist in Clapton's band in 2004.

He also played on *Me and Mr. Johnson*, *Sessions for Robert J*, and *Clapton*, which he also coproduced.

He has become a fixture with Clapton, having played on his '06 and '07 world tours, '07 North American and Eastern tours; '08 U.S./Canadian tour; '08 European tour; '09 Japan, Australian, and New Zealand tour; and '09 U.K./Ireland tour. He also continues to play on his own and with the Arc Angels.

Derek Trucks

Derek Trucks was born on June 8, 1979, in Jacksonville, Florida. His uncle Butch Trucks was a founding member of the legendary Allman Brothers, with whom he continues to perform. As a teenager, he played with Bob Dylan, Joe Walsh, and Stephen Stills.

In 1999, Derek Trucks officially joined the Allman Brothers as a guitarist and remains a band member to the present day. This began an ambitious decade, as he was also fronting his own Derek Trucks Band, had formed an association with Eric Clapton, and was playing dates with his wife, blues singer Susan Tedeschi.

Clapton hired him as a session musician for *The Road to Escondido*. He and his wife were then invited to play at the 2007 Crossroads Festival, where they opened for Clapton, supported Johnny Winter, and backed Clapton. He then accompanied Clapton on his world tour.

Trucks would balance being a part of different bands for a number of years. In 2006, he played with three different bands in seventeen countries.

His 2009 album, *Already Free*, reached #19 on *Billboard*'s Top 200 chart, #11 on the Blues chart, #1 on the Internet chart, and #4 on the Rock chart.

He and Tedeschi formed the Soul Stew Revival in order to tour together.

Both Trucks and Tedeschi curtailed their schedules in 2010 to concentrate on home and family. Trucks did, however, contribute to *Clapton* (2010).

30

Way-Out Willie and Rocking Millie

Singles—Hits and Misses

Brittle 78s dominated the music industry as the format of choice for the first half of the twentieth century. These one- and two-sided records could fit about three minutes of music per side.

While the LP format was invented during the previous decade, the Columbia label honed the format in the late 1940s. In 1948, they began releasing recordings, which contained five or six tracks per side. The best part was that the vinyl did not break if it was dropped or abused in any way.

The RCA label countered with the 45-rpm record. RCA argued that their little records with the big hole were easier to handle and store, plus you could stack them on a spindle on your record player so they would drop down one after the other for continuous play.

The LP and the 45 would complement each other and dominate the music industry for close to forty years, until the advent of the CD.

Singles (45s) were originally issued as a commercial entity in their own right but as time passed, transitioned to bringing attention to the artist's albums, which cost more and initially sold in smaller quantities. Singles also dominated radio airplay during the fifties, sixties, and into the seventies, which would keep the artist in the public eye and increase his or her fan base.

During the late sixties and early seventies, album-only radio began to make inroads into the 45's radio dominance. As time passed, artists began to issue fewer singles, and mainstream rock stations began to proliferate over the airwaves. Still, during the late seventies, eighties, and nineties, the little classic single remained an important music form.

Trivia note: a reissue of "Banquet of Roses"/"Texarkana Baby" by Eddy Arnold carries the RCA 0001 number. It was one of ten 45s issued on the same day but in many circles is recognized as the first modern single.

Eric Clapton released dozens of singles during his career, with bands and as a solo artist. Some were huge successes and remain among his best-known songs, while others quickly disappeared with little notice.

The following is an extensive but ultimately incomplete list of Clapton's singles. Many countries had releases that were unique to them, and when you add in picture sleeves and B-sides, you are left with hundreds of variations. Enjoy and collect them if you feel adventurous.

Yardbird Singles

I still have some old Yardbird singles in my record collection. The yellow Epic labels may have faded a little, but they still play, with a hiss here and a crackle there. They represent some of the earliest recordings of Eric Clapton.

"I Wish You Would"/"A Certain Girl"

"I Wish You Would" was a typical early Yardbird song and an appropriate choice for their first single release.

Billy Boy Arnold was a Chicago blues musician born on September 16, 1935, and remains active today. At a young age, he played harmonica on Bo Diddley's "I'm a Man." By the mid-fifties, he had signed his own contract with the Vee-Jay label. One of his first releases was his composition "I Wish You Would."

"I Wish You Would" was released during the transition period between 45s and 78s and so was issued in both formats. The 78 version remains very difficult to find today and is a highly prized collectible.

The song fit the early traditional style of the Yardbirds well. The single was released in May 1964 in the United Kingdom and three months later in the United States. It found tough sledding on both sides of the Atlantic, initiating few sales and receiving no chart action whatsoever. It was a raw and bluesy production and was lost in the pop/rock of the early British Invasion releases, especially in the United States. It received some airplay in the United States when it was included on the *For Your Love* album in 1965.

The Yardbirds' version clocked in at only 2:19 but manages to retain the melodic quality of the original. Both Jeff Beck and Jimmy Page recorded live versions of the song during their time with the group.

The single came with a picture sleeve in the United States, which is extremely rare. When you combine that fact with it also being an early Clapton-related single, you have a collectible of value.

"Good Morning Little Schoolgirl"/"I Ain't Got You"

The Yardbirds' second single, "Good Morning Little Schoolgirl," was released in October 1964, in the United Kingdom. It was the first chart single of their and Eric Clapton's career when it reached #44 on the singles chart.

The song originated with the first Sonny Boy Williamson in 1937. It was titled "Good Morning, School Girl" in its first incarnation. It featured Williamson's vocal backed by guitarists Big Joe Williams and Robert McCoy. Smokey Hogg had a rhythm and blues hit with it but changed the title to "Little School Girl." The duo of Don and Bob recorded the song under the well-known title, "Good Morning Little Schoolgirl."

The song was a staple of the early Yardbirds' concert act. It served as one of the first vehicles for the young Eric Clapton to impress people with his developing guitar skills.

The single, while not released in the United States, did appear on their *For Your Love* album and again on *Five Live Yardbirds*. The live version is a rare Yardbird song sung not by Keith Relf, but rather by Clapton and Paul Samwell-Smith sharing the lead vocals.

The song has been inducted into the Blues Hall of Fame and remains a very heavily covered song.

"For Your Love"/"Got to Hurry"

As has already been discussed, "For Your Love" was the song that drove Eric Clapton out of the Yardbirds, as he was appalled at its pop nature. While it may not have been truly a pop song, its odd melody made it unique at the time. Released as the band's third single, it was their first by a contemporary writer, Graham Gouldman.

The song became the Yardbirds first big hit single, peaking at #3 in the United Kingdom and #6 in the United States. Clapton may not have loved the song, but it brought him his first taste of fame.

All was not lost, however, as the obscure B-side of the single, "Got to Hurry," caught the attention of John Mayall. When Clapton became available, Mayall immediately fired his guitarist and hired Clapton.

John Mayall and the Bluesbreakers Singles

John Mayall was an album guy, and since Clapton's time in his band was short, his singles with Clapton are a treasure trove for the collector of his music.

"I'm Your Witchdoctor"/"Telephone Blues"

If Eric Clapton was upset by the pop turn of the Yardbirds, he would have no such worries with John Mayall and his first single released as a part of the Bluesbreakers.

"I'm Your Witchdoctor"/"Telephone Blues" was issued in October 1965, with no impact on the British charts. In addition to Mayall and Clapton, the song featured bassist John McVie and drummer Hughie Flint. Jimmy Page produced the session.

"I'm your witchdoctor, got the evil eye, got the power of the devil, I'm the conjurer guy. Gonna teach you love at the midnight hour," was an original composition by Mayall and was blues enough even for the hardcore Clapton, whose guitar playing provided just the right touch and a more complex sound than any of his work with his former group.

"Lonely Years"/"Bernard Jenkins"

The year 1966 saw the release of a second Bluesbreakers single featuring Eric Clapton. Unfortunately, "Lonely Years"/"Bernard Jenkins" traveled the same path as the first, receiving little attention and no chart success. The Yardbirds, on the other hand, had gone on to commercial popularity and produced a series of successful singles.

"Lonely Years" was another blues-based release. "I got to face five lonely years/everybody got a trouble/I got to live with mine right now/everybody got a trouble."

It was a single that flew under the radar and did not appear on the original release of *John Mayall's Bluesbreakers Featuring Eric Clapton*. It has been issued on some recent CD reissues.

The song finds the twenty-one-year-old Clapton at the height of his Bluesbreakers career and on the cusp of becoming a genuine guitar god. It's worth the price of the remastered album for this performance and the obscure flip side.

The reissue attributes the song to Eric Clapton, while "Bernard Jenkins" is listed as by John Mayall and the Bluesbreakers. The odd part of that is "Lonely Years" was written by Mayall and "Bernard Jenkins" by Clapton.

"Parchman Farm"/"Key to Love"

The Mississippi State Penitentiary is still baking in the hot southern sun. It was known as the Parchman Farm for many years as it was where varied inmates served hard time. It was the temporary home for the likes of Bukka

White and Son House. There were a number of blues songs written about the old prison.

The version recorded by Mayall was by blues/jazz pianist Mose Allison. Mayall and Clapton interpreted it from a strict blues perspective. The single and its B-side, "Key to Love," would be a part of the legendary *Bluesbreakers with Eric Clapton* album.

"Parchment Farm"/"Key to Love" is the last of three singles Clapton recorded with John Mayall and like the other two failed to chart on either side of the Atlantic.

Cream Singles

Cream was at heart an album and live band, but their record company was savvy enough to promote them with a series of single releases. The importance of these old 45s is affirmed by the fact that "White Room" and "Sunshine of Your Love" remain two of their more memorable and recognizable songs.

"Wrapping Paper"/"Cat's Squirrel"

"Wrapping Paper" was an odd choice for Cream's first single. There was a lot of hype surrounding this new supergroup at the time. Clapton, Baker, and Bruce were held in high esteem, but "Wrapping Paper" was not the type of song their fans had been expecting.

The composition had a light and jazzy feel rather than the blues/rock sound people had been expecting. The song was not included on their debut album in the United States or England, although it did appear on some other worldwide versions. The flip side was an instrumental interpretation of the traditional blues piece "Cat's Squirrel," which was included on the release everywhere.

Jack Bruce and Pete Brown wrote "Wrapping Paper." Clapton and Baker have not been kind about their feelings for the song over the years. One legend has it that Bruce released it without the knowledge or permission of the other two. Fans were sort of neutral about the song, and it only reached #34 in the band's home country despite the anticipation. It did not chart in the United States.

"I Feel Free"/"N.S.U."

The second Cream single, "I Feel Free," more than made up for the mediocrity of the first. It was also written by Bruce and Brown, and while more pop sounding than much of their material would be, it was brilliant pop.

"I Feel Free" was the first track on their debut album, *Fresh Cream*. It was an excellent introduction of the group to the music world that had been waiting for them.

The single reached #11 on the British charts. I am always amused that it reached #116 in the United States. *Billboard* had a Bubbling Under chart at the time that was reserved for singles that had not yet or never would reach the top 100. It deserved much better, but that is where it remained.

"I Feel Free" also had the distinction of being the first Cream single to contain a Clapton solo, however brief.

Jack Bruce released a solo single of the song in 1981 that spent one week on the U.K. singles charts. It may not have been successful, but at least it was not #116.

"Strange Brew"/"Tales of Brave Ulysses"

"Strange Brew" was released in June 1967 and introduced the world to the *Disraeli Gears* album. It peaked at #17 on the British charts and did not even bubble under in the United States. It was a rare Cream song to feature an Eric Clapton vocal rather than that of Jack Bruce.

The flip side, "Tales of Brave Ulysses," was a signature performance by Cream as it was one of the songs that established their sound. It was written by Eric Clapton in conjunction with lyricist Martin Sharp. The song featured Clapton using a wah-wah pedal for his guitar for the first time. His guitar playing is some of the best of the psychedelic era.

"Sunshine of Your Love"/"SWLABR"

Rolling Stone ranked "Sunshine of Your Love" as the 65th Greatest Song of All Time. It was also Cream's breakout single in North America, reaching #5 in the United States and #3 in Canada. Oddly, it was less popular in their home country than some of their lesser-known songs, topping out at #25.

The song's authorship was a rare collaboration among Bruce, Brown, and Clapton.

Clapton's guitar riffs here would ring down through rock history. When you add in Bruce's bass lines and Baker's slow, modified drumming, you have one of the superior performances of the psychedelic rock era. Musicians have tried to copy the style and sound of this performance for over forty years with little success.

When Clapton performs the song live, he makes it all look so effortless. If you want to study a history of the guitar and Eric Clapton as a guitarist, this is one of the places to start.

"Spoonful Part 1"/"Spoonful Part 2"

I have always thought "Spoonful" was an odd choice for release as a single, especially following "Sunshine of Your Love." While it's a memorable Cream song and is directly rooted in the blues, it is more renowned as an expanded, improvisational, live piece rather than one that fits on a small 7″ record. The A-side was 2:45, while the live version from *Wheels of Fire* clocked it at almost 17 minutes. Fans would prefer the longer version, as the "Spoonful" single did not chart despite following the most popular single of Cream's career.

Willie Dixon wrote the tune, and Howlin' Wolf first recorded it in 1960, but like many blues songs, it traces its lineage back to another era.

Charley Patton wrote "A Spoonful Blues" in 1929, which in turn looked back to "All I Want Is a Spoonful" by Charlie Jackson in 1925.

The Rock and Roll Hall of Fame listed it as one of the 500 Songs That Shaped Rock 'n' Roll. Howlin' Wolf's recording was inducted in the Blues Foundation Hall of Fame. Wolf recorded the song with guitarist Hubert Sumlin, guitarist Freddie Robinson, pianist Otis Spann, drummer Fred Below, and bassist/writer Willie Dixon.

Cream's version has become the most recognized, but it's the live, not the single version at less than three minutes that has gained that status.

Today those little 7″ 45 rpm records have disappeared from the music landscape, but in their day, they were an important part of the music industry. Many AM radio station only played singles.   *Author's collection*

"Anyone for Tennis"/"Pressed Rat and Warthog"

"Anyone for Tennis" remains one of the more unusual songs in the Cream catalog and an even stranger single release. It was pulled from the film *The Savage Seven* and seems to have appeared from nowhere. It reached #40 in the United Kingdom, #64 in the United States, and #37 in Canada. It was another song written by Clapton and Martin Sharp.

The Savage Seven was a biker flick and not a very good one. It was a quickly made B movie and mercifully disappeared. It you do watch the film, look for rock 'n' roll guitarist Duane Eddy and a young Penny Marshall in acting roles.

The original soundtrack was only a half hour in length. A second Cream song was also included, the short, 1:23, "Desert Ride."

"Anyone for Tennis" has an unusual melodic quality and moves toward a pop sound that was far different from what was being produced elsewhere at the time. It retrospect, it is more fascinating than good.

The best music on the soundtrack, for what it's worth, were the four Iron Butterfly Tracks, particularly "Iron Butterfly Theme," which took that group in a psychedelic rock direction as opposed to their usual heavy rock proclivities.

"Anyone for Tennis" was only available as a single or as a part of this poor-selling and obscure soundtrack at the time of its release but now can be found on a number of compilation albums.

"White Room"/"Those Were the Days"

"White Room" was Cream's second most successful single behind "Sunshine of Your Love." It was released in early 1969 and reached #28 in Britain, #6 in the United States, and almost made it all the way to the top of the charts in Canada, stopping at #2.

The song was another Jack Bruce and Peter Brown collaboration, with lyrics revolving around drugs and a railway station.

It is Clapton's guitar solos that connect the different parts of the song and provide its foundation. Bruce may have written the music, but there is no way he could have envisioned Clapton's guitar playing. The use of a wah-wah sounds so smooth but is very difficult to reproduce unless you are Eric Clapton.

The single release was two minutes shorter than the one included on *Wheels of Fire*. Felix Pappalardi plays the viola on the track. *Rolling Stone* listed it as one of the 500 Greatest Songs of All Time.

"Crossroads (Live)"/"Passing the Time"

"Crossroads (Live Version)"/"Passing the Time" was the first single released after Cream's demise. It was only released in North America and was a moderate hit in the United States, reaching #28. It was more successful in Canada, checking in at #13.

"Cross Road Blues" was a song by one of Clapton's heroes and a writer/ performer he would return to many times throughout his career. Robert

Johnson's original recording can be found on his 1990 *The Complete Recordings*. It was the song that the legend of Johnson selling his soul to the devil centered on.

"Crossroads" became an important part of Cream's live shows. The four-minute live take on *Wheels of Fire* is probably their most famous version. Released as a single, it was a tight performance that served the song's original intent well. Live tracks are difficult sells as singles as they are removed from their original context.

Clapton brought the song with him from his brief time with Powerhouse. Cream's take put the emphasis on Clapton's guitar, while Powerhouse centered on the harmonica as the lead instrument.

"Badge"/"What a Bringdown"

Cream has split up before *Goodbye* was released. It was their only album to reach #1 in Britain, while it hit #3 in the United States.

"Badge," written by Clapton and friend George Harrison, was pulled from the album for release as a single. It became a minor hit in the United States and Canada, charting at #60 and #49 respectively. It reached #18 in England.

Clapton was supposed to have had a song written and ready for the *Goodbye* recording sessions but had no ideas. He turned to George Harrison for inspiration. The story is that they were sitting across the table from one another, and Harrison wrote the word "Bridge"; reading it upside down, Clapton thought is said "Badge."

While the duo shares the writing credit, it is a George Harrison type song more than a Clapton/Cream song. Harrison as L' Angelo Misterioso plays rhythm guitar on the track, with Pappalardi on keyboards. Clapton contributes the lead guitar parts.

Clapton has continued to play the song live at various points during his career. The best version can be found on his live *24 Nights* album.

"Badge" remains interesting as it pointed Clapton in a direction and style that would be a part of his future solo career.

"Lawdy Mama"/"Sweet Wine"

Cream singles continued to be released throughout the seventies and eighties and really only slowed down with the advent of the CD.

"Lawdy Mama"/"Sweet Wine" was a single release from 1969 that brought the career of Cream to a mundane end as it received little notice and no chart action.

Both tracks appeared on the *Live Cream* album, although "Sweet Wine" was in an elongated form at 15:16.

"Lawdy Mama" was a traditional tune arranged by Clapton and was originally an old studio recording from the *Disraeli Gears* sessions of 1967. "Sweet Wine" was cowritten by Ginger Baker and recorded from a 1968 concert at Winterland in San Francisco.

Delaney and Bonnie Singles

Delaney and Bonnie were a working band who were always on the cusp of stardom. They were wise enough to capitalize on their newly acquired backing guitarist's fame by issuing as much product as possible and touring constantly while he was with the band. It proved to be a wise decision as they would reach the pinnacle of their popularity while he was with them.

"Comin' Home"/"Groupie (Superstar)"

"Comin' Home" is really a Delaney and Bonnie single release, although it was cowritten by Eric Clapton. At 5:30, it was longer than the normal single of the day and was an edited version taken from their *On Tour with Eric Clapton* album. The single was a fair-sized hit in England, reaching #16.

"Comin' Home" was a Delaney and Bonnie group effort, and while it did not contain a truly memorable Clapton performance, he was there playing as a member of the band. Most importantly, his time with the group allowed him to recharge his engines before moving on again.

Derek and the Dominos Singles

Derek and the Dominos were another band that concentrated on album sales. Their label, however, did a good job in selecting the material as many of their singles represent the best of their music.

"Tell the Truth"/"Roll It Over"

"Tell the Truth" was the A-side of the first single issued by Derek and the Dominos. It appeared as a 6:59 track on their studio album *Layla and Other Assorted Love Songs*.

The song is attributed to both Clapton and Bobby Whitlock, but it was the latter who was primarily responsible for its creation. It has a unique vocal as Whitlock and Clapton alternated verses.

"Tell the Truth" was the first song recorded by the group, and Dave Mason was the second guitarist on the original recording. Phil Spector was the producer, intending the song be released as a single. The records were pressed, and they were sent out to various outlets for delivery. But wait!

In August 1970, the Dominos went into the studio to rerecord "Tell the Truth." This time Tom Dowd was at the production helm, and Duane Allman was on hand as the second guitarist. Allman's slide technique combined with Clapton's solos to create a superior recording to the already issued single. Clapton was so impressed with this new take that he called executives at his record label to halt the release of the first single and substitute this one in its place. A few of the earlier pressings managed to survive and remain rare and very collectible.

This interesting story did not have a happy ending; "Tell the Truth" did not become a hit, as it received no chart action and few sales.

Both recordings of the song were issued on the 1972 *History of Eric Clapton* and Mr. C. was indeed correct, as the Duane Allman version is decidedly better.

"Bell Bottom Blues"/"Keep on Growing"

"Bell Bottom Blues" was an inauspicious chart debut for Derek and the Dominos on the American singles chart, peaking at #91 and only lasting two weeks. The reaction in England was even less, as it failed to chart at all.

"Bell Bottom Blues" is one of the Derek and the Dominos tracks that did not include Duane Allman, as it was recorded before he joined the band. Clapton played both the rhythm and lead guitar parts, and Tom Dowd combined them.

Clapton stated in his autobiography that the song originated when Pattie Boyd requested he bring her a pair of bell-bottom jeans from the United States that were popular at the time. The blues addition to the title probably sums up his enthusiasm for the task.

Despite its origin and his feelings, "Bell Bottom Blues" is filled with emotion, while musically it sums up Clapton at this point in his career.

"Layla"/"I Am Yours"

"Layla" was the nickname for Pattie Boyd, who was married to George Harrison (1966–1974) and Clapton (1979–1988). It remains one of his best-known songs from the Derek and the Dominos period and in a different form from his solo career as well.

It was released twice in rapid succession in the United States. The first time, with a length of 2:43, it met with moderate success, reaching #51 in mid-1970. A year later, it retuned in a long form, 7:10, and climbed to #10 and spent fifteen weeks on the chart.

The song was a bigger hit in England, where in 1972 it was paired with "Bell Bottom Blues" and reached #7.

"Layla" is one of rock's most memorable love songs, propelled by the guitar interplay of Clapton and Allman. It was ranked #27 on *Rolling Stone*'s 500 Greatest Songs of All Time.

Clapton originally wrote "Layla" as a ballad, and to a ballad it would eventually return. But with Duane Allman on hand, it became a rocker. It was a multitracked affair with twelve different guitar parts consisting of leads, rhythm, harmonies, and even Clapton and Allman playing duplicate solos. Dowd managed to splice them all together into a calliope of guitar sound.

The song would have ended there except for the fact that Clapton heard Jim Gordon noodling at the piano. His piano lines formed the foundation of the famous second part of the song where Clapton switches to an acoustic guitar with Allman playing bottleneck slide. Dowd then combined the two sections. Gordon's contribution earned him a cowriter credit on one of the lasting love songs of the rock era.

As mentioned in another chapter, the sophisticated technical creation of the song made it virtually impossible for one guitarist to perform alone, which was how Derek and the Dominos usually performed live.

While his 1992 *Unplugged* performance is now the best-known rendition of the song, on September 20, 1983, at the ARMS Charity Concert for Multiple Sclerosis in Royal Albert Hall, Eric Clapton, Jeff Beck, and Jimmy Page combined to perform the song as it should be heard.

"Bell Bottom Blues"/"Little Wing"

"Bell Bottom Blues" only reached #91 when it was originally released in the United States, but because of "Layla's" success as a reissue, it too received a second chance. Lightning did not strike twice, however, as it was only marginally more popular the second time, reaching #78.

What made the single different was the inclusion of "Little Wing" as the flip side. "Little Wing" was a Jimi Hendrix composition from his *Axis: Bold as Love* album and was ranked among *Rolling Stone*'s 500 Greatest Songs of All Time.

Clapton had always been attracted to the song and recorded it for his *Layla* album plus consistently performed it live. It is always interesting to compare his and Hendrix's versions.

Commercial copies sold in the millions. Notice the BB hole in the label. That meant the record was returned to the distributor as unsold. They punched a BB hole in the label, and resold the record at a reduced price. The hole made it so the record could not be sold as new.

Author's collection

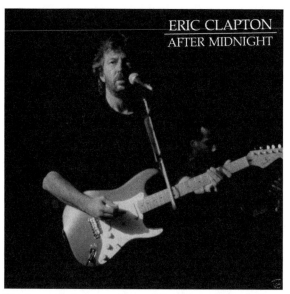

Singles came in many forms. When I was buying 45s as a teenager, I always looked for a picture sleeve.

Author's collection

Eric Clapton: Solo Singles

Eric Clapton's solo singles span the decades. He continued to release singles even after they had lost their commercial viability. While the following list is extensive, I'm sure there are a few that have slid under the radar.

"After Midnight"/"Easy Now"

Clapton's first successful solo single actually occurred in 1970 between "Comin'" Home" by Delaney and Bonnie and his Derek and the Dominos releases.

"After Midnight," taken from his first solo album, reached #18 in the United States and #10 in Canada but was largely ignored in England.

It was a J. J. Cale composition, and Clapton remained true to the style and intent of the 1966 original. The release proved to be a breakthrough for Cale. In addition to the royalty payments, it began his lifelong association with Clapton. His career was revitalized and he released his own single of the song that became a moderate hit at #42.

Many times radio stations received records with a different label. Also, most promo copies had the same song on both sides so that the stations would not play the flip side.   *Author's collection*

Clapton was backed by Delaney and Bonnie's basic band at the time. Whitlock, Radle, and Gordon were joined by Leon Russell, trumpet player Jim Price, and saxophonist Bobby Keys.

"Let It Rain"/"Easy Now"

"Let It Rain" was released in the fall of 1972 and can best be described as a filler single that almost worked. It was pulled from his two-year-old self-titled debut album and reached #48 in the United States.

It remains a very smooth performance that unfortunately has disappeared into his vast catalog. It probably deserved better at the time, but when compared to his Derek and the Dominos output, it sounded a bit antiquated at the time of its release.

"I Shot the Sheriff"/"Give Me Strength"

"I Shot the Sheriff" was Eric Clapton's first #1 single, group or otherwise, in the United States and also reached #1 in Canada. It managed to enter the top ten in England at #9.

I have always been amused that the song's narrator admits to killing the sheriff but is indignant that he has been accused of killing the deputy. The original was a Bob Marley reggae creation that Clapton moves toward a rock 'n' roll format while maintaining the style of the original.

George Terry is the second guitarist, and he shines along with backing singer Yvonne Elliman, who fills in the sound and makes it all come together.

Nearly forty years after its initial release, it stands out as a unique stop in Eric Clapton's musical journey. There are a lot of elements fused together—blues, rock, reggae—that coalesce into a wonderful mix. It makes one wish he could have recorded more material in the same vein as it was a perfect single release.

"I Shot the Sheriff" also served its purpose as a single well as it pushed its parent album, *461 Ocean Boulevard,* to the top of the charts in the United States and #3 in England, cementing Clapton's status as a superstar solo artist.

"Willie and the Hand Jive"/"Mainline Florida"

Willie and the Hand Jive has traveled from Johnny Otis to Eric Clapton to Grease to Sha Na Na, and at each stop it has been a joyful tune that makes listeners want to tap their feet and even dance if they are so inclined.

Clapton's version is peppy, energetic, and guitar based. The words are somewhat inane, but it was a dance song, so it does not really matter.

I guess they don't hand jive very much in the United Kingdom, as it received no chart action. It reached #26 in the United States.

Most of Clapton's covers were blues tunes, but here he reached back into 1950s rock 'n' roll history. It may not be Clapton at his very best or what was expected of him, but it certainly is enjoyable. A little fun, every once in a while, is good even for a guitar god.

"Swing Low, Sweet Chariot"/"Pretty Blue Eyes"

Every once in a while Clapton would travel in a gospel direction, but "Swing Low, Sweet Chariot" was a surprising choice for the lead single from *There's One in Every Crowd.*

"Willie and the Hand Jive" did not chart in Britain, but "Swing Low, Sweet Chariot" did reach #19. On the other hand, "Swing Low, Sweet Chariot" did not chart in the United States. What it all added up to was that England was more religious but there were better dancers in the United States (or maybe not).

The song is an old spiritual and was first recorded in 1909 by the Fisk Jubilee Singers. It actually goes further back to the American Civil War period and is attributed to Wallis Willis, a Choctaw freedman.

The song has crossed boundaries and styles: big band (Benny Goodman, Tommy Dorsey, Glenn Miller), country (Johnny Cash, Willie Nelson, Loretta Lynn, Barbara Mandrell), folk (Joan Baez, the Brothers Four, Glenn Yarbrough), jazz (Louis Armstrong, Dizzy Gillespie), easy listening (Johnny Mathis, Patti Page), blues (B. B. King, Etta James), rhythm and blues (Stevie Wonder, Solomon Burke) and rock (Elvis Presley, the Grateful Dead).

Clapton's take on the song is economical and restrained, which fits the style of the album but may not have been the best choice for singles radio. If you want to hear some nice acoustic guitar, turn the record over and give a listen to "Pretty Blue Eyes."

"Knockin' on Heaven's Door"/"Someone Like You"

As most people are aware, "Knockin' on Heaven's Door" was written by Bob Dylan for the film *Pat Garrett and Billy the Kid*. He included the song on the soundtrack album and released it as a single, which climbed to #12 on the *Billboard* Hot 100 Pop charts. It also was a hit in England at #14. *Rolling Stone* ranked it #190 on their list of the 500 Greatest Songs of All Time. It remains one of Dylan's most beloved songs.

Clapton's single was released two years later in 1975. Albhy Galuten, who produced eighteen #1 singles during his career, was in charge of the session. He is credited with inventing the drum loop, first used by the Bee Gees, which he mercifully left behind for his work with Clapton.

Clapton's version probably falls into the reggae/pop category, although it is difficult to pigeonhole. It reached #38 in England. It has graced a number of his live albums, including *Crossroads 2: Live in the Seventies* (1996). It was also a part of *Time Pieces: The Best of Eric Clapton* (2002).

While Clapton's version did not equal Dylan's original, it nevertheless fit the laid-back style of his life and music at the time and was a complementary single to "Swing Low, Sweet Chariot,"

"Hello Old Friend"/"All Our Past Times"

No Reason to Cry, released in 1976, yielded two singles. The first, "Hello Old Friend," reached #24 in the United States, #37 in Canada, but nada in the United Kingdom. While the single was ignored in his home country, the album did reach #8.

The album found Clapton in his Dylan/Band phase, and the music reflects their rustic quality and style.

"Hello Old Friend" certainly fits the flow of the album, as it is pop/country. It has a simple and direct beauty that may have been a bigger hit for him several decades later. The B-side, "All Our Past Times," featured a vocal duet with Rick Danko and was a strong song itself.

"Carnival"/"Hungry"

"Carnival" was the first Clapton solo single not to chart in either England or the United States. It did not chart in Canada either, for that matter.

It is one of the better and certainly more interesting concoctions on *No Reason to Cry* as it is based on Latin rhythms that are both percussive and funky. An excellent album track that was not suited for singles radio at the time.

"Lay Down Sally"

"Lay Down Sally" was released in late 1977 in the United Kingdom with "Cocaine" as the flip side. This combination should have propelled it to the top of the charts, but it stalled at #39.

"Lay Down Sally" was paired with "Next Time You See Her" in North America and released in early 1978 with much better commercial results, as it rose to #3 in both the United States and Canada.

The track was written by Clapton, backing singer Marcy Levy, and guitarist George Terry. It can best be described as Clapton's blues meeting American country. It became his highest-charting country song in the United States, reaching #26 in April 1978.

The lyrics revolve around the narrator trying to get Sally to lie down in bed instead of leaving. The guitar style was a cross between some precise picking and a chuga-chuga rhythm.

"Lay Down Sally" may have lost some of its surprise and impact due to the fact it has been played to death on AOR and recently Adult Contemporary Radio, but it remains one of Clapton's better single releases.

"Wonderful Tonight"/"Peaches and Diesel"

"Wonderful Tonight" was another noncharter in England and continued the trend of Clapton's albums selling well and charting high while his singles were only intermittently successful.

The song would finally become a big single hit in England but not for him. The group Damage took it to #3 in 1997.

"Wonderful Tonight" was another song written for Pattie Boyd, which would become part of the title of her post-divorce book; *Wonderful Tonight: George Harrison, Eric Clapton, and Me.* The story is that Clapton was about to attend a Buddy Holly tribute with Paul and Linda McCartney. Pattie was not ready, and Clapton quickly wrote the song while he was waiting for her.

It is a mellow affair that has stood the test of time. While the music of Eric Clapton is not usually associated with weddings and proms, this song has proved to be the exception.

All was not lost in the United Kingdom, however, as a live version from *24 Nights* was released as a single in 1991 and reached #30.

"Promises"/"Watch Out for Lucy"

"Promises" was another top ten hit in North America in late 1978, reaching #9 and #7 in the United States and Canada respectively. It even managed to crack the top forty in England at #37.

"Promises" remains one of my favorite Clapton singles. It is a laid-back country/pop tune with a restrained vocal. Despite its somewhat melancholy nature, it was catchy in an odd sort of way. It also stayed with you, which was important for a single; plus you could actually sing along with it.

"Watch Out for Lucy," which inhabited the flip side, is a nice pop shuffle tune and remains a good listen in its own right.

"Cocaine (Live)"/"Tulsa Time (Live)"

"Cocaine" and "Tulsa Time" were both taken from the live album *Just One Night* issued in April 1980. They were recorded at Japan's Budokan Theatre in Tokyo and remain two of his finest performances. The single only reached #30 in the United States but was a huge hit in Canada at #3.

Clapton's basic band of the time consisted of guitarist Albert Lee, keyboardist Chris Stainton, bassist Dave Markee, and drummer Henry Spinetti. These two tracks are testament to their excellence as his backing band.

Both songs have an excellent sound, especially for a live single release of the time. Clapton recorded many of his concerts through the years with varying technical results, but his crew got this one just right.

"Cocaine" is a typical strong performance, and while the solos have been reduced due to the length of the 45-rpm format, they still ring out in short sound bites.

"Tulsa Time" is presented as a rollicking rock/country song. By this time in his career, Albert Lee was well on his way to becoming one of the better country guitarists, of the day and his influence shows here.

One of his most controversial and best singles.
Author's collection

"Cocaine"/"Tulsa Time" remains not only a single for collectors but a good listen as well.

"Blues Power (Live)"/"Early in the Morning"

"Blues Power" was the second single released from *Just One Night*. The song was originally released on his 1970 solo debut album and was a part of the remastered live album of his *Rainbow Concert*. It has remained a part of his concert act ever since.

"Blues Power" makes one wonder why a particular track was selected for a single release. As the title suggests, the song has a blues orientation that was better suited for album-only airplay rather than top forty radio. It was a disappointing release, reaching only #76 in its five weeks on the charts before disappearing into the collector's market.

"I Can't Stand It"/"Black Rose"

It was with the release of "I Can't Stand It" that singles radio became more complicated, and would become more so as time passed.

Billboard introduced their Top Tracks Chart for Rock Songs, which would become their Mainstream Rock chart. No longer were hits songs just measured by the singles charts; now album tracks had a radio life of their own. Many Clapton songs were released as singles plus received extensive play on album-only radio stations and would chart high on this chart as well. The single remained an important music format for the time being, but now it had company in determining hits.

"I Can't Stand It" by Eric Clapton was the first track to top the newly created Mainstream Rock chart on March 21, 1981, and would remain there for two weeks. Clapton would be followed by the Who, Tom Petty, Joe Walsh, the Moody Blues, Foreigner, Blue Öyster Cult, the Rolling Stones, Foreigner (again), the Police, and Quarterflash through the rest of the year.

What this new chart proved was that more people were listening to certain songs than were buying the singles. "I Can't Stand It" was a successful pop single as well, reaching #10 in the United States, but its place in music history remains tied to its #1 status on the first of what would become Mainstream Rock chart.

"Another Ticket"/"Rita Mae"

"Another Ticket" was the second single released from the album of the same name. It had limited success on the pop charts at #78 for five weeks. While Clapton would continue to regularly release traditional singles, they would usually, and I do say usually, be more popular on the *Billboard* Rock charts than on the Pop charts, which were based on 45-rpm sales and their radio airplay.

"Another Ticket" may have been a failed single, but its rock-oriented B-side, "Rita Mae," was more successful as it reached #10 on the Mainstream Rock chart.

"I've Got a Rock 'N' Roll Heart"/"Man in Love"

"I've Got a Rock 'N' Roll Heart" is a rare 1980s Clapton single that charted in the United States (#18), the United Kingdom (#83), and Canada (#17).

The song today is remembered for its use as a touch-tone phone commercial in which Clapton appeared.

It reached #24 on the Mainstream Rock chart and also moved Clapton onto the Adult Contemporary Chart at #6, which reflected the direction his music was gradually moving at the time.

"The Shape You're In"/"Crosscut Saw"

"The Shape You're In" was the second single from *Money and Cigarettes*. It achieved minor success in England at #75.

It was the flip side, "Crosscut Saw,' that was the gem of the release, as it returned Clapton to his blues roots.

Originally titled "Cross Cut Blues," it was first released by Tommy McClennan in 1941. It was filled with sexual references; "Now I'm a cross cut saw, drag me 'cross yo' log." Albert King's version, which cleaned it up a bit by substituting a couple of guitar solos in place of some of the saw lyrics, became a rhythm and blues hit in 1966. King used Booker T. and the MG's as his backing band, which gave the old blues song a fuller and somewhat funky sound.

Clapton's version is tight and economical at three and a half minutes and relied on King's interpretation as a jumping off point as he created a blues/rock fusion piece.

"Slow Down Linda"/"Crazy Country Hop"

This was another single that should have been turned over, to use the terminology of the day.

"Slow Down Linda" was the third single from *Money and Cigarettes* and was basic competent blues/rock. It received no chart action.

"Cross Country Hop" was a Johnny Otis song, which is always positive. Otis was best known for his hit "Willie and the Hand Jive" and other high-energy R&B singles. His music may not have been essential to the history of music but was always a fun ride. Otis passed away January 17, 2012, as one of the grand old men of American rock music.

"Crazy Country Hop" finds a relaxed Clapton rather than a serious or laid-back one. At the time I remember thinking I wish he had covered more of his music, as this one and "Willie and the Hand Jive" were both excellent. Clapton missed an opportunity when "Crazy Country Hop" was consigned to the B-side.

"Forever Man"/"Too Bad"

Behind the Sun, released March 11, 1985, was an album assembled for commercial success as Clapton wanted to produce some hit songs. The first single, "Forever Man," written by Jerry Lynn Williams, accomplished that goal when it #26 on the *Billboard* Hot 100 and was #1 for two weeks on the Mainstream Rock chart. It also was a middling hit in England at #51.

The song was coproduced by Phil Collins, which gave the music an eighties feel as he brought in synthesizers and ramped up the bass sound. Clapton's vocal, however, retains a bluesy quality.

Time was passing and times were changing, "Forever Man" was Clapton's first music video. It featured him performing the song backed by Donald "Duck" Dunn, Jeff Porcaro, Michael Omartian, Tim Renwick, Shawn Murphy, plus backing singers Yvonne Elliman and Marcy Levy.

Clapton performed the song at some of his 2009 and 2010 concert stops.

"She's Waiting"/"Jailbait"

"She's Waiting," written by Clapton and Peter Robinson, was the second single pulled from *Behind the Sun*. It was another Clapton single to receive no pop action.

It was far more successful on the Mainstream Rock chart, where it rose to #11, while receiving considerable airplay.

"See What Love Can Do"/"She's Waiting"

What do you do with a failed pop single? You make it the B-side of your next pop single release, of course.

"See What Love Can Do" was the third single from *Behind the Sun* and was another Jerry Lynn Williams composition recorded for commercial success. It may have only reached #89 on the pop charts, but it was another solid rock track and climbed to #20 on the Mainstream Rock chart.

"Behind the Mask"/"Grand Illusion"

Behind the Mask had a schizophrenic nature when it came to the music charts. It produced four Mainstream Rock chart hits in the United States and charted four pop singles in England. The album's title song was Clapton's first top twenty single in his home country since 1975's "Swing Low, Sweet Chariot." It reached #15 in early 1987.

The song was originally written by Chris Mosdell and Ryuichi Sakamoto for the Yellow Magic Orchestra, which was a Japanese electro-pop group of which Sakamoto was the keyboardist. Quincy Jones had Michael Jackson record the song, but it did not make the final cut for his *Thriller* album. Jackson wrote new lyrics that allowed him to take a writing credit for the revamped tune.

The story might have ended there except for the fact that Greg Phillinganes was Jackson's keyboardist at the time, and he recorded the song for his own solo album *Pulse,* which was released in 1984. Two years later he brought the Jackson version to the attention of Clapton, who recorded it for *August*. It is an interesting evolution to follow from the Yellow Magic Orchestra, to Jackson, to Phillinganes, to Clapton.

"It's in the Way You Use It"/"Bad Influence"

"It's in the Way You Use It" was a minor hit in England, reaching #77. In the United States, it received extensive airplay and received the added boost of being featured in the Paul Newman/Tom Cruise movie *The Color of Money*, for which Newman won the Academy Award for Best Actor. Martin Scorsese directed the film, and the original score was by Robbie Robertson. The soundtrack album also featured Don Henley, Willie Dixon, B. B. King, Mark Knopfler, and Warren Zevon, in addition to Clapton.

The song was cowritten by Clapton and Robertson, and that combined with the film's popularity boosted it to the top of the Mainstream Rock chart on January 10, 1987.

"Tearing Us Apart"/"Hold On"

"Tearing Us Apart," cowritten by Clapton and Phillinganes, was another track from *August* to receive massive airplay in the United States.

The lyrics were about a group of Pattie Boyd's friends who Clapton believed was interfering with their relationship. Released in both the 7″ and 12″ single formats on June 8, 1987, it reached #4 on the Mainstream Rock chart.

"Tearing Us Apart" is notable for its duet with Tina Turner, whose voice fit surprisingly well with Clapton's. Turner recorded her own version of the song, with Clapton reprising his role on guitar and vocal, for her *Tina Live in Europe* album.

The single clocked in at 3:38, compared to the album track at 4:14. It managed to reach #56 in England.

Clapton has performed the song live with a number of singers substituting for Turner, including Katie Kissoon, Tessa Niles, and Sheryl Crow.

"Holy Mother"/"Tangled in Love"

"Holy Mother" remains one of the more obscure singles in the Clapton lexicon. It appeared on no chart in the United States. "Miss You" at #9 and "Run" at #21 both charted Mainstream Rock in the United States and would have been better choices for a single release.

"Holy Mother" was written by the odd combination of Clapton and Stephen Bishop. The connection may have been Phil Collins, who would produce Bishop's 1989 album *Bowling in Paris*.

By the time the single was released, *August* had pretty much run its course, and so the B-side was the Marcy Levy cowritten "Tangled in Love" from his previous album *Behind the Sun*.

"Pretending"/"Journeyman"

"Pretending" was another song written by Jerry Lynn Williams. It continued the successful commercial relationship between Williams and Clapton, as it topped the Mainstream Rock chart for six weeks beginning November 25, 1989. It also reached #55 on the pop charts during an eleven-week run. It flopped to #96 on the English singles chart.

"Pretending" is a classic Clapton vocal, with backing vocals by Chaka Khan. It has been resurrected on some of his recent tours.

"Bad Love"/"Journeyman"

"Bad Love" reflects the dual blues/rock nature of its parent album *Journeyman*. It was also one of Clapton's better vocal performances of the decade but may have only been his second best on the album, as "Pretending" was one of the best of his career.

It made a short appearance on the U.S. pop charts (#88 in five weeks) but had a long stay on the Mainstream Rock chart, where it was #1 for three weeks. It also won Clapton a Grammy for Best Rock Vocal.

The song was composed by Clapton and Foreigner's Mick Jones, with old friend Phil Collins on drums and harmony vocals.

"Tears in Heaven"

Just when Eric Clapton's singles had become staples on the Mainstream Rock chart rather than the Pop chart, along came "Tears in Heaven." The song exemplifies the modern pop side of Clapton's music and career, which has proven to be very successful.

The song was in the *Rush* film and soundtrack and was released on Clapton's famous *Unplugged* album. It won three Grammy Awards and returned Clapton to the upper regions on the *Billboard* Top 100 Chart at #3. It also reached the top of the Adult Contemporary chart for three weeks.

His presence as an Adult Contemporary artist signaled a change in those charts and the artists who would inhabit it. Barry Manilow, Barbra Streisand, and Neil Diamond now found themselves sharing the chart with the likes of Genesis, Elton John, Rod Stewart, Tina Turner, Billy Joel, and Eric Clapton. It all proved that these former rock and pop stars were aging and their music was finding new niches. It also demonstrated their original fan base was aging as well.

Much has been written here and elsewhere about the song being about the loss of Clapton's son. The personal nature of the song and its emotional vocal and impact made it an important part of the Clapton catalog.

Clapton stopped performing the song (and "My Mother's Eyes") in 2004. He noted he had moved on from the grief attached to each song, and if he resumed performing either of them, it would be in a more detached form.

"Layla (Unplugged)"

"Layla" was and is one of the great rock songs in music history as originally recorded by Derek and the Dominos. It returned in acoustic form on Clapton's *MTV Unplugged* performance and subsequent album release.

The song is ranked #27 on *Rolling Stone*'s list of the 500 Greatest Songs of All Time. The acoustic "Layla" won the 1993 Grammy for Best Rock Song.

The two interpretations, issued twenty years apart, are both brilliant in their own way, and part of that is their difference. The single reached #12 on the pop charts and still receives considerable airplay.

"Motherless Child"/"Driftin'"

In the middle of his adult contemporary, soundtrack, pop career, Clapton issued the single "Motherless Child" from his blues album *From the Cradle*.

While the song is listed as traditional in the writing credits, there was an old blues tune that contributed to its evolution—"Motherless Child Blues," which was first performed by Robert "Barbecue" Hicks and Elvie Thomas— although they were very different songs both musically and lyrically.

Clapton's is more in tune with the Hicks version, although he changed the approach and dropped the word "blues" from the title.

It joined the ranks of odd single choices, as it was not among the best tracks on the album. It was a minor hit in England at #63 but nothing in the United States. It was in Canada that it became a hit, reaching #9.

The flip side, "Driftin'," was a stronger performance. It was originally recorded by Johnny Moore's Three Blazers and became one of the huge blues hits of the 1940s. The Blues Hall of Fame and the Rock and Roll Hall of Fame have honored it.

This was Clapton's second recording of the song. He played it live with his full band on the live *E. C. Was Here*. It is his acoustic performance here that retains the feeling of the original.

"Change the World"

"Change the World," from the film and soundtrack *Phenomenon,* won three Grammys. It went to #5 on the *Billboard* Pop chart. That was just a warm-up for its performance on the Adult Contemporary chart, where it remained in the #1 position for thirteen weeks. It charted at #33 in England.

If you want to hear a different take of the song, check out Babyface's live album, *Babyface MTV Unplugged NYC* with Clapton providing the covocals and guitar work.

Wynonna Judd recorded a version on her #2 country album *Revelations.* The album was released on February 13, 1996, before Clapton's version.

"I Ain't Gonna Stand for It"/"Losing Hand"

"I Ain't Gonna Stand for It," released in 2001, bears the distinction of being the last traditional Clapton single. It was a Stevie Wonder composition, taken from the album *Reptile,* and quickly disappeared with no chart action.

Clapton's popularity allows him to remain commercially successful through the release of his albums and constant touring. The demise of the 45 has not affected his career, but many of those little 7″ records with the big hole remain not only collectible, but when taken as a whole, provide a nice history of his career.

31

Drink Some Brew and Find a Safe Place

Album Art

lbum art, or album covers if you will, have been an important component of drawing attention to, and selling, albums since their invention.

Some covers just pass by the senses with little notice, while others immediately grab your attention and make you want to explore the music inside. A very few covers are considered art in their own right and become a well-known part of the music scene.

Eric Clapton's covers run from average to spectacular and memorable. Due to space constraints, I have limited my comments to the more interesting or unusual covers. The mundane will not be covered here but await your individual exploration should you so choose.

Finally, the 12″ vinyl LP was more conducive to artwork than the small CDs of today but that, as they say, is progress.

Bluesbreakers with Eric Clapton

The first thing that strikes me about *John Mayall: Bluesbreakers with Eric Clapton* is not the picture but the words at the top of the cover.

John Mayall was nobody's fool. He now had Eric Clapton as his guitarist, and they had just created one of the seminal blues albums of the era. Mayall slapped his own name right in the middle of the album's title. It was, of course, in bigger letters than the rest of the title.

Now that he had established who the boss was, he added Eric Clapton, which would draw attention to the album and actually sell copies. He accomplished his goal, as it rose to #6 on the British charts.

The photo shows a very young Bluesbreakers comprised of John Mayall, Eric Clapton, Hughie Flint, and John McVie.

The picture is notable for Clapton reading a copy of *Beano,* which was a British comic book geared toward children. Why Clapton had a copy handy at the photo sessions remains unexplained.

It seemed Mr. C. was an unhappy rock star that day at being imposed upon to actually sit down for an album picture. Feeling cantankerous, he grabbed the copy of the comic and pretended to read it. What he did was create a memorable picture to adorn the album, which is still many times referred to as *The Beano Cover.*

Another interesting fact about the cover was the *Bluesbreakers* title. At this point it was the name of the album and not Mayall's backing band. After the album's release, it became his band's moniker for decades.

Which came first, the album or the nickname?

Author's collection

I wonder how much that copy of *Beano* would bring on ebay?

Fresh Cream

Fresh Cream was released on December 9, 1966, and showed the serious side of the three musicians, at least on the cover. Given the three studio album covers that would follow, it remains their simplest by far.

Expectations for Cream at the time were exceedingly high, but the cover goes against that grain in its simplicity. The group is dressed in flight jackets and accoutrements, which may represent Cream taking off, and take off they did.

While the album is ranked as the #101 album of all time by *Rolling Stone,* the same cannot be said for the cover, which is solid and well thought out but not spectacular.

Disraeli Gears

Disraeli Gears, and the album that followed it, *Wheels of Fire,* may be the best back-to-back album covers by the same group in music history. The LP versions are suitable for framing.

To be a little repetitive, a roadie named Mick Turner named the album by calling it *derailleur* gears, which were used on high-tech racing bicycles; it then became Disraeli gears after the Victorian-era prime minister. Clapton and Baker had been having a serious discussion about bikes, but the comment so amused them that they used it for the title of their second album. The original working title has been simply *Cream,* which seems very mundane in retrospect.

The album art that adorns the cover has been synonymous with *Disraeli Gears* since its release. It is a perfect psychedelic rock creation and matched many posters of the day such as those being produced by the Fillmore East and West, the Jefferson Airplane, and the Grateful Dead. Cream's advantage was that *Disraeli Gears* got the release into the hands of the millions of buyers, which brought it to the attention of millions more friends, family members, and acquaintances. The famous cover is still being produced to adorn countless CDs, even if it does lose something in the translation.

The cover originated from the fertile mind of Australian artist Martin Sharp, who at one time had lived in the same building as Clapton. Sharp's artwork became eternally associated with Cream and Eric Clapton. Sharp also took his relationship with Clapton beyond just the art, as he cowrote "Tales of Brave Ulysses" and "Anyone for Tennis."

Bob Whittaker took the photography that appears on the back cover. His greatest claim to fame was a big one, as he created the famous and controversial cover that originally adorned the Beatles' *Yesterday and Today* album. The "butcher cover" was withdrawn and remains one of the supreme Beatles collectibles.

Disraeli Gears remains one of those rare albums that is a delight to both the ears and the eyes.

Wheels of Fire

The tile of *Wheels of Fire* may not have been the inside joke of its predecessor, but it perfectly described the music inside.

The artwork of *Disraeli Gears* was so well received that Martin Sharp was invited back for a second project in a row. He came through once again and created another spectacular cover that remains unique in its own right. When displayed next to the *Disraeli Gears* cover, they complement each other without being repetitive. Sharp won the New York Art Directors Prize for Best Album Art in 1969.

I have always thought the design would have made nice wallpaper. Just turn on a black light and have at it.

Goodbye

Goodbye has such a cheesy cover that it remains amusing four-plus decades after its release. The band members' smiles seem genuine, making one think their happiness at the time was due to the fact their Cream journey had come to an end.

Unless they actually had those gold lamé suits in their respective closets, the cover was a planned affair. It was right out of vaudeville as they danced across the stage for one last bow.

Blind Faith

Many Americans missed the controversy surrounding the original Blind Faith album cover, as it was quickly replaced with a picture of the band and life went blissfully along.

The initial album cover carried a photo of a young girl nude from the waist up and holding a model airplane in her hands, which many people interpreted as a phallic symbol. Today, the cover would not have made it past the idea stage, if that far, and even in the liberal atmosphere of 1969 it was too tactless for release in the United States.

The photograph was courtesy of Bob Seidermann, who was another former flatmate of Clapton's.

He originally approached a young girl in a London railway station about modeling for the cover, which today would probably have ended with a trip to a police station. Seidermann met with the girl's parents but ultimately determined she was too old for the cover. She did have a younger sister, however.

Mariora Goschen would be immortalized on the album jacket. She originally wanted a pony for her picture but settled for a small fee. Given what happened when the album was released, she probably deserved the pony.

Rumors followed the cover for years, including that she was Ginger Baker's daughter and that she was a young love slave of the band.

Clapton did not want to print the name of the group on the cover. Instead, it would be on the wrapper, and when it was removed, so was the name.

Interestingly Seidermann planned to sell lithographic prints of the cover (Martin Sharp, were you listening?) and even sent out advertising to publicize the event. It was straight out of the late sixties.

"I could not get my hands on the image until out of the mist a concept began to emerge. To symbolize the achievement of human creativity and its expression through technology, a spaceship was the material object. To carry this new spore into the universe, innocence would be the ideal bearer, a young girl, a girl as young as Shakespeare's Juliet. The spaceship would be the fruit of the tree of knowledge and the girl, the tree of the fruit of life."

Wait, there's more!

Mark Milligan, a jeweler at the Royal College of Art, could make the spaceship. The girl was another matter. If she were too old, it would be cheesecake, too young and it would be nothing. "The beginning of the transition from girl to woman; that is what I was after. That temporal point, that singular flare of radiant innocence. Where is that girl?" So said the literature of the day.

What it all added up too was a banned album of a half-nude young girl. Today, the cover still makes many people very uncomfortable. It was definitely an attention-getter in its day, and rightly or wrongly, it served the album well.

On Tour with Eric Clapton

The album cover for Delaney and Bonnie's *On Tour with Eric Clapton* was perfect for Clapton's time with the group. It pictured a parked car with two feet sticking out of the side window. It projected a very relaxed feel. After the pressure of two high-profile bands, Cream and Blind Faith, Clapton was content to disappear into a working band for a while. It was about the relationships more than being the star.

Barry Feinstein, who was serving as the Delaney and Bonnie manager at the time, took the photo. It was shot in 1966 when he was working as a photographer covering Bob Dylan's U.K. tour. Legend has it that those feet are actually Bob Dylan's. Whether this is true or not, only the shoes know for sure.

Layla and Other Assorted Love Songs

Derek and the Dominos came into being with a little help from Delaney and Bonnie's backing band as Eric Clapton took three of its members with him. Jim Gordon, Carl Radle, and Bobby Whitlock would become famous for being a part of the short-lived group.

The album title, *Layla and Other Assorted Love Songs,* came from his passion for Pattie Boyd. At the time, she was still married to George Harrison, and it would still be several years before she and Clapton would come together romantically and marry.

"Layla" was one of the grand love songs of all time but was unlike just about any other love song in rock history.

The tale originated as the story of Layla and Majnun, written by the Azerbaijani poet Nizami. It was about an unavailable woman, which Clapton equated to his Pattie Boyd situation at the time. His reaction to the story was "Layla."

The cover painting or collage was more surrealistic than psychedelic. It remains a memorable and instantly recognizable piece of art.

The artist was Frandsen De Schonberg. The liner notes attribute the art to Frandsen-de Schonberg with thanks to son Emile. Legend has it that the original artwork hung in George Harrison's recording studio.

This Derek and the Dominos cover has a simple beauty.   *Author's collection*

461 Ocean Boulevard

The unassuming house on the cover of the *461 Ocean Boulevard* album was the actual home where Eric Clapton and his band stayed while recording it. All the photos were taken at this house, located in Miami, Florida.

It was a simple title for an excellent album that produced such songs as "I Shot the Sheriff" and "Willie and the Hand Jive."

The album was recorded in April–May 1974, so it was only a short-term home for Clapton and crew. The house and the album have gone down as memorable stops in Clapton history.

There's One in Every Crowd

There is a track on the third disc of George Harrison's *All Things Must Pass* titled "I Remember Jeep," which was an eight-minute-plus improvisational piece. This jam is credited to Ginger Baker, Klaus Voormann, Billy Preston, George Harrison, and Eric Clapton. Jeep was the name of Clapton's Weimaraner dog that was missing/stolen at the time, and the song was dedicated to his memory.

Jeep made a triumphant return, at least his picture did, when it adorned the cover of *There's One in Every Crowd*. It looks like he is resting his nose on a coffin.

The inside of the gatefold sleeve contains an original sketch by Clapton. Photographer Robert Ellis took the picture on the back of the jacket.

The album was originally going to be called *The Best Guitarist in the World: There's One in Every Crowd*, but his record company thought it would be taken the wrong way. They feared it would be interpreted as Clapton proclaiming himself the best guitarist in the world. In a later interview Clapton would, somewhat seriously, say that was indeed the message.

As far as the cover is concerned, I haven't changed my mind; I still like the dog.

No Reason to Cry

The album title got it wrong. Clapton and Marcy Levy cowrote "Innocent Times," which appeared as the eighth track on the original release. The lyrics actually say, "No Reason to Laugh, More Reason to Cry." It seems simple and straightforward enough, but somehow it ended up on the album cover as "No Reason to Cry."

Clapton is seated at a table with his back reflected in the mirror. There is booze on the table in front of him. The word "Shangri-La" is written on the mirror in back.

Backless

The title of the *Backless* album is said to have originated with old friend Bob Dylan.

Dylan had a habit of turning his back on the audience and facing the band when things weren't going well at one of his concerts. Clapton always thought Dylan was so aware of what was happening onstage that he must have eyes in the

Not a spectacular cover but on of my favorites, as it shows a relaxed Clapton.   *Author's collection*

back of his head. The title, *Backless,* emerged from those thoughts.

The cover finds Clapton still in his beard phase, calmly seated while strumming his guitar, which fits the laid-back nature of the music perfectly.

Another Ticket

The title and cover of *Another Ticket* grew out of another inside joke.

Countless people have asked Clapton for concert tickets through the years. He had one friend who seemed to be always scrounging tickets from him, so he named the album in his honor (sort of).

Clapton even pictured a copy of a ticket on the album cover, and only the ticket, which served to enhance the level of the joke. I wonder if it was an actual ticket given to his friend.

Money and Cigarettes

The title referred to the two most important things in his life and all he had left.

The cover pictures Clapton standing next to a melted guitar and when combined with the title, makes for a depressing scene.

The thought of a melted fender Stratocaster is still appalling. Hey, he still had Pattie Boyd, which brings us back to the money and cigarettes.

Behind the Sun

The *Behind the Sun* album saw the light of day title-wise from the song "Louisiana Blues" by Muddy Waters, where the phrase is used in the lyrics. Clapton is a walking encyclopedia of the blues, but to pull this partial line from such an obscure tune is impressive.

Larry Vigon drew the pictures on the front and back covers. He is a noted graphic artist who remains active in the music world.

The album contains a photo of Clapton by Pattie Boyd Harrison, and she is listed in the credits.

August

The original working title was *One More Car, One More Driver,* but in celebration of the birth of his son, Clapton retitled it *August*. The album was actually released in November.

The cover photo does not portray a happy Clapton, especially one who was celebrating the birth of a son. Happy or not, it was his biggest-selling studio album up to that point.

Crossroads

I have already gushed over *Crossroads* as being the best chronicle of Clapton's career despite its advancing age.

A little-known fact is that Ronnie Wood of Faces and Rolling Stones fame drew the portrait that graces the front cover, and it is really very good. The fact should be better known as his signature appears on the bottom right side of the cover.

He found the picture in the archive of the Star File Photo Agency and used it as his model.

24 Nights

Peter Blake at the time, now Sir Peter Blake, drew the cover art for Clapton's *24 Nights* and worked with Clapton again on *Me and Mr. Johnson*. He contributed the artwork inside the jacket as well.

Despite his work with the high-profile Clapton, Blake's best-known work was the *Sgt. Peppers* cover for the Beatles, for which he was paid a flat fee of £200 with no royalties.

While he is a noted fine artist, he designed a number of other album covers as well such as the Who's *Face Dances* and Pentangle's *Sweet Child*. He also designed the Band Aid picture sleeve for the single release "Do They Know Its Christmas?"

In 2002, Blake received a knighthood for his services to the arts and became Sir Peter Blake.

From the Cradle

Clapton wrote a poem that contained the phrase "from the cradle to the grave." The "From the Cradle" part fit Clapton's blues album perfectly and became its title. Clapton was returning to his roots and the music that inspired him and continues to do so.

He used his own photo for the cover. He snapped a shot of light coming in under his front gate. He must have been feeling very ambitious at the time as he also hand lettered the title plus the quote on the inside of the jacket.

Pilgrim

Clapton had a vision of how he wanted the cover of his new album, *Pilgrim,* to look. He entrusted Yushiyuki Sadamoto, who is a Japanese anime artist to bring his vision to fruition. He was the perfect choice to create the surrealistic, dreamy landscape.

Riding with the King

There was nothing terribly creative about the album cover of *Riding with the King*. What I did like was that it finally portrayed a smiling Clapton, chauffeuring a blues legend.

Me and Mr. Johnson

Sir Peter Blake returned to create the cover for *Me and Mr. Johnson.*

Blake worked exclusively from photos of Clapton in order to match the image of Robert Johnson. There are only two or three authenticated photographs of Johnson, and the most famous hangs behind Clapton. Blake painted Clapton in somewhat the same pose to create a lasting image.

Live from Madison Square Garden

The professional relationship between Steve Winwood and Eric Clapton extended back to the sixties and was solidified with their time in Blind Faith together. They were both part of the psychedelic era with the bands Cream and Traffic.

When they reunited for a series of concerts at Madison Square Garden, February 25–28, 2008, the resultant CD release cover art bore that psychedelic stamp.

The artwork was conceived and drawn by Donny Phillips, a former member of the hard-core rock group the Warriors. He is also one of the best graphic designers for WB records.

32

Oh Lordy Lord

Guest Appearances

E ric Clapton's guest appearances, both live and in the recording studio, are almost too many to count, and new ones are always being discovered. He has networked his way through nearly a half-century of artists and shared his talents and skills with the famous and not so famous alike.

Some of his guest appearances have gone down in history, and others have quickly disappeared. Here are some of the more stellar, and not so stellar, as recorded on vinyl and CD.

George Harrison

Clapton has probably been a guest on more George Harrison projects than on those of any other artist. They remained friends through thick and thin, and even with Pattie Boyd, until Harrison's death.

"While My Guitar Gently Weeps"

"While My Guitar Gently Weeps" originally appeared on the Beatles' *White Album*. *Rolling Stone* ranked it at #135 on their list of the Greatest Songs of All Time and #7 on their list of the 100 Greatest Guitar Songs of All Time. It is that ranking near the top of the guitar list that brings us to Mr. Clapton.

The Beatles were in the habit of recording their songs a number of times in the studio, tinkering with them until they sounded right. Such was the process for "While My Guitar Gently Weeps." Harrison even tried playing the guitar solo backwards.

The dramatic day occurred September 6, 1968, when Harrison asked Clapton to play the lead guitar part. Clapton was at first reluctant to play the lead on a Beatles tune but showed up in the studio with guitar in hand and that evening recorded the legendary solo. His performance would not be common knowledge, but eventually the solo was attributed to him and recognized as one of the best ever created.

All Things Must Pass

All Things Must Pass was George Harrison's musical coming-out party, and he was joined by Eric Clapton and assorted friends.

The album's sound owes a lot to producer Phil Spector, who kept his excesses under control while enhancing the beauty of Harrison's music. He treated the all-star band as a pop orchestra, with excellent results.

Curiously, Harrison had the most to gain from the breakup of the Beatles. Lennon and McCartney lorded over the rock world through their writing skills and recorded work with the group. Ringo Starr was along for the ride and was swept along in the wave of massive popularity. Harrison was known as the quiet Beatle who was mainly a background figure. He had difficulty getting his songs on their album releases given the quantity and quality of the Lennon-McCartney writing team. As it turned out, he had quite a number of songs tucked away. The quality of the material showed just how much his career had been hindered.

Clapton was a guitarist of the highest caliber, but Harrison still recruited him as a second guitarist, and when Clapton plays the guitar, he is second to none.

He significantly contributed to the following tracks: "My Sweet Lord," "Wah-Wah," "Isn't It a Pity," "What Is Life," "Run of the Mill," "Beware of Darkness," "Waiting on You All," plus the third-disc jams "Out of the Blue," "Plug Me In," "I Remember Jeep," and "Thanks for the Pepperoni."

While the album will always be remembered as George Harrison's greatest creation and one of the most significant rock albums in history, Eric Clapton did play a large part in its creation, and it remains one of his most important guest appearances.

Dark Horse

Dark Horse was released on December 20, 1974. It was during the time that Harrison was separating from his wife Pattie Boyd Harrison, who was in the process of switching over to Eric Clapton.

Both Clapton and Boyd are listed in the credits among a long list of musicians. Mick Jones, Billy Preston, Ringo Starr, Steve Winwood, Ron Wood, Nicky Hopkins, Klaus Voormann, and a host of others joined Clapton and Boyd. Pattie Harrison is listed as a vocalist.

The gem of the album was his imaginative parody of the Everly Brothers' "Bye Bye Love," which came complete with some new lyrics that referred to the Boyd/Clapton relationship. One of the great rumors associated with the album was that Clapton and Boyd appeared on the track, but to date they remain unfounded. The track remains one of his important nonguest appearances.

George Harrison (Album)

Eric Clapton returned to the recording studio with George Harrison for a brief session in 1978. He contributed the guitar introduction at the beginning of "Love Comes to Everyone," which was released on Harrison's self-titled 1979 album.

Clapton recorded the song as a posthumous tribute on his own 2005 *Back Home* album to bring the composition full circle.

Cloud Nine

Cloud Nine was the last solo studio album released by George Harrison during his lifetime, and it was nice to have old friend Eric Clapton on board to lend a hand.

The album reestablished Harrison as a commercial force and provided the impetus for his participation in the Traveling Wilburys project. Clapton played on the title track, "That's What It Takes," "Devil's Radio," and "Wreck of the Hesperus."

Otis Spann

Otis Spann was only fifteen years older than Eric Clapton, having been born March 21, 1930, in Jackson, Mississippi. He may have been a son of the South, but by the age of twenty, he had relocated to Chicago.

It was in the Windy City that he made his name as a vocalist/pianist. While he would record as a solo artist, it was as the piano player for Muddy Waters, 1952–1968, that he became famous. He did not form his own full-time band until the late sixties.

The young Eric Clapton must have thought he had died and gone to heaven when he was asked to perform with Spann on his 1964 album, even if it was only for two tracks.

This brings us to the 2005 CD reissue *Blues of Otis Spann/Cracked Spanner Head*. The CD cover makes it look like two different albums, but that is only partially true, as it is two versions of the same release.

The first disc presents the original 1964 record, *Blues of Otis Spann*. It was a typical Chicago blues album of the day and features Muddy Waters on guitar. Regardless of Eric Clapton, it is worth a listen on its own as it is a mid-sixties blues lesson.

The second disc, titled *Cracked Spanner Head,* is a remix of *Blues for Otis Spann* with reverb added plus some extra instruments, including horns, to give it a fuller sound. The real oddity was that the songs were retitled, which was probably done to fool buyers into thinking this was a new release. Thus, "Keep Your Hand out of My Pocket" became "Crack Your Head," and "Rock Me Mama" was now known as "Wagon Wheel." While interesting in a macabre sort of way, it is inferior to the original.

The important thing for Clapton fans is tucked in among the four bonus tracks: "Pretty Girls Everywhere," featuring Eric Clapton on guitar. It is one of the first, if not the first, paid guest appearances of his career. It does make one other appearance, so read on.

The recording session took place in West Hempstead, London, on May 4, 1964. Besides Spann and Clapton, on hand were drummer Little Willie Smith, bassist Ransom Knowling, and Muddy Waters himself. The session produced the song "Stir It Up," which would be relegated to the B-side of an obscure single. Muddy Waters was the vocalist and Clapton the guitarist. It's out there, but it's a tough one for any Clapton collector.

Aretha Franklin

One of Clapton's guest appearances that many times floats under the radar is the one with the queen of Soul in 1968.

Aretha Franklin had been recording since the late fifties, but it wasn't until she switched from the Columbia label to Atlantic that she became a star of the brightest magnitude. In 1967, her albums *I Never Loved a Man the Way I Love You* and *Aretha Arrives* at #2 and #5 in the United States. It was her third album that would bring her into contact with Eric Clapton.

Lady Soul was recorded in 1967 and released in January 1968. When you read the list of credits, the name Eric Clapton—guitar is almost lost in the mix with the likes of Joe South, Bobby Womack, Ellie Greenwich, King Curtis, and engineer Tom Dowd.

Clapton's contribution was limited to "Good to Me as I Am to You," which was the only solo composition by Franklin herself. Her only other writing credit was as coauthor of "(Sweet Sweet Baby) Since You've Been Gone."

It may be an obscure song on the second side of *Lady Soul,* but it was an occasion when the Queen of Soul crossed paths with the King of the Guitar.

Champion Jack Dupree

Jack Dupree was born somewhere between 1908 and 1910 and passed away January 21, 1991. He was not a traditional blues artist but rather combined the blues with a barrelhouse/boogie-woogie style of piano playing. He also won over one hundred bouts as a boxer, which was how he acquired the name Champion Jack, which he used professionally the rest of his life. His recording career extending back to pre–World War II but was interrupted by two years in a Japanese prison camp.

Eric Clapton contributed to two tracks on Dupree's 1966 album *From New Orleans to Chicago*. "Third Degree" and "Shim-Sham-Shimmy" are both typical of Dupree's raw style, which was more energetic than technically proficient. He was a blues player but not the type on which Clapton modeled his career. Both tracks can be found on the CD reissue *From New Orleans to Chicago/Champion Jack Dupree and His Blues Band*.

Clapton's other track with Dupree was "Calcutta Blues," which can be found on *Raw Blues*. The album was a 1980s release, which has since been reissued on CD. It was a compilation album of sorts as John Mayall, Eric Clapton, Otis Spann, Dupree, Curtis Jones, Peter Green, and Steve Angelo were all involved.

Raw Blues was probably a John Mayall–fueled project. "Calcutta Blues" can be found on the album. As an added treat for Clapton collectors, Otis Spann's "Pretty Girls Everywhere" is also included.

The interesting fact is that "Long Night" by Steve Anglo was really written by Steve Winwood under an assumed name.

Jackie Lomax

Jackie Lomax has been associated with the Beatles more than with Eric Clapton. He recorded a dozen or so albums, was associated with some of the elite of the rock world at the time, but only had limited commercial success on his own. He was also signed to the Beatles' Apple label, for which he recorded *Is This What You Want* in early 1969. It was his only chart success in the United States at #145.

Lomax's career extended back to a number of early 1960s British groups such as Dee and the Dynamiters and the Undertakers, which also included Chris Huston, who would go on to become a successful producer with the Young Rascals and engineer for the likes of Led Zeppelin and Todd Rundgren. The Brian Jones in the group was not of Rolling Stones fame. The band recorded and toured heavily but with little success and disbanded in 1965. Lomax embarked on a solo career that ultimately brought him to Apple.

Is This What You Want is Lomax's best album, which may be due to the stellar cast of characters that surrounded him at the time.

The gem of the album is a single release that undeservedly and amazingly failed to gain any exposure. George Harrison wrote "Sour Milk Sea," but it was the backing band that couldn't be beat. Eric Clapton and George Harrison were the guitarists, Paul McCartney played bass, Ringo Starr was the drummer, and Nicky Hopkins played piano. Anytime you start with three Beatles and Eric Clapton, you really have something.

In addition to the aforementioned superstars, three of the top session players were on hand for the album: drummer Hal Blaine, keyboardist Larry Knetchel, and bassist Joe Osborn.

"Sour Milk Sea" featured the double lead guitars of Clapton and Harrison. Clapton played on the B-side of the single as well, "The Eagle Laughs at You."

"New Day" was the second single, and again Clapton was the guitarist. "New Day" was not included on the original vinyl issue but has been added to many CD releases. Harrison plays rhythm guitar on the track. Clapton also plays lead on "You've Got Me Thinking."

The album title, *Is This What You Want,* was aimed at the music-buying public after years of Lomax trying to find the right commercial formula for success. While it was not the hit he wanted, it remains memorable as one of Clapton's better outside projects.

John Lennon

"Cold Turkey" was the first song to bear a writing credit by John Lennon alone. The Beatles had rejected it, so Lennon recorded it with the Plastic Ono Band, consisting of lead guitarist Eric Clapton, bassist Klaus Voormann, and drummer Ringo Starr. Released as a single, it reached #30 in the United States and #14 in the United Kingdom. It was a part of Lennon and Clapton's performance captured on the *Live Peace in Toronto 1969* album.

Note: "Give Peace a Chance" was issued prior to "Cold Turkey" but bore the traditional Lennon/McCartney credit. Lennon later removed McCartney's name and claimed it as his own.

The song was played live along with "Don't Worry Kyoko" at the Lyceum Ballroom in London, where, on December 15, 1969, John Lennon was performing at a UNICEF Concert. "Cold Turkey" at 8: 35 and "Don't Worry Kyoko" at 16:01 both featured Eric Clapton on lead guitar under the name Derek Claptoe. Other credited musicians were Jim Boredom (Jim Gordon), Sticky Hopkins (Nicky Hopkins), Billy Presstud (Billy Preston), and on it went, which proved John Lennon had way too much time on his hands. Another version of "Don't Cry Kyoko" appeared on Yoko Ono's *Fly*.

Vivian Stanshall

Vivian Stanshall was a member of the Bonzo Dog Doo-Dah Band or the Bonzo Dog Dada Band or the Bonzo Dog Band if you will. Whatever their name, they were one of the oddest of the late sixties British bands. Their biggest hit was "I'm Your Urban Space Man," which reached #5 in the United Kingdom in 1968. They also released two top forty albums, *The Doughnut in Granny's Greenhouse* (1969) and *Tadpoles* (1969). Stanshall was the lead vocalist and trumpet player. He participated in a number of reunions through the years before passing away in 1995. The remaining members reunited in 2006.

Stanshall may have been the most eccentric performer with whom Clapton guested. At times, the guy wore pink rubber ears and violet glasses while performing. He was a close friend of Keith Moon, which probably explains a lot.

He began his solo career in 1970, and while he did not release an album until 1974, he did issue three singles prior to that.

The first single was "Labio-Dental Fricative"/"Paper Round." He was backed by the Skin Head Show Band. He also coerced Eric Clapton into playing lead guitar on the single. It may all have been a little weird, but it was still Eric Clapton.

Ringo Starr

Clapton shared the stage on a number of occasions with Ringo Starr, most notably *The Concert for Bangladesh* and at the other end of Harrison's life, *The Concert for George*.

"It Don't Come Easy" was a song written for Starr by George Harrison. It became Starr's first solo hit, reaching #4 in both the United States and Britain.

There were a number of versions recorded. The first included Harrison as the guitarist plus Stephen Stills, Klaus Voormann, Badfinger members Pete Ham and Tom Evans as the background vocalists, with Starr as the drummer and lead vocalist. Starr would tinker with the song over the ensuing months, which is where Clapton came in. Starr rerecord the song in the studio, and Clapton may have participated (or not).

Clapton officially helped Ringo on a number of projects. *Rotogravure* featured the Clapton-penned "I'll Still Love You," on which he provided the guitar work. Starr returned to the studio for his *Old Wave* album. "Everybody's in a Hurry but Me" was cowritten by Clapton and features him on lead guitar, bassist John Entwistle, keyboardist Chris Stainton, and drummer Ray Cooper.

It would be twenty years before he joined Ringo in the studio again, this time for 2003's *Ringo Rama*. "Never Without You" was a tribute to their old friend and bandmate George Harrison, who had passed away. The song, with Clapton's lead guitar, was released as a single but failed to chart.

Doris Troy

Doris Troy, 1937–2004, only had one chart single during her long career when "Just One Look" reached #10 in 1963. In addition to her long solo career, she was a backing singer of note, working with such artists as Solomon Burke, the Rolling Stones, Pink Floyd, Dusty Springfield, and George Harrison, among others. *Mama, I Want to Sing* was a musical based on her life that ran for 1,500 performances off-Broadway and was performed in London as well. In 1970, she signed to the Apple label, for which she released a self-titled album on November 9, 1970. Eric Clapton contributed to six tracks during the recording sessions. The album has just been remastered and released as a part of the Apple series of reissues.

The recent CD contains an important single B-side, at least for Clapton fans: "Get Back" with his guitar work included.

The original release was an important one for *Slowhand* aficionados. Clapton appears on "Ain't That Cute" and "Give Me Back My Dynamite," which are both George Harrison compositions. His other contributions were on "You Give Me Joy Joy Joy," also cowritten by Harrison, and "Don't Call Me No More" and "I've Got to Be Strong," which were cowritten by Jackie Lomax.

If you have not been exposed to the music of Doris Troy, this album will be a treat, with Eric Clapton as an added bonus.

Leon Russell

Leon Russell began his career while a teenager back in 1946 and for the past half century-plus has been a noted session musician, producer, songwriter, and solo artist in his own right. He has played with such artists as the Byrds, Gary Lewis and the Playboys, Joe Cocker, and Herb Alpert. He served as a member of Phil Spector's house band and played at the legendary T.A.M.I. Show. He was also a part of the late sixties/early seventies group Asylum Choir with Marc Benno.

He and Clapton were both a part of Delaney and Bonnie's sprawling band, which toured and played during the *Live on Tour with Eric Clapton* era.

His self-titled 1970 album featured assistance from a number of Delaney and Bonnie stalwarts plus some other well-known faces. George Harrison, Mick Jagger, Charlie Watts, Bill Wyman, Chris Stainton, Steve Winwood, Joe Cocker, Jim Gordon, and Eric Clapton were all present in the studio to lend a hand.

Clapton recorded a number of tracks with Russell during the second half of 1969, but only "Prince of Peace" made it onto the original vinyl release. His other contributions remained unissued until the album was reissued as a CD with bonus tracks.

"Sweet Home Chicago" is played at a faster tempo and renamed "The New Sweet Home Chicago." There is also a Russell-Clapton jam titled "Blue Jam" or "Jammin' with Eric."

In 1971, Clapton assisted Russell again, this time on *Leon Russell and the Shelter People*. The first track was a Leon Russell song titled "Alcatraz. The second was an energetic cover of George Harrison's "What Is Life."

The remastered CD is notable for three Bob Dylan covers; "It's All Over Now, Baby Blue," "Love Minus Zero/No Limit," and "She Belongs to Me."

Billy Preston

Billy Preston is another musician more noted for his work with the Beatles and George Harrison than with Eric Clapton, although their paths would often cross.

In addition to his own successful career, he was one of the ultimate session musicians, as he backed Harrison, the Beatles, the Rolling Stones, the Band, Little Richard, Ray Charles, Johnny Cash, Neil Diamond, and dozens of others. He was credited on the Beatles' "Get Back" single, which read "The Beatles with Billy Preston."

Clapton appears on both sides of Preston's single "That's the Way God Planned It"/"Do What You Want," which was also included on the album *That's the Way God Planned It*. It was a minor hit in the United States at #62 but charted much higher in the United Kingdom at #11.

Clapton returned to lend another helping hand to Preston on his next album, 1970's *Encouraging Words*. George Harrison coproduced the disc as Preston covered his "My Sweet Lord" and "All Things Must Pass," in addition to the Lennon/McCartney song "I've Got a Feeling." Clapton guests on the title song and "Right Now."

A forgotten fact is that Billy Preston, with Janis Ian, was a music guest on the premier episode of *Saturday Night Live* on October 11, 1975. He died on June 6, 2006.

Not all of Clapton's guest appearances have been high profile. Such was the case when he supported Martha Velez.
Author's collection

Martha Velez

Martha Carmen Josephine Hernandez de Velez is an American singer and actor. She began her career with the early sixties folk group the Gaslight Singers.

Fiends & Angels was her first blues/rock album, and she managed to attract such artists as Christine McVie of Fleetwood Mac, Mitch Mitchell of the Jimi Hendrix Experience, Jack Bruce, Jim Capaldi, Al Anderson, and Eric Clapton to lend a hand.

The album is a nice slice of late sixties rock history. Velez had a big, powerful voice that was not overwhelmed or intimidated by the illustrious people who surrounded her.

The music is basic British blues that was very similar to what McVie had been producing with her first group, Chicken Shack.

Clapton appears on four tracks, and you can easily hear his clear guitar lines shining through. The tracks are "It Takes a Lot to Laugh, It Takes a Train to Cry," "I'm Gonna Leave You," "Feel So Bad," and "In My Girlish Days."

Fiends & Angels by Martha Velez is one of the more obscure guest appearances by Eric Clapton, but it will be worth the time and energy to seek out a copy. The CD version is currently available on Amazon.

Bobby Whitlock

After the demise of Derek and the Dominos, keyboardist Bobby Whitlock released two solo albums in rapid succession in 1972.

His first, self-titled album lists all the members of his former group in the credits but never on the same track at once. Many of the tracks credit George Harrison and his perennial sideman bassist Klaus Voormann. There is also a Delaney and Bonnie connection, as many of the musicians who played with the duo while he was a member are present.

As discussed earlier in this book, one of the main questions regarding the album is the level and the when of Clapton's involvement. Clapton and Whitlock's relationship had deteriorated after the Dominos had destructed, as Whitlock was not pleased with the situation, to say the least. There are conflicting reports, but Clapton may have recorded his parts before the breakup and the others afterwards. Given the animosity between the two, this may be the correct version of the story.

Clapton appears on "Where There's a Will," "A Day Without Jesus," "Back in My Life Again," and "The Scenery Has Changed." The first three also feature George Harrison. The second number on the original album, "Song for Paula," was written for the sister of Pattie and Jenny Boyd. Harrison appears on the track but not Clapton.

The album *Raw Velvet* appeared six months later. Credit is given to the Dominos but not to Radle, Gordon, and Clapton individually. Clapton's involvement is limited to "Hello L.A., Bye Bye Birmingham."

The Crickets

The Crickets achieved their greatest fame as the backing band for Buddy Holly. After his death, they continued to perform together with a rotating cast of musicians. Some of the best known and longest surviving are Jerry Allison, Sonny Curtis, Joe B. Mauldin, and Glen Hardin. Old Eric Clapton sidekick Albert Lee spent time with the group.

Clapton's first contribution was in 1972. He can be heard on "Rockin' 50's Rock 'N Roll" and "That'll Be the Day" from the *Rockin' 50's Rock 'N Roll* album.

He appeared with the band again in 2004 when he guested along with Waylon Jennings, Nancy Griffiths, J. D. Souther, Johnny Rivers, and Bobby Vee for *The Crickets and Their Buddies* album. Albert Lee was on hand as a guitarist, which explains the Clapton connection. Clapton backs Curtis, Allison, and Mauldin on "Someone, Someone."

Freddie King

Freddie was one of the three Kings of the Blues along with B. B. and Albert. His career was cut short on December 28, 1976, when he died at the age of forty-two from heart failure. His first wave of popularity occurred in the early sixties with such popular songs as "Have You Ever Loved a Woman" and "Hide Away."

Clapton entered the studio with King to help out on one track for his 1977 album *Burglar Alarm*. This was a little different from a traditional blues affair as it was a little funky in places, plus he used some brass to enhance the sound. Clapton and his backing band at the time supported King on "Sugar Sweet." E. C. plays the rhythm part, while King provides the lead.

There is more Clapton on the posthumous release *Freddie King: 1934– 1976*. The second side of the original vinyl release is comprised of Clapton and King from their *Burglar Alarm* sessions together. The aforementioned "Sugar Sweet" is joined by "TV Mama," "Gambling Woman Blues," and "Further on up the Road (Live)," which contains dual solos. The tracks have also been issued on a number of Freddie King compilations CDs.

Arthur Louis

Arthur Louis was born in Jamaica on June 21, 1950, attended Michigan State University in the United States, and is now based in London. He is a guitarist/singer who specializes in fusing rock and blues with reggae.

Louis and Clapton crossed paths due to Bob Dylan's "Knockin' on Heaven's Door." Louis's 1975 debut album was named after the song, which was recorded with help from Eric Clapton. E. C. would use Louis's interpretation as the basis for his own recording of the song. They both released single versions in July 1975, but Clapton's became the more successful. Louis's album had some commercial success internationally.

The album is actually credited to "Arthur Louis featuring Eric Clapton," who plays on five of the nine tracks. He can be heard on "Plum," "The Dealer," "Still It Feels Good," and "Come On and Love Me." The last two were released as a second single.

It should also be noted that soul artist Gene Chandler is on hand as a guest vocalist.

Stephen Stills

Stephen Stills's career goes back to the Rock and Roll Hall of Fame group the Buffalo Springfield with Neil Young, and his seminal composition "For What It's Worth." While he has built a credible solo career, he will always be tied to Crosby, Stills, Nash, and sometimes Young.

Stills's first two solo albums are arguably his strongest. His stature at the time was such that many of the leading musicians of the day would take part in these two projects.

His self-titled 1970 solo debut album featured Clapton on the fifth track, "Go Back Home." The fourth track, "Old Times, Good Times," had Jimi Hendrix providing the guitar work, which is about as good back-to-back guitarists as can be found. The best-known song from the album was the hit "Love the One You're With."

Clapton returned for a one-song appearance on Stills's second album. He provides guitar on the track "Fishes and Scorpions,"

Stills, Young, and Richie Furay reunited in late 2010 for a mini Buffalo Springfield reunion.

Howlin' Wolf

The London Howlin' Wolf Sessions remains one of the key collaboration albums of Eric Clapton's career.

Wolf was fifty-one when he arrived in London with his personal guitarist, Hubert Sumlin, in tow.

While Clapton, Steve Winwood, Bill Wyman, and Charlie Watts are mentioned on the album cover, there are a number of other musicians involved both credited and uncredited. Ian Stewart, Phil Upchurch, Ringo Starr, Klaus Voormann, and nineteen-year-old harpist Jeffrey Carp, who would die shortly after the album's release, were all on hand for the May 2–7 recording sessions.

Clapton and Sumlin handle the guitar duties on all the tracks. A 2003 deluxe edition adds three bonus tracks plus a second disc of rehearsals and outtakes, which are essential for any Clapton collection.

Wolf was not a well man at the time, and his voice did not have the power of his youth, but the emotion and authority were still present.

Clapton plays and then plays some more. It may not be definitive blues, but it is good blues that have stood the test of time. The definitive Howlin' Wolf will always be his original material. If you want to immerse yourself in the traditional blues, this is an album that will open the door, acquaint you with the style, and point you toward Chicago and the American Delta.

As good as this album is, beware of *London Revisited* by Muddy Waters and Howlin' Wolf, which was released to cash in on some unissued material from their respective London recording sessions. The Clapton-Wolf tracks are "Going Down Slow," "Killing Floor," and "I Want to Have a Word with You" and were all added to the *London Howlin' Wolf Sessions* CD as bonus tracks.

Dr. John

Malcolm John Rebennack is an eclectic American singer/songwriter who has entertained the music world since the 1950s. He was originally a guitar player but is now recognized as a master of the piano. His style is a cross between New Orleans swamp music and psychedelic rock.

His solo career began in 1968 with the release of *Gris-Gris*. It was his fourth 1971 solo album, *The Sun, Moon, & Herbs*, that was notable for Clapton's involvement. Clapton appears on six of the seven tracks, and more were actually recorded than appeared on the original release.

The album was Dr. John's coming-out party, as it began his transformation into an eternal and brilliant rock character. The music is original, funky, New Orleans–based rock, and Clapton's guitar work shines through it all.

Clapton's contributions include "Black John the Conqueror," "Where Ya at Mule," "Craney Crow," "Pats on Fiyo (File Gumbo)"/"Who I Got to Fall On (If the Pot Gets Heavy)," "Zu Zu Mamu," and "Familiar Reality—Reprise."

Jesse Ed Davis

Jesse Ed Davis was born in Norman, Oklahoma, on September 21, 1944. He is now a somewhat forgotten rock artist and guitarist.

During the mid-sixties, he left college to tour with Conway Twitty. He eventually moved to the West Coast and joined Taj Mahal, whom he backed on his first three albums. He also appeared with Taj Mahal on the album *The Rolling Stones Rock and Roll Circus*, which introduced him to John Lennon and George Harrison, with whom he would work in the future.

Davis recorded his first, self-titled album in 1971. It featured Eric Clapton on all eight tracks. Davis was one of the lead guitarists with Clapton at the Concert for Bangladesh.

His voice may have been a little gruff at times, but he more than made up for it with his guitar prowess and especially his slide technique. When you add Eric Clapton to the mix, you have an album of note.

Their tracks together include "Reno Street Incident," "Tulsa Country," "Washita Love Child," "Every Night Is Saturday Night," "You Belladonna You," " Rock and Roll Gypsies," "Golden Sun Goddess," and "Crazy Love."

Buddy Guy and Junior Wells

When Buddy Guy and Junior Wells came a-knockin' in 1971, Eric Clapton was quick to respond.

Junior Wells, 1934–1998, was born in Memphis, Tennessee, and by the age of seven was well on his way to becoming a harmonica virtuoso. He produced over a dozen solo album albums during a career that began in 1965. Wells's last major appearance was in the motion picture *Blues Brothers 2000,* which was released a month before his death.

This 45 is an example of Clapton's willingness to help out friends
in the studio. *Courtesy of Robert Rodriguez*

Wells began working with Buddy Guy in the sixties, and his guitar was a
good match for Wells's harp. In 1971, they came together to record *Buddy
Guy & Junior Wells Play the Blues*, which is where Eric Clapton came in.

Clapton was in his Derek and the Dominos phase and was an excellent
combination for Guy's guitar and Wells's harp. Also on hand were Dr. John
and J. Geils. It added up to a raw and powerful blues album. Wells brought
a unique aspect to the guitar playing of the two masters.

Clapton appears on "Man of Many Words," "My Baby Left Me (She Left
Me a Mule to Ride)," "Come On in This House"/"Have Mercy Baby," "T
Bone Shuffle," "A Poor Man's Plea," "Messin' with the Kid," "I Don't Know,"
and "Bad Whiskey."

Clapton formed a professional relationship with Guy that has lasted to
the present day.

Stephen Bishop

Stephen Bishop may have had a long and successful career, and Eric Clapton
may have played on three of his albums, but for better or worse I will always
remember him as the folk singer in the film *Animal House* whose guitar John
Belushi destroys in a frenzy.

Bishop's style can best be defined as folk/pop, and Clapton's appearances on his album were clearly not the blues.

Clapton guested on Bishop's 1976 debut album, *Careless*, with appearances on the hit song "Save for a Rainy Day" and "Sitting in an Ocean of Tears." *Red Cab to Manhattan* (1980) contained "Little Moon" and "Sex Kittens Go to College." Finally, 1989's *Bowling in Paris* contained "Hall Light," which completed Clapton's trifecta of Stephen Bishop album appearances.

Marc Benno

Marc Benno was born on July 1, 1947, to a father who managed the Texas State Fair's Music Hall Garden. Artists such as the Drifters, Lloyd Price, Paul Anka, Sam Cooke, and many others performed there during his formative years.

Benno gained experience as a session musician, working with the Doors on their *L.A. Woman* album. He formed a relationship with Leon Russell, and they would found Asylum Choir together and release *Look Inside the Asylum Choir* (1968) and *Asylum Choir II* (1971), which reached #70 on the American album charts.

It was through his partnership with Russell that he was introduced to Eric Clapton, who played on Benno's 1979 album *Lost in Austin*. He was living in Leon Russell's closet when he met Clapton. Who knows, it may have been a big closet.

Lost in Austin was recorded in England. Clapton definitely played on "Last Train" and "Chasin' Rainbows." Some sites list Clapton as having appeared on all ten tracks, but I have not found any verification of that fact. It is interesting listening to the album and trying to pick out the parts Clapton might have played.

Bob Dylan

Bob Dylan and Eric Clapton have crossed paths a number of times, which is natural given the stature and length of their careers plus the company they have kept.

Their first time in the studio together for a Dylan album was for *Desire*. Early in the sessions, Clapton found himself as one of five guitarists and a seemingly endless parade of musicians. He advised Dylan to pare the backing musicians down to a manageable number.

As with many Dylan albums, there were multiple takes of just about every song plus material that would not see the light of day. Who knows how much stuff Dylan has salted away in his archives, but it must be massive as his *Bootleg Series* is now up to volume 9.

Clapton can be heard on "Romance in Durango" but actually played on a number of takes not included on the original release. "Oh Sister," "Mozambique," "Hurricane," "Catfish," "Honey Blues," and "Wiretappin'" were all recorded, both with and without Clapton's participation.

Dylan's film *Hearts on Fire* and its resulting soundtrack also had a Clapton connection, although the less said about the actual movie, the better. It received poor reviews in England upon its release and went directly to video in the United States. The original soundtrack remains extremely difficult to track down.

The *Hearts on Fire* sessions took place on August 27–28, 1986, with Clapton on hand for a number of tracks. "The Usual" and "Had a Dream About You" were released on the soundtracks, and "Five and Dime" has since been issued. "To Fall in Love with You" remains unissued.

Clapton's last contribution to a Dylan album was more up front as he was actually listed in the credits. He recorded the guitar parts for "Had a Dream About You Baby," which was issued on 1988's *Down in the Groove*.

Kinky Friedman

Kinky Friedman (Richard S.) was born on November 1, 1944, in Chicago, Illinois, but moved to Austin, Texas, at a very young age.

Friend's music traveled in some unusual directions, and, once, he took Eric Clapton along for the ride. *Author's collection*

He music career began while a music student at the University of Texas. His style can best be described as a sort of weird folk music that has comedic elements while maintaining a critical edge. In 1971, he formed Kinky Friedman and the Texas Jewboys, who were representative of his developing musical style.

His third studio album, *Lasso from El Paso*, features Eric Clapton on the Dobro guitar. The Dopyera Brothers formed the Dobro Guitar Company in 1928. They produced mainly resonating guitars, originally with inverted cones. Gibson bought the company and the rights to the design in 1994. Clapton can be heard on "Kinky" and "Ol' Ben Lucas."

The album also contains a cover of the old Ray Stevens hit "Ahab the Arab," plus "Men's Room L.A.," which features Ringo Starr as the voice of Jesus. Those two sings provide a good summary of his musical approach.

Ronnie Lane and Pete Townshend

Pete Townshend of the Who and Ronnie Lane of Faces came together in late 1966 and early 1977 to record *Rough Mix* together. They were joined by such luminaries as John Entwistle, Charlie Watts, John Bundrick, and of course Eric Clapton, who was among the dozen or so musicians listed in the credits. The overall style of the album is a nice balance between Lane and Townshend.

Clapton contributed lead guitar, 6-string acoustic guitar, and Dobro on four of the tracks: "Rough Mix," "Annie," "April Fool," and "Till the River Runs Dry."

The title song emerged from a jam, with Clapton supplying the guitar leads and some fine keyboards by Bundrick. "April Fool" is a good example of Clapton's Dobro work and an excellent introduction to the instrument itself. "Till the River Runs Dry" is more Dobro work by Clapton, which combines well with Townshend's acoustic play.

Clapton aside, it was probably the best of Townshend's projects outside of the Who. It was fairly successful, reaching #44 in Britain and #45 in the United States.

Clapton also contributed to Lane's 1980 album, *See Me*. It was during the *Rough Mix* sessions that Lane was diagnosed with multiple sclerosis, which would ultimately claim his life in 1997 at the age of fifty-one.

See Me would be Lane's last true studio album. In addition to Clapton, he was joined by Ian Stewart, Alun Davies, Mel Collins, and Henry McCullough. Clapton appears on three tracks: "Lad's Got Money," "Barcelona," and "Way Up Yonder."

John Mayall

Back to the Roots was an ambitious two-disc album recorded by John Mayall in January 1971, in London and California. It featured former Bluesbreakers Eric Clapton and Mick Taylor as the guitarists on many of the tracks. A word of warning may be in order as Mayall remixed the album with new drum and bass parts and released it as *Archive to the Eighties*. It is better to stick to the original.

The album contains excellent guitar work by both Clapton and Taylor. Clapton's best performance is "Prisons on the Road." He also performs on "Accidental Suicide," "Home Again," "Force of Nature," and "Goodbye Tomorrow."

While Clapton is brilliant, and Mayall does bring out the best in him, Mick Taylor's guitar solo on "Marriage Madness" is one for the ages. Consider it a wonderful bonus for any fan of Clapton's.

Roger Waters

Roger Waters will never escape the shadow of Pink Floyd. *Dark Side of the Moon* and *The Wall* remain two of the most creative and commercially successful in music history. *The Dark Side of the Moon* stayed on the *Billboard* Top 200 Album chart for 741 consecutive weeks, 1973–1988. It sold in excess of forty million copies worldwide, and Pink Floyd has exceeded the two hundred million mark.

Waters's first solo album was 1984's *The Pro and Cons of Hitchhiking*, which is where Eric Clapton came in. The theme of an impending mid-life crisis was first developed in 1977, when it was considered for a possible Pink Floyd album. The band rejected the idea in favor of *The Wall*, which in retrospect was an extremely wise decision as it would sell twenty-three million copies.

Clapton is the lead guitarist throughout the album and provides backing vocals as well. He subsequently toured with Waters but left the group before it reached America, reasoning that the music was too restrictive and confining. He was probably correct in his assessment, but one wonders if he had been listening to the music of Waters through the years.

The album was successful in the United States (#13), the United Kingdom (#13), and worldwide as well.

Bob Geldof

Today, Bob Geldof is more recognized for his humanitarian efforts and political activism than for his music.

He began his career as a member of the Boomtown Rats. In 1984, he assembled the supergroup Band Aid to raise money for famine relief in Ethiopia. He has organized numerous charity events.

He recorded his first solo album in 1986 after leaving the Boomtown Rats. *Deep in the Heart of Nowhere* featured guitarists Eric Clapton, Brian Setzer, and Dave Stewart. Clapton's tracks are "Love Like a Rocket"; "August Was a Heavy Month," which features a restrained but clear solo; and "Good Boys in the Wrong." This is an album of the eighties, but the synthesizers never overwhelm the guitar work.

Carole King

Carole King is one of the legendary names in the music world. She has written or cowritten 188 songs that have reached the singles charts in the United States. She has also released three solo albums that have reached number one in the United States. Her best-known release is the eternal *Tapestry*, which has sold in the neighborhood of eleven million copies. Despite these accomplishments, she seems an odd choice for an Eric Clapton pairing.

She had stated that Clapton was her dream guitarist, and so in 1989 he provided the lead for two tracks on her *City Streets* album. He can be clearly heard on "Ain't That the Way" and the title song.

If you want a real treat, go to YouTube and plug in Eric Clapton/Carole King "City Streets." Make sure you have the full five-minute video version, and then sit back and enjoy. Clapton's solo is near the end. It is worth the wait. You cannot get a better tone or sound from a guitar.

Rod Stewart

Rod Stewart has gone from rock star with Faces and Jeff Beck, to pop star with such #1 hits as "Tonight's the Night" and "Do Ya Think I'm Sexy," to the interpreter of the Great American Songbook Series, which has now reached five volumes.

The third album in the series contains his collaboration with Eric Clapton on the Richard Rodgers/Lorenz Hart standard "Blue Moon." The song has had many interpretations through the years including Django Reinhardt, Harpo Marx, Billie Holiday, Elvis Presley, Sam Cooke, the Supremes, and perhaps the most famous, a doo-wop version by the Marcels that topped the American and English singles charts in 1961.

Stewart's take, the traditional approach with a piano up front and Clapton playing subtle guitar, runs until about the two-minute mark, when he embarks on a laid-back solo. It is not earth-shattering but is nevertheless pleasant.

Les Paul

Les Paul died at the age of ninety-four on August 12, 2009. His career stretched back to the mid-forties as a recording artist, with and without Mary Ford; inventor; and guitar virtuoso. He is recognized as one of the important figures in twentieth-century music.

Paul helped develop the solid-body electric guitar, which was an important part of the development of the rock 'n' roll sound. He also experimented with overdubbing, tape delay, and multitrack recording.

At the age of ninety, he released his first new studio album in over a quarter of a century. *Les Paul & Friends: American Made World Played* was a duet album featuring the likes of Keith Richards, Rick Derringer, Sting, Joss Stone, Peter Frampton, Richie Sambora, Jeff Beck, and Eric Clapton. When Les Paul went into the studio, the guitarists of the twenty-first century followed. Clapton appears on "Somebody Ease My Troublin' Mind Tonight."

Hubert Sumlin

Hubert Sumlin was born on November 16, 1931, and was listed as the 65th best guitarist of all time by *Rolling Stone*. He was Howlin' Wolf's guitarist from 1955 until Wolf's death in 1976. Sumlin then embarked on a solo career. He performed at Clapton's recent Crossroads Guitar Festival, but deteriorating health forced him to use an oxygen tank while onstage. He and Clapton crossed paths in the studio during *The Howlin' Wolf London Sessions*.

Sumlin was a major influence on such guitarists as Keith Richards, Stevie Ray Vaughan, Jimi Hendrix, and Eric Clapton himself.

About Them Shoes was a throwback to the Chess era. Clapton joins in on two tracks. "Long Distance Call" finds him in his blues comfort zone. He also contributes to "I'm Ready."

This is an album of Howlin' Wolf covers, which may not be the right word as Sumlin played on the originals. His only composition here, "This Is the End, Little Girl," is also the only one that features his own vocal. The guitar play between Sumlin and Richards is first-rate.

Clapton has literally contributed to dozens and dozens of albums, which may be a huge understatement. He has recorded tracks with Gary Brooker, Jim Capaldi, Joe Cocker, Phil Collins, King Curtis, Rick Danko, Jools

Holland, Bruce Hornsby, Johnnie Johnson, Corky Laing, Cyndi Lauper, Paul McCartney, Christine McVie, Willie Nelson, Shawn Phillips, David Sanborn, Sting, Taj Mahal, Brian Wilson, Bill Wyman, and a host of others that goes on ad infinitum.

His willingness to help out friends, whether in the studio or live, has always been one of the most positive aspects of his career and personality.

33

I'll Sleep in This Place with the Lonely Crowd

Guitars

There are many types of addictions in life. Eric Clapton's drug addictions have been well chronicled by countless journalists and writers, including himself. His addiction to the blues has been a more positive influence in his life and has brought joy to millions.

It can be argued that guitars and women fall into the addictive category as well. Clapton has been attracted to all types and styles during his lifetime and has brought passion to his dealings with both. Both have been dominating influences throughout his career and lifetime.

The following is an examination of the guitars and women that have been active in his life.

Guitars

The guitar has been an important part of Eric Clapton's adult life. He received his first Hoya guitar as a teenager, and it quickly became a lifelong passion. He would quickly become recognized as one of the masters of the instrument.

The guitar as an instrument has been around for close to a thousand years in an acoustic form. Acoustic guitars have hollow bodies. When the strings are plucked, strummed, or picked, a sound and tone are produced and amplified by the body of the guitar.

The electric guitar was first seriously developed during the early thirties, and without it, rock, blues, jazz, and country music as we know them would have not have developed.

The need for an electrified guitar arose during the Big Band era when the guitar sound was lost and overwhelmed by the brass.

Clapton has been and will always be associated with his instrument of choice. Some of his guitars have become among the most famous in guitar history.   *Courtesy of Robert Rodriguez*

While acoustic guitars are hollow, electric is solid body. The first documented performance by an electric guitarist was by Gage Brewer in 1932. Brewer was a rare orchestra leader who made the guitar his instrument of choice, so he was always experimenting with its sound.

Gibson produced its first electric guitar in 1936. Many big band guitarists began using the electrified instrument during the decade or so that followed, as did blues artists such as Howlin' Wolf, Muddy Waters, T-Bone Walker, and Memphis Minnie. By the early fifties, electric guitars were becoming common and were waiting for the onset of rock 'n' roll.

Clapton was born just about the right time as the guitar was beginning to evolve rapidly at the time of his birth. By the time he was a teenager, it was an accepted part of the music world.

Fender Telecaster

Clapton played a number of guitars during his short stint with the Yardbirds, proving he was experimenting with his sound and always trying to improve himself, even at this early point in his career.

His first guitar with the group was the workmanlike Fender Telecaster, which is a dual pickup, solid-body guitar. It was one of the first guitars of its type to be produced on a large scale, meant for the commercial market. It also made guitar repair much easier as parts were continually being produced and could also be scavenged from discarded instruments.

It produced an excellent sound for a fairly simple construction design. It was the perfect guitar for the young Clapton as it produced a warm and bluesy sound when played with skill, which Clapton had no problem doing even at a young age.

Elvis Presley, Ricky Nelson, and James Burton all played Telecasters during the period. Muddy Waters, Steve Cropper, and Mike Bloomfield would use them shortly after.

It was a mass-produced guitar that was readily available, and many musicians of the day gravitated toward it.

Fender Jazzmaster

Clapton must have been making a few bucks from his time with the Yardbirds, as his Fender Jazzmaster was a more upscale and pricey instrument than his Telecaster. It was also a fairly new model at the time, having first been produced in 1958.

It was originally marketed as a jazz guitar but quickly became an instrument of choice to a generation of surf guitarists in the United States. Eric Clapton also used it for a spell, and he was definitely nowhere near a surf guitarist sound. Fender quickly developed a Jaguar model that catered to the growing surf movement.

The original run of Jazzmasters was discontinued in 1977, but by that time Clapton had long since moved on many times over.

Gretsch 6120

The Gretsch 6120 is a legendary hollow-body electric guitar. It is difficult to imagine Eric Clapton playing this instrument with the Yardbirds, as it is a rather large and ornate model.

I did not realize it at the time, but I saw a Gretsch 6120 long before I had ever heard of Eric Clapton. Early rock 'n' roll guitarists Eddie Cochran and Duane Eddy both used the model. Its visibility and prominence grew during that time through its association with Chet Atkins. For a brief period, it was one of the most popular guitars on the market.

Brian Setzer, during his Stray Cats days, can be seen playing one of the early models. They are still being produced in many variations today.

Gibson ES-335

The Gibson ES-335 is still being produced and has been an instrument of choice for everyone from Trini Lopez to B. B. King to Alex Lifeson of Rush.

It is an arch-top semiacoustic electric guitar. Early Gibsons had produced feedback when played too loud. The second generation of Gibsons solved the feedback problem, but their instruments lost some of their tone-producing capabilities. The semihollow body solved both problems and quickly became the choice of many blues, jazz, and rock artists. It also had a slim neck that made it much easier to play.

The guitar made a dramatic comeback when Clapton took it out of the closet and began using it again. It thus began a journey through rock history.

He used it at the last Cream concert, then again with Blind Faith. It became his guitar of choice during the 1970s when he wanted to employ a slide technique. It reappeared again at a Hyde Park concert in 1996. He used it when recording his blues album *From the Cradle*. It was finally auctioned for charity in 2004 for over $800,000.

Gibson Les Paul Sunburst

By the mid-sixties, Clapton had settled on the Les Paul Gibson as his instrument of choice. He followed Keith Richards, who had bought a used one in 1964 and had played it regularly. Freddie King and Hubert Sumlin were also coaxing sound from their Les Pauls that had impressed Clapton.

Clapton played a standard Sunburst Model and as a recognized guitar god, initiated a sales run on it. Peter Green, Jeff Beck, Mick Taylor, and Jimmy Page soon followed.

Only 1,700 of the guitars were made between 1958 and 1960 and any in good condition today would sell in the $100,000-plus range.

Clapton's first Les Paul was stolen, but he managed to replace it by purchasing one from Andy Summers. He continued to use a Gibson during his time with Cream.

1964 Gibson SG

In 1967, he switched to a 1964 Gibson SG. It became one of his more memorable guitars.

Enter the Fool! The Fool was a group of Dutch artists who were popular for their psychedelic art during the late sixties. Some of their best-known clothes creations were worn by the Hollies on their *Evolution* album cover. They also made apparel for the Move, Procol Harum, and the Incredible String Band. The Fool really missed the brass ring when their cover design was rejected by the Beatles for the *Sgt. Pepper's* album, although it worked out fine for the Beatles. They did decorate George Harrison's car and even released their own album in 1968, cajoling Graham Nash into being their producer. It was reissued in 2005.

They designed many of Cream's clothes during the era, which brings us to Cream's instruments. The Fool decorated Jack Bruce's Fender Bass, Ginger Baker's personal drum set, and Clapton's Gibson SG. The instrument was christened "the Fool Guitar."

The famous guitar ended up in the hands of Jesse Ed Davis, who sold it to Todd Rundgren for $500. It was a good investment for Rundgren as he sold it for over a $100,00 in 2000. It now rests in the hands of a private collector.

Fender Stratocaster

In late 1969, Clapton switched to a Fender Stratocaster. He had attained his godlike status playing a Gibson, but times were changing.

Clapton has probably appeared in thousands of ads for guitars, amps, and other related paraphernalia. *Author's collection*

Buddy Guy was using one at the time, but it was Steve Winwood who convinced Clapton to give it a try.

Brownie

Clapton named his Fender Stratocaster Brownie and used it during the early seventies, including live performances with Derek and the Dominos plus in the studio for the *Layla* sessions.

The guitar had an alder body, tobacco sunburst finish, maple neck, skunk stripe routing, and black dot inlays. It was a 1956 model he bought for $400. It can be seen on the cover of his solo debut album, *Eric Clapton*. As time passed, it was relegated to backup status to his more famous Fender Telecaster, Blackie.

Clapton parted with his old friend at a June 24, 1999, charity auction at Christie's Auction House in New York City. The proceeds went to his Crossroads treatment center. The final sale price was $450,000.

Brownie can be viewed at the Experience Music Project in Seattle, Washington.

Blackie

In 1970, Eric Clapton went on a shopping expedition to the Show-bud Guitar Shop in Nashville, Tennessee. He bought six Fender Stratocasters, which must have made the owner think he had died and gone to heaven. Clapton gave George Harrison, Pete Townshend, and Steve Winwood one guitar apiece. He disassembled the other three and built one guitar from the parts. The name Blackie came from the color of the finish.

The guitar was first used live at the famous 1973 Rainbow Concert. It would also be used at the Band's The Last Waltz concert. Clapton retired the guitar in 1985 due to use and age, which resulted in mounting problems, although it has been unretired a few times since.

In 2004, Clapton auctioned the guitar at Christie's as he had done with Brownie several years earlier. It was another charity affair to benefit his Crossroads Rehab Center. Blackie sold for $959,500, which at the time was a guitar record.

In the fall of 2006, Fender produced a limited number of 275 Blackie reissues, which quickly sold out. They were identical to the original. Clapton used one of the reissued models at his Royal Albert Hall concert on May 17, 2006.

The Eric Clapton Stratocaster

James Burton and Jeff Beck were both given the opportunity to go down in guitar history but turned it down. They were the first guitarists to be offered their own Stratocaster signature model. Burton finally received his model in 1990, and Beck followed in 1991.

It fell to Eric Clapton to be the first recipient of his own Stratocaster Signature Model. Clapton agreed to the deal in 1985, as long as the guitar was built to his specifications. It would be marketed under his name.

He used Blackie as the foundation for the first model. They were issued in red, green, and pewter. Black followed in 1991 and white in 1994. Clapton used the model live and in the studio from 1988 to 1993.

Gold Leaf Stratocaster

Eric Clapton gave Fender a special order in 1996. His original Gold Leaf Stratocaster was built by guitar master craftsman Mark Kendrick. Clapton used the guitar regularly from 1997 to 2001. It would be another charity auction piece, fetching $455,000.

The guitar was reissued eight years later in a very limited run of fifty pieces. Clapton has continued to use Fender Stratocasters including Clapton's Blue Stratocaster, which will be auctioned in 2011.

Woman Tone

Woman Tone is a term used to describe the sound Clapton produced and perfected from his guitar playing during the mid- to late sixties. Clapton has related that he achieved the sound by turning the tone control all the way off and the volume all the way up. The result was a distorted or fuzz-laden sound. A wah-wah pedal is also employed.

If you want to hear one of the best examples of this sound, just turn "Sunshine of Your Love" up real loud on your stereo system. Also check out Cream's performance of the song at their Rock and Roll Hall of Fame induction, where Clapton reproduced the sound effortlessly. In the final analysis, it has more to do with Clapton's style and skill than it does with the technique.

Guitar Auctions

Clapton's vision and dream for a rehabilitation center began in 1993. He had visited Antigua a number of times and felt it would be a good and safe place to bring his dream to fruition.

The Crossroads Rehabilitation Centre opened in 1998. It quickly became a recognized treatment facility for addictive behavior. Patients participate in a twenty-nine-day residential, 12-step program, while the center keeps the costs as low as possible.

Clapton has been very active in raising funds to support the center. His three Crossroads Guitar Festivals, in 2004, 2007, and 2010, have attracted many of the world's best guitarists as performers and raised millions of dollars. There is another auction scheduled for April 2013.

He has also parted with many guitars from his collection/accumulation to support Crossroads. He joined with Christie's Auction House in New York City in 1999 and 2004 to raise millions of dollars.

June 1999

Clapton's first guitar auction was held on June 24, 1998. A total of 105 guitars were auctioned, which may seem like a lot but was actually only the tip of the iceberg as far as his collection was concerned. The illustrated catalog cost $40.

The final bid total for the auction was just short of $4,500,000. When you add in the premiums, over $5,000,000 changed hands.

Some of the more famous guitars to find new homes were as follows:

- 1959 Gibson ES-335 TDN (Natural)—$45,000
- 1919 Martin 0-18 (Natural)—$44,000
- 1996 Fender Stratocaster Eric Clapton Signature Model (Black/Green) —$52,000
- 1959 Gibson ES-335 TD (Sunburst)—$70,000
- 1991 Fender Stratocaster Eric Clapton Blackie Signature Model— $68,000
- 1986 Fender Stratocaster Eric Clapton Signature Model (Pewter)— $95,000
- 1959 Gibson T-200 (Sunburst)—$78,000
- 1958 Gibson Explorer (Natural) used in ARMS concert—$120,000
- 1974 Martin 000-28 (Natural) Rodeo Man Sticker—$155,000
- 1954 Fender Stratocaster (Sunburst)—$190,000
- 1952 Fender Telecaster (Natural) gift from Carl Radle—$90,000
- The last lot number 105 was his famous Brownie 1956 Fender Strato-caster used on the *Layla* album—$450,000.

June 2004

His first auction was only a warm-up for the second. Clapton returned to Christie's in New York City with a new batch of guitars for auction. The proceeds would again go to his Crossroads Rehabilitation Center.

Some of the more impressive sales were as follows:

- 1966 C. F. Martin style 000-28-45 Conversion Acoustic Guitar—$166,000

- 1939 Style 000-42 Martin Acoustic used by Clapton for *MTV Unplugged* —$500,000

- 1996 Fender Custom Shop 50th Anniversary Goldleaf Stratocaster made for Clapton—$455,500

- A circa 1965 and later Composite Stratocaster named Lenny by Stevie Ray Vaughan after his first wife—$550,000

- 2004 Master Built Stratocaster Concept Model used recently by Clapton —$280,000

- Blackie started at $100,000 and the final bid was $850,000 ($959,000 after fees)

- 1964 Gibson ES-335 TDC—$750,000

- 1939 Martin Style 000-42 used for *MTV Unplugged*—$700,000

2011

Eric Clapton held his third guitar auction for his Crossroads Centre in the spring of 2011 at Bonham's in New York. It was originally announced that 64 lots of guitars and 46 lots of amps would be up for auction. When all was said and done, 175 lots of guitars, amps, and memorabilia were auctioned for a grand total of just under $2.2 million.

Some of the results included:

- Gene Autry Style d-45GAC.F Martin and Company Guitar ($25,000)

- C. F. Martin and Company Guitar—Brazilian Rosewood Style ($37,500)

- 1939 C. F. Martin and Company Guitar, Style 000-42 ($86,500)

- Fender Electric Company Solid-Body Electric Stratocaster Guitar ($12,500)

- Fender Electric Company Solid-Body Telecaster Electric Guitar ($37,500)

- Fender Electric Company Solid-Body Broadcaster Electric Guitar ($56,250)

- Gibson Incorporated Solid-Body Flying V Electric Guitar ($74,500)
- Two Gibson Incorporated Solid-Body Les Paul Electric Guitars ($22,500 and $23,750)
- 1926 Barcelona Francisco Simplicioa Classical Guitar ($18,750)
- Gibson Mandolin-Guitar Company from 1927. Mandolin Style F-5 $60.000)
- C. F. Martin and Company Guitar Style D-28 from 1942 (32,500)

As I mentioned earlier, there are more to come, so save your pennies.

34

I'll Really Sleep in This Place with the Lonely Crowd

Women

Eric Clapton has had a number of important romantic relationships during the course of his life and career. Some have definitely worked out better than others, which make him a very human person.

Pattie Boyd

It is doubtful that Pattie Boyd could have guessed what lay ahead for her when she was growing up in Taunton, Somerset, England. She was the eldest child born to Colin Ian Langdon Boyd and Diana Frances Drysdale.

The Boyd family moved to Nairobi, Kenya, 1947–1954, as her father was a member of the military. When her parents divorced, her mother brought the children back to England.

Pattie would marry two of the legends of the rock world: George Harrison (1966–1977) and Eric Clapton (1979–1989). As is well known, both marriages ended in divorce. Her younger sister Jenny, married, divorced, married, and divorced Mick Fleetwood.

Pattie met Harrison on the set of the film *A Hard Day's Night*. She was almost an extra but did have one word of dialogue when she uttered "Prisoners" with great emphasis. When she married Harrison January 21, 1966, Paul McCartney was the best man.

Pattie Boyd must have had that rare allure as Mick Jagger pursued her for years, and she had a brief affair with Ronnie Wood when her marriage to Clapton was coming to an end.

Clapton's marriage to Boyd was filled with infidelity and drugs. The couple had no children together. It seems that for Clapton the chase was better than the conquest.

Clapton also had an affair with her younger sister Paula, who left him after hearing the song "Layla." She was seventeen at the time and realized that she was serving as a substitute for her older sister. Paula met Clapton when Pattie took her to a Delaney and Bonnie concert in London. After her breakup with Clapton, Paula dated Bobby Whitlock for a spell. He composed "Song for Paula" for her. Paula finally married engineer Andy Johns and then David Philpot. Both marriages centered around drugs, and while there were three children, the years proved difficult. Pattie Boyd proved to be a good caretaker until Paula's death on November 8, 2008, at the age of 58.

Pattie Boyd has in a sense left behind quite a discography herself. George Harrison wrote "Something" and "Isn't It a Pity" for her, while Clapton composed "Layla," "Bell Bottom Blues," and "Wonderful Tonight" in her honor. These songs may be the best testament to Harrison's and Clapton's genuine passion and addiction for Boyd.

Lory Del Santo

Lory Del Santo will always be associated with the most tragic event of Eric Clapton's life, the death of his son Conor.

She was born on September 28, 1958, the second daughter of very strict Catholic parents. Her first experience of loss with a loved one was the death of her father at a young age.

During her early twenties, she embarked on a successful modeling career and was seen on the arm of a number of high-profile men. She became a regular of the concert scene, where she met Eric Clapton at a time when his marriage to Pattie Boyd was in a state of deterioration. It was also the period when Clapton was moving from drug addiction to alcoholism. Their relationship led to a pregnancy and the birth of their son Conor. Pattie cited Del Santo as part of the divorce proceedings.

Conor's death in 1991 will always be a pivotal point in both their lives. Unfortunately for both, accidents do happen. The funeral was held in St. Mary Magdalene's Church in his hometown of Ripley, Surrey, England. Friends such as George Harrison, Phil Collins, and former wife Pattie Boyd were present to support Clapton.

Del Santo resides in her native Italy today. She runs a gym, works in real estate rentals, and is active on Italian television. She was a part of the cast of Italian *Survivor*.

Melia McEnery

In many ways, Melia McEnery is less known than either Pattie Boyd or Lory Del Santo, yet history will probably designate her as the central woman of Eric Clapton's romantic life.

She and Clapton met in 1999, and in June 2002 invited friends to join them at St. Mary Magdalene's Church in Surrey for the christening of their six-month-old daughter and Clapton's older daughter from another relationship. After the ceremony, they were called forward by the Reverend Christopher Elson to exchange wedding vows, which was a surprise to everyone present.

The couple currently has three children together; Julie Rose (June 13, 2001), Ella May (January 14, 2003), and Sophie Belle (February 1, 2005). The song "Three Little Girls," featured on *The Road to Escondido* album, is a tribute to his children and the contentment of married life with Melia.

McEnery is of Korean-Irish descent and was twenty-three when she met the then fifty-four-year-old Clapton. She was working as a waitress at the time but today has a career as a graphic designer.

It seems Clapton has found the home life that eluded him as a child and during his first marriage. One can only wonder if any of the girls have inherited a certain guitar gene.

Charlotte Martin

Charlotte Martin was a French model who had a two-year relationship with Clapton in the mid-late sixties. She was the person who introduced Clapton to Martin Sharp, who produced the covers for *Disraeli Gears* and *Wheels of Fire.*

Martin met Clapton at the Speakeasy Club while he was touring with Cream. She was born on September 19, 1948, in Paris, France. Pictures of her at the time certainly show why she was attractive to Clapton. That she managed to stay with him during this rock-star period of his career is testament to her affection for him

After their breakup, she remained a friend of many rock stars of the day. She attended a concert at the Royal Albert Hall with her friend Heather and then-boyfriend and future husband Roger Daltrey. She met Jimmy Page on his twenty-sixth birthday. Thus began a sixteen-year relationship, which produced a daughter, Scarlet. While the relationship ended in 1986, she and Page have remained on good terms and in 2007 became the grandparents of Martha Alice.

Martin married landscape painter Ernest Riall in 2005. Scarlet works as an accomplished photographer.

Alice Ormsby Gore

Alice Magdalen Sarah Ormsby Gore was born on April 22, 1952. She was the youngest daughter of William David Ormsby Gore, who was the 5th Baron Harlesch KCMG PC. What it all means is that he was a member of the Most Distinguished Order of Saint Michael and Saint George, which was a chivalry award bestowed for important services to the British Empire.

He was a longtime member of parliament, plus was the British ambassador to the United States during the early sixties. He was a friend of the Kennedy family and served as a pallbearer at the funeral of Robert.

In 1968, the very young Alice met rock star Eric Clapton though designer David Mlinaric, who had been hired by Clapton. He was a friend of some of Alice's older siblings and took her along when he visited Clapton's home. The attraction between schoolgirl Alice and the twenty-three-year-old rock star was immediate and intense.

They announced their engagement on September 7, 1969, and in 1970, she moved into his Hurtwood Edge home.

Their relationship took place during the stage of Clapton's life when his heroin use was on the increase and his obsession with Pattie Boyd was growing. Alice became hooked on heroin as well. They remained together for four years but never married. When Clapton finally kicked his heroin habit with the help of her family, he ended the relationship.

Life has not ended well for some of Clapton's old girlfriends. Her older brother Julian (thirty-three) committed suicide in 1974. Her father died in a car accident in 1985.

Alice Ormsby Gore was found dead in her one-room apartment in April 1995. The cause of death was a heroin overdose. She was just shy of her forty-third birthday.

Yvonne Kelly and Ruth Clapton

Yvonne Kelly was the daughter of an RAF father and a Duncaster mother. She moved to Montserrat, in the Caribbean, with her husband Malcolm, when he was hired to manage a restaurant. She was then hired to run the Air Recording Studio by its owner, George Martin.

Eric Clapton was married to Pattie Boyd when he arrived on the island to do some recording in 1985, and Yvonne was married to Malcolm. Despite their spouses, they entered into an affair. The result was daughter Ruth, whose existence he kept from Boyd for a number of years.

When Ruth was nine, she moved back to Duncaster, England, with her mother. She maintains that Clapton was a good and attentive parent when in London. She also maintains that the fact that she was the daughter of Eric Clapton was not hidden as she was growing older.

She tried the guitar as a teenager but realized she had not inherited her father's talent for the instrument. Still, today she is a member a band called the Alyscamps. The name is taken from a Van Gogh painting. They currently play on the club/pub circuit.

I find it interesting that of all the women in his life, Ruth has the best things to say about him over the longest period of time. Now in her mid-twenties, she maintains a close relationship with her father. At the age of sixteen, she officially changed her name to Ruth Clapton.

And So It Goes

Clapton has had a number of short relationships and shorter encounters during the course of his life. The period between his divorce from Pattie and his marriage to Melia was particularly fruitful in that regard.

His women have ranged from the famous to the infamous. Carla Bruni, Naomi Campbell, Vivian Gibson, Debra Hunter, Janis Joplin, Cathy James, Rosanne Cash, Davina McCall, Sharon Stone, Sheryl Crow, Marianne Faithfull, Jennifer McLean, Michelle Pfeiffer, Barbie Hunter, Barbie Epps, and many others have been linked to Clapton and succumbed to his charms and rock star appeal.

35

Deep Down in the Dead of Night, I Call Out Your Name

Whatever Happened To

Martin Sharp

It was Eric Clapton who put Martin Sharp on the path to one of his eclectic lifelong passions. Sharp was a lover of old songs, and Clapton suggested he see Tiny Tim perform at the Royal Albert Hall. Sharp was mesmerized by the performance. It would initiate a lifelong professional relationship between the two.

Sharp would design many of the artist's costumes. His Tiny Tim opera house concert poster was one of his most memorable and famous.

His grand Tiny Tim project took him nine years to complete. It was a 108-minute documentary film titled *Street of Dreams*. It remains the best and most complete look at Tiny Tim's life.

Sharp also had the good fortune to become independently wealthy through an inheritance. He established the *London OZ* magazine and became its editor and chief cartoonist. His work with *OZ* cemented his reputation as an artist. He did not leave the music world behind as he created posters for Bob Dylan, Donovan, and Jimi Hendrix. His work of the period remains highly collectible today.

By the mid-seventies, he had become a renowned artist and designer in England and Australia.

His other long-term passion was his commitment to Luna Park in his home country of Australia. He was hired as a designer and artist to oversee its renovation.

Luna Park was constructed at the foot of the Sydney Harbor Bridge in 1935 and quickly became the leading amusement park in the country. It was famous for the huge face that was and is located at the entrance. Sharp gave the face a new design.

The project struck a sour and tragic note when arson caused extreme damage to the facility in addition to taking seven lives. He believed the fire was set to destroy the park so the land could be used for modern development. Today, the historic part is protected by the Australian government.

Sharp continues to celebrate his work at exhibitions. His most recent was a major retrospective of his work, which ran from October 2009 through March of 2010 at the Museum of Sydney.

He is now far removed in time and distance from his famous work with Eric Clapton and Cream, but his covers for *Disraeli Gears* and *Wheels of Fire* will always be an immortal part not only of his artistic legacy but of rock history as well.

Otis Spann

Otis Spann was one of the old bluesmen who played hard and lived hard. He died at the age of forty from liver cancer on April 24, 1970. His stint as the piano player for Muddy Waters, 1952–1968, dominated his professional life and remains his last will and testament to the music world.

The solo album he recorded with Eric Clapton and Waters in support was the exception to the rule during his career, as he remained the ultimate sideman until just before his death. It was not until 1968 that he formed his own band, and by then he only had two years to live.

The best example of his style can be found on 1966's *The Blues Is Where It's At*. While it was a studio recording, it has a raw and spontaneous feel that captured the meaning of the blues perfectly.

Spann did branch out on occasion and can be heard on albums by Buddy Guy, Fleetwood Mac, and Peter Green.

Today his legacy is overshadowed by that of Muddy Waters, but many consider him to have been the most important post–World War II blues pianist.

Jackie Lomax

Jackie Lomax's main claim to fame, fortunately or unfortunately, was his time spent as a recording artist for the Beatles' prestigious Apple label. While his album for the label, *Is This What You Want,* only had moderate commercial success, it did show promise and was interesting for its inclusion of some of the rock luminaries of the day.

After the breakup of the Beatles, Apple became less of a priority, and interest in the artists who were signed to it diminished. The label released its last record in 1975, casting Lomax and others to the four winds. The company is still in operation and continues to reissue albums.

During the 1970s, he became a musical vagabond, joining and quickly leaving a number of bands, all with little commercial impact. He first joined the group Heavy Jell, with bassist Alex Dmochowski, guitarist John Moorshead, and drummer Carlo Little. They managed to issue one single, but their album of original songs by Lomax remained unreleased.

In 1971, Lomax was in Woodstock, New York, for a reunion of his early career group the Undertakers. He also released two solo albums for the Warner Brothers label, *Home Is in My Head* and *Three*.

By early 1974, he was back in England, where he joined Badger with former and future Yes keyboardist Tony Kaye. It was a progressive rock band that initially took Lomax somewhat out of his comfort zone.

He only recorded one album with the group, but it contained ten songs written or cowritten by him. Allen Toussaint was brought in as the producer. The result was more of a Lomax album than the type of release Kaye had envisioned, which may shed light on the short-term relationship between the two. Jeff Beck plays guitar on the title track.

During the mid-seventies, Lomax was on the move again, recording two more solo albums, *Livin' for Lovin'* and *Did You Ever Have That Feeling?*

He moved to America in 1978, and there he would remain for the next twenty-two years. He became a session player and backup musician. His lifelong passion for soul music prompted him to serve in the backing bands of such early soul and vocal groups as the Drifters, the Diamonds, and the Coasters. In between touring with these groups, he continued to make some appearances of his own. During this period, his sound also began to move in a blues direction.

In 2001, he released his first solo album in twenty-four years, *The Ballad of Liverpool Slim*. He finally returned to England in 2003 and performed at the famous Cavern Club in Liverpool, bringing his career full circle. He continues to tour and be active in the music industry.

Leon Russell

Anyone who has played with Gary Lewis and the Playboys, the Shindogs, George Harrison, Eric Clapton, and Bob Dylan must have stories to tell.

The career of Leon Russell has woven itself through the music scene for almost fifty years. While he is primarily remembered for his association with other artists, he had a number of very successful solo albums in the United States. *Leon Russell and the Shelter People* from 1971 (#17), 1977's *Carney* (#2), and 1973's *Leon Live* (#9) were all huge successes. All told, he has had fifteen solo albums reach the *Billboard* Top 200 album chart.

My first exposure to him was during the *Mad Dogs and Englishmen* tour, 1969–1971, with Joe Cocker, where he was the pianist and bandleader. It was a legendary and larger-than-life tour with thirty members, who partied and played together for close to two years. The title of the tour and resulting album was taken from an early song by Noel Coward.

Mad Dogs & Englishmen made Joe Cocker a star as it reached #2 on the *Billboard* album chart. Its energy and musicianship help it remain one of the better albums from the era. "Honky Tonk Women," "Cry Me a River," "Let's Go Get Stoned," "She Came in Through the Bathroom Window," and "Delta Lady" are all exuberant and passionate rock/soul performances. Cocker and Russell were joined by Rita Coolidge, Chris Stainton, Jim Gordon, Jim Keltner, Carl Radle, and many of the other characters who inhabited the music world at the time and entered Eric Clapton's world on occasion. A deluxe CD edition was issued in 2005 and another in the fall of 2010. The most spectacular document of the day is a six-CD set issued in 2006, which contains two complete Fillmore East concerts for both March 27 and 28 dates recorded in 1970.

Leon Russell was back in the news recently for his collaboration album with Elton John. Released October 19, 2010, in the United States, it quickly climbed to the #3 position. Guest musicians included Neil Young and Brian Wilson. Russell wrote or cowrote six of the songs.

The album proved Leon Russell is alive and well and that you are never too old to create good music and enjoy life. He received his due on March 14, 2011, when he was inducted into the Rock and Roll Hall of Fame.

Billy Preston

William Everett Preston died at the age of fifty-nine from kidney failure. Despite his long and successful solo career that produced thirty gospel/rock/R&B albums, he is often remembered as a Beatles sidekick and one of the ultimate session musicians.

Preston was many times referred to as the Fifth Beatle, and it reached the point during the "Get Back" sessions that John Lennon proposed to make the designation official. Paul McCartney brought the idea to an abrupt halt by commenting that it was bad enough with four.

At the conclusion of his Beatles career, Preston became a regular with the Rolling Stones. He appeared on *Sticky Fingers, Exile on Main Street, Goats Head Soup, It's Only Rock 'N Roll*, and *Black and Blue*. He also toured with the Stones in 1973 and 1976. He returned for 1981's *Tattoo You* and again for 1997's *Bridges to Babylon*.

He had his own addiction problems in the eighties, but in the nineties he would become active again touring with the likes of Ringo Starr and Eric Clapton. In 2004, he toured with both Eric Clapton and Steve Winwood.

His final session work was with Neil Diamond for his *12 Songs* album and the Clapton/Cale collaboration *The Road to Escondido*.

Preston's final public performance was a three-song set in support of an appearance for the rerelease of *The Concert for Bangladesh* movie. This final song, "Isn't It a Pity," featured Ringo Starr on drums.

His final resting place is in the Inglewood Park Cemetery, Inglewood, California.

Martha Velez

After her collaboration with Eric Clapton, Martha Velez headed for Jamaica to become the only American artist for whom Bob Marley agreed to be musical producer. The result of the pairing was *Escape from Babylon*.

Her output as a solo artist was meager in the years ahead. There was *American Heartbeat* (1977) and a compilation album, *Angels of the Future Past* (1989).

Velez became active as an actor. She had a role in the short-lived Norman Lear sitcom *AKA Pablo*. This was followed by a role in the hit TV series *Falcon Crest* during the 1988 season. She has appeared in films with Samuel L. Jackson, Halle Berry, Julianne Moore, and Dennis Hopper.

She has not released a studio album in twenty years as of late 2010.

Arthur Louis

Since Arthur Louis's adventure with Eric Clapton on "Knockin' on Heaven's Door," he has gone on to a successful and critically acclaimed solo career, especially in Europe and Japan.

Louis has established himself as a reggae/rock crossover artist. He received international exposure, the United States being an exception, for his interpretation of Bob Dylan's "I Shall Be Released."

He has released two solo albums during the last dozen years. *Back from Palookaville* (1998) and *Black Cat* (2009) were both commercially successful in Europe and Japan.

Dr. John

Dr. John is one of those musicians who can make a person smile.

His career the last three-plus decades has revolved around a fusion of various styles of music with his New Orleans roots.

He has remained an in-demand session musician and has worked with such diverse artists as the Rolling Stones, Carly Simon, James Taylor, Neil Diamond, Maria Muldaur, Van Morrison, and Rickie Lee Jones. He even wrote the theme song, "My Opinionation," for the TV sitcom *Blossom*.

Dr. John branched out into movies with appearances in *The Last Waltz*, *Sgt. Pepper's Lonely Hearts Club Band,* and *Blues Brothers 2000.*

He has released twenty-five solo albums during his career. His 1968 debut, *Gris-Gris,* was ranked #143 on *Rolling Stone'*s list of the 500 Greatest Albums of All Time. His latest album, *Tribal,* was released in 2010. He has won five Grammys along the way.

Jesse Ed Davis

After Jesse Ed Davis's brush with history, he went on to play with John Lennon, Ringo Starr, Leonard Cohen, Keith Moon, Steve Miller, Harry Nilsson, Van Dyke Parks, and Jackson Browne. Next time you listen to the guitar solo on Browne's "Doctor My Eyes," be aware you are listening to the skill of Jesse Ed Davis.

Like many of his contemporaries, he descended into alcohol and drug abuse, which caused him to virtually disappear at the beginning of the eighties. He reappeared in the middle of the decade as a member of the band Graffiti, which combined his music with the poetry of Native American John Trudell.

His drug addiction was never fully dealt with, and on June 22, 1988, he died of a heroin overdose. He was forty-three at the time.

Today he is remembered as a footnote of the era, but the man could play the guitar with the best of them.

Marc Benno

Marc Benno has had a long and varied career in addition to his early professional relationship with Leon Russell as a member of Asylum Choir.

In early 1971, he was hired as a session musician by the Doors for their *L.A. Woman* recording sessions, where he formed a friendship with Jim Morrison. He can be heard on "Been Down So Long," "Cars Hiss by My Window," "L.A. Woman," and "Crawling King Snake."

After his *Lost in Austin* album with Eric Clapton, he returned to Texas and formed Marc Benno and the Nightcrawlers. The group featured guitarist Stevie Ray Vaughan, drummer Doyle Bramhall (whose son would become a member of Clapton's backing band), bassist Tommy McClure, and keyboardist Billy Etheridge. *Crawlin'* was the only album they recorded together, but their label, in all its wisdom, decided not to release it. Benno finally issued it privately in 2006 and internationally in 2009.

During 1974–1975, Benno had a job that would have made even Eric Clapton envious: he was the second guitarist in Lightnin' Hopkins's backing band.

He remains very active in the studio, as he has released eleven albums in the last twenty years.

Kinky Friedman

Friedman's association with Eric Clapton may have been brief, but his story is too good to pass up. Anybody who produces a song with the title "They Ain't Makin' Jews Like Jesus Anymore" deserves to have his story told. His most famous song is probably "Asshole from El Paso," which was a take on Merle Haggard's "Okie from Muskogee." He has also toured with Dylan, appeared on *Saturday Night Live,* and performed at the Grand Ole Opry.

His interests have traveled far beyond his music. He authored two successful detective novels and wrote a regular column for *Texas Monthly.*

Friedman mounted a 2006 campaign for governor of Texas. One of his goals was the dewussification of Texas. He received a little over 12 percent of the vote cast. I'm not sure what that says about the other 88 percent of the state's voters.

Pattie Boyd

Many people, rightly or wrongly, have portrayed Pattie Boyd as a villain in the lives of Eric Clapton and George Harrison. She is an easy person to blame for many of the ills and low points of their lives. But the fact cannot be ignored that both men pursued her, and Clapton did so relentlessly for a number of years. Both men also married her of their own free will.

Today, Boyd is a photographer and writer. She lives in a cottage built in the 1600s in West Sussex.

She has exhibited photographs taken during her time with Harrison and Clapton; first in August–September 2008 in Dublin and Toronto, next November–December in Australia, and then December 2009–January 2010 in Barbados.

Her recent high-profile claim to fame was her autobiography, *Wonderful Tonight: George Harrison, Eric Clapton, and Me.* It reached #1 on the *New York Times* best-seller list.

Boyd has stated she did not tell all, but she did tell enough to be both reviled and praised by fans of both musicians.

Like her or not, she remains a fascinating character who was part of an important musical era and the lives of two of its leading figures.

One thing is certain: she has lived an interesting life!

36

Tell Me Who's Been Fooling You

Boots

No matter what a person's feeling about bootlegs, they exist, and have existed since technology enabled people to create their own recordings.

In the 1960s, before cassettes became the norm, bootlegs were few and far between. To create a bootleg recording, you had to produce or cut a record, which was not the easiest thing to do at the time. Cassettes made bootlegs far easier to produce and copy.

CD technology was a giant leap in quality over those old vinyl records, but one of the unforeseen results was that the ability to reproduce CDs in the home became widely available. The mass production of computers quickly followed, which opened up the bootleg market to just about anyone with the will and a little technological savvy.

Concerts by just about any major artist are recorded and many times filmed these days. Technology makes it virtually impossible to stop this process. When thousands of fans attend a concert, each one cannot be checked thoroughly. The house lights go down, and the performance is on the Internet within hours. As time passes, more and more concerts and material by major artists continues to appear. Many major artists come close to having every concert on a tour chronicled in this way.

Bootlegs can be of terrible quality or quite good. A rare few seem to have better quality than the official releases. The general rule is the older the bootleg, the worse the quality. Bootlegs are also bootlegged and go through a number of reissues, which tends to reduce the quality even further.

Eric Clapton is nearly fifty years into his career, and has been continually active in the studio and especially on the road. His bootleg recordings now number probably close to a thousand, and that may be an underestimate. A number of huge sites offer them for trade. Some also sell them, which remains a federal offense as it deprives the artist, who owns the

A Blind Faith bootleg.   *Author's collection*

music, of royalties. A very few bands, and I mean very few, have encouraged their fans to record their concerts. The Grateful Dead were a prime example of this.

Below are some of Clapton's more interesting bootlegs. I do not have any bootlegs in my music collection, thus these are not for sale or trade. They are intriguing on paper in that they shed light on some of his performances, which have disappeared. Some of this has already been covered in the performance chapter.

The Steampacket: The First British R&B Festival

This bootleg reaches far back into the career of Eric Clapton. I can't say that it is the oldest Clapton material that has been preserved, but it probably comes close. Since the concert included other acts, there are a number of early performances by others as well.

The festival itself took place on February 28, 1964, at the Birmingham Town Hall in England. While it was advertised as the first R&B festival, I have my doubts, although some festival had to be first.

Eric Clapton's participation was as a member of the Yardbirds, who were backing Sonny Boy Williamson at the time. There are five tracks: "Slow Walk," "Highway 69," "My Little Cabin," "Bye Bye Bird," and the closing jam of "Mojo Working." The material has been issued a number of times over the years.

Also included was the seven-song set by the group Steampacket. Brian Auger was the keyboardist, and vocalists included Long John Baldry, Rod Stewart, and Julie Driscoll. The Spencer Davis Rhythm & Blues Quartet is also on hand for several tracks. This was before they became famous and include a very young Stevie Winwood.

Beano's Boys by John Mayall and the Bluesbreakers

The major problem that artists encountered when appearing live on the radio was that tape recorders were rolling in the homes of their listeners, and a few of these would be used to create bootlegs.

The BBC attracted many of the major artists of the day into their studio for performances that would later be broadcast free over the airwaves. Cream performed multiple times. Since they were a national organization, without a great deal of competition, the exposure was huge.

Beano's Boys gathered BBC performances by John Mayall's Bluesbreakers into one place. His boys were Peter Green (four tracks), Mick Taylor (two tracks), and Eric Clapton (three tracks). Clapton is represented by "Crawling up a Hill," "Crocodile Rock," and "Bye, Bye, Bird." The recording finishes with a live four-song set from Bremen, Germany, featuring Mick Taylor.

As much as I love Eric Clapton, Mick Taylor was every bit as proficient as Clapton during his time with Mayall. It makes me realize why the Rolling Stones selected Taylor as Brian Jones's replacement. It can be argued that his time with the Stones was the best and most productive of their career. His solo career has been somewhat disappointing, which may say that he is best served in a group setting.

John Mayall's Bluebreakers with Eric Clapton: Bluesbreaking 1965–1966

This release purports to contain every known recorded performance by Eric Clapton during his time with the Bluesbreakers. Whether it's officially recorded material, BBC performances, singles, club dates, it's all here. I have my doubts as to the completeness even at the time of its release, as the band was very active and played numerous small clubs. One also needs to remember that it is a bootleg, and the truthfulness of anything its creators claim is open to a great measure of doubt.

Still, the song lineup is a treat. There are twenty tracks listed, and the final four were advertised as never having been unreleased before. "Hideaway," "Little Girl," "Tears in My Eyes," and "Parchment Farm" make the release alluring, at least on paper.

Steppin' Out: Radio Sessions 1966–1968

I wrote earlier that Cream performed a number of times of BBC Radio, more than one would expect from one of the world's most popular bands.

This release gathers six of their performances from November 1966 to January 1968 and bundles them together in one place. The interesting thing is that the only song to appear twice is "Steppin' Out," which may be one of the reasons it was used for the album title. Also of note is that neither "Sunshine of Your Love" nor "White Room" appears on the album.

Included are "I'm Your Witchdoctor," "Riding on the L+R," and "Sitting in the Rain." The last two were not included on the above review, which claimed to contain the complete Eric Clapton output from his John Mayall days. *Steppin' Out* ends with a John Mayall's Bluesbreakers performance with Eric Clapton on the BBC from 1965.

Big Black Loading Zone

Cream pulled into the Oakdale Music Theatre in Wallingford, Connecticut, on June 15, 1968. I have probably attended twenty-five to thirty concerts at this venue through the years but not this one, despite living in the area. I was a big Cream fan at the time, so the question remains, what was I doing at the time?

The theater was unique in that the stage continued to rotate throughout the concert. This meant that for 25 percent of the show you had the band in front of you, and for another 25 percent you viewed them from behind. I can't imagine what it was like for the performers, although I never saw a problem. I think the place seated several thousand, so it was an excellent place to view a concert, at least part of the time.

The track list was a typical set from their career. The first seven tracks— "White Room," "Politician," "I'm So Glad," "Sitting on Top of the World," "Crossroads," "Sunshine of Your Love," and "Traintime"—all clocked in at between three and a half and seven minutes. The show concluded with an eighteen-minute "Spoonful" and a ten-minute "Toad."

All of this begs the question again: what was I doing on June 15, 1968?

Lost Farewell Masters

Anything to make a buck!

While some bootlegs were well thought out, others were hastily thrown together strictly for financial reasons, as they made little sense.

This release takes concerts from Oakland, California, October 4, 1968; San Diego California, October 19, 1968; and Stockholm, Sweden, on March 7, 1967, and just pastes them together. There is a lot of repetition, and the concerts do not seem complete. They are not lost, nor were they the group's farewell.

Blind Faith: Compensation for Betrayal

There are short bootlegs, there are poorly conceived bootlegs, and then there are bootlegs that go on and on. Such is the case with *Blind Faith: Compensation for Betrayal*. It is made up of six discs of live material from the summer of 1969.

The first disc is a concert from Sweden, performed on June 18, 1969. The other five are from the band's U.S. tour. Stops in New York City, Milwaukee, Oakland, Santa Barbara, and San Antonio each occupy one disc. All seem complete except for the Oakland concert of August 14th. The set also highlights the main problem of the band: they just did not have enough original material. "Sunshine of Your love" and "Crossroads" are called on to fill in upon occasion. They even reach back to the Rolling Stones songbook for a rendition of "Under My Thumb."

This set is only for fans who want everything, as many of the songs appear five and even six times. How many performances of "Well All Right," "Sleeping on the Ground," and "Can't Find My Way Home" are necessary? The answer is, for many Clapton fans, all of them.

Blind Faith: Rehearsals

Sometimes it's easy to know how a bootleg comes into being. If it's a concert, the simplest way is to bring a portable recording device. A radio or television program is easy. However, releases such as *Rehearsals* look back to different sources.

Blind Faith grew out of Eric Clapton and Stevie Winwood jamming together. Early on, Ginger Baker joined them. Stevie Winwood handles the bass parts as Ric Grech had not joined the band at this point.

Obviously the principals involved had the tape machine running during their rehearsals or jams together, but how were the tapes leaked? One would assume that Clapton, Winwood, or Baker was not involved in their use for bootleg recordings, so it had to have been someone who had access to them either at the time or later on.

Does a person really need ten takes of "Well All Right" or five of a track labeled "Instrumental Song"? Maybe not, but it gives a rare look at the evolution of a legendary band and finds Clapton in a relaxed setting, which was also rare during this period of his life.

Eric Clapton with Delaney and Bonnie and Friends: Far from the Maddening Crowd

This concert was recorded on December 10, 1969, in Denmark. It was the classic band with Clapton, Harrison, Mason, Gordon, Radle, Whitlock, and the rest of the gang.

I've always considered this to be Clapton's mental health time as he was recovering from being the central part of two of the most popular bands in the world, Cream and Blind Faith. For better or worse, he would leave the band after a short stint and form Derek and the Dominos.

This is very representative of their concert style. There are eight songs bookended by "Poor Elijah/Tribute to Robert Johnson" and the "Little Richard Medley."

Fillmore East, New York City, New York: Delaney & Bonnie & Friends with Eric Clapton

This release was taken from two shows performed at the Fillmore East in New York City. Most of the usual band is present, but George Harrison is not listed.

While many of the tracks are from their usual repertoire, there are some nice additions. Both "Crossroads" and "Will the Circle Be Unbroken" make appearances at the first show and "They Call It Rock and Rock Music" and "Soul Shake" at the second.

The Fillmore East and West were a breeding ground for bootlegs during the late 1960s and early 1970s.

Derek and the Dominos: Electric Factory Theatre, Philadelphia, Pennsylvania

So who was the better band, Cream or Derek and the Dominos? I think the general consensus would be Cream, but every once on a while I have to wonder. On the rare occasions when Duane Allman played with the band, the decision becomes very difficult indeed.

This October 16, 1970, seven-song set probably finds the band at its best. When Clapton is the only guitarist onstage, the results are usually good to spectacular. Bobby Whitlock may not have been associated with Clapton for very long, but they matched extremely well. It is nice to see them associating with one another again after years of estrangement. Carl Radle is a more than competent bass player, and Jim Gordon was one of the better drummers of his era. Any material from this period of their career is worth a listen or two.

Derek and the Dominos Featuring Duane Allman: Live at Tampa

Duane Allman only played a few gigs with Derek and the Dominos, which was a shame as his studio contributions to the band were excellent and important. He was onstage at Curtis Dixon hall in Tampa, Florida, on December 1, 1970, and no doubt the tape machines were running, both legally and otherwise.

When Clapton was the only guitarist onstage, he found it virtually impossible to perform "Layla" at this point in his career, due to the guitar interplay. When Duane Allman was on hand, "Layla" was rolled out in all its glory as the two original studio guitarists could perform the guitar parts.

Budokan, Tokyo, Japan: 11/2/74

Bootlegging was not limited to the United States. It was prevalent in just about every country Clapton visited.

The Budokan in Tokyo is a venue many artists have played. It is probably the most famous concert theater in Japan. Clapton has played there on numerous occasions in the course of his career and many times has performed a series of concerts.

This particular recording is a chronicle of his first tour of Japan and probably of his last performance in Tokyo. It was originally a vinyl release but has since been moved to the CD format. Again, modern technology has made it easy to mass produce just about any recording or film and to clean up the originals.

The twelve-song set is representative of this early period of his solo career. Songs such as "I Shot the Sheriff," "Key to the Highway," and "Willie and the Hand Jive" share the stage with older material like "Badge," "Presence of the Lord," and "Layla."

The Slowhand Master File (Part 20)

This recording was taken from an August 14, 1975, performance at the Forum, in Inglewood, California. There were three special guests on hand that evening: Keith Moon, Carlos Santana, and Joe Cocker. The three artists take part in "Why Does Love Got to Be So Bad," "Teach Me to Be Your Woman," "Badge," and "Eyesight to the Blind."

If there's anything that whets the appetite of fans of an artist, it's guests of this caliber, as they change the dynamics of a concert or recording.

While such songs as "Layla," "Further On up the Road," "Knockin' on Heaven's Door," and "Tell the Truth" are always welcome, the guests give the affair an extra allure.

Happy Happy Birthday Eric

My birthday parties pale in comparison to this one. Clapton was at the Shangri-La Studios, in Malibu, California, working on a new album. March 30 is his birthday, so he and a few friends decided to do what they do best. The tape was rolling for guitarists Robbie Robertson, Jesse Ed Davis, and Ron Wood; keyboardist Billy Preston; and vocalist Van Morrison; plus Bob Dylan, Richard Manuel, Garth Hudson, drummer Levon Helm, and Bob Dylan.

"Who Do You Love," "Stormy Monday," "Adios Mi Corazon," "Big River," and other songs are all played by various members of the band.

The only thing to keep in mind is that the information comes from a bootleg and thus needs to filtered by that fact. Clapton was, however, in the studio, and it was his birthday.

Civic Center: Providence, Rhode Island: April 28, 1979

The only reason I include this concert is that it's from a stop in Rhode Island, which was my state of origin and my home base for a number of years.

There was nothing different or outstanding about this show. It was merely a leg on one of his North American tours. It featured his basic late 1970s band of guitarist Albert lee, which is always a good thing; bassist Carl Radle; drummer Jamie Oldaker; and keyboardist Dick Sims. The thirteen-song set is typical except for Albert Lee's "Setting Me Up" and a long cover of "Double Trouble."

What this set does prove is that by this time, just about every live performance was being recorded by someone. Whether they would ever see the light of day or be consigned to some closet and forgotten or destroyed was not the point. It was virtually impossible to stop the process. Old performances by Clapton and other artists are constantly appearing; again because the technology of today allows them to be resurrected.

Eric Clapton—The California Stars

Two shows from the west portion of his *Money and Cigarettes* North American tour are spread over four discs. The first was taken from Clapton's stop at the Universal Amphitheatre in Los Angeles on February 8, 1983, and the second from his concert a day later in Long beach, California.

His backing band at the time was guitarist Albert Lee, bassist Duck Dunn, keyboardist Chris Stainton, and drummer Roger Hawkins.

The sets are very similar, which is part of the appeal. I am always interested in the differences Eric Clapton brings to his performances of the same songs, especially when they are close together.

Page and Collins

Just by the title, you can tell this is another show with guests, in this case Jimmy Page and Phil Collins. Collins has produced and performed with Clapton on a number of occasions, but Page less so.

The release was taken from a performance at the Civic Hall, Guilford, Surrey, in the United Kingdom.

The first fourteen tracks are the usual combination of Clapton's well-known hits and blues covers. It is the last six tracks that made the concert special.

Collins and Page join Clapton and his band for "Further On up the Road," "Cocaine," "Roll Over Beethoven," "You Win Again," "Matchbox," and "Goodnight Irene," Anytime you have two of the old Yardbird guitarists onstage together, good things are bound to happen.

Three Yardbirds in the Hall

This release was taken from the Arms Benefit Concert Series, September 20 and 21, 1983, at the Royal Albert Hall. On hand were Eric Clapton, Jeff Beck, Jimmy Page, Andy Fairweather-Low, Stevie Winwood, Charlie Watts, Bill Wyman, Chris Stainton, and a host of supporting characters.

This four-disc set captures both performances in their entirety and is one of the reasons bootlegs have an appeal. It presents material that is otherwise unavailable at the time and often pushes the artists and companies involved to release official versions.

The set centers around Clapton's material, but in the middle are such songs as "Hound Dog," "Road Runner," "Gimme Some Lovin'," "People Get Ready," and "Stairway to Heaven."

The two sets are similar, but again, anytime you have guitarists of the caliber of Clapton, Page, and Beck, there are bound to be differences.

August Outtakes and Different Mixes Volume 1 and 2

I can understand how concert material is recorded and released without permission. It is difficult to control thousands of fans and concertgoers. In the studio is another issue, as there are not thousands, hundreds, or in some cases even dozens of people who have access to the tapes.

This release taken from Clapton's *August* album outtakes is a case in point. It was material not released on the album but was recorded in the studio. Its appeal is limited, as it was studio material not intended for release, usually because there was a better take on the song. However, there is always curiosity about what is not included and about the evolution of songs themselves.

The gems are songs that are not included on the release. All artists have material that just disappears for various reasons, some of it bad and some quite good. Bob Dylan comes to mind as he continues to resurrect unreleased and forgotten material through his multivolume *Bootleg Series*.

It all comes back to the issue of how it is leaked?

White Rome

There is bootlegging going on in Italy as well. Clapton performed in Rome on January 29, 1987, and the tape machines were rolling.

Every once in a while I bow down to cleverness, and such was the case with the title of the recording, a play on words of the famous Cream hit "White Room."

Also interesting is that the set contains a lot of Clapton's older material. "Crossroads," "White Room," "I Shot the Sheriff," and "Badge" join the newer material. It is also a very basic backing band of bassist Nathan East, keyboardist Greg Phillinganes, and drummer Steve Ferrone.

Eric Clapton—Ex-Serviceman's Charity Show

This is one of those year-end charity shows that fans would pay almost any amount to attend, as they were by invite only. This one occurred on December 23, 1989, in Chiddingford, England.

The appealing thing about this show and many of Clapton's private charity performances is that he plays unusual material. I believe he just plays what comes to mind at the time as he is not forced to play what his fans have come to expect (and in fairness have paid to hear).

The nineteen-song set contains such gems as "Lucille," "Midnight Hour," "Let the Good Times Roll," "Too Much Monkey Business," "Ubangi Stomp," and "Little Queenie."

The band is listed as vocalist/pianist Gary Brooker, drummer Henry Spinetti, guitarist/vocalist Andy Fairweather-Low, bassist Dave Bronze, sax player Frank Meade, and guitarist Eric Clapton.

It always nice to know that E. C. returns to the roots of rock 'n' roll on occasion.

Complete Montevideo 1990

I know, say it ain't so, but there is even bootlegging in South America, and according to comments about this recording, it has a pristine sound.

The concert was recorded on October 3, 1990, in Montevideo, Uruguay. The backing band consists of guitarist Phil Palmer, bassist Nathan East, drummer Steve Ferrone, keyboardist Greg Phillinganes, percussionist Ray Cooper, and support singers Katie Kissoon and Tessa Niles.

As I look at the set list, I can only wonder how many times Clapton has played "Cocaine," "Layla," "Crossroads," and "Sunshine of Your Love" onstage. I'm sure somebody out there is keeping track.

Interestingly, a third disc is included, which contains a five-song Mick Taylor set.

Cream: Reunion Party

Cream was inducted in the Rock and Roll Hall of Fame on January 12, 1994. The last four tracks of this release are the readily and legally available induction and reunion performances of "Sunshine of You Love," "Born Under a Bad Sign," and "Crossroads."

The first twelve tracks are basically rehearsals from the day before at the Power Plant Studios in Los Angeles, California. If you want six takes of "Sunshine of Your Love," three of "Born Under a Bad Sign," and two of "Crossroads," this set should pique your interest.

The Hall of Fame performance remains historic, as it was the first time Cream had performed together in a quarter of a century. However, if you look at it from a different angle, these rehearsals were actually their first performances together since their dissolution.

The Complete Japanese Tour 1995—10 Days

This set is one of the most ambitious bootlegs to ever be put together. It gathers ten shows at three different concert halls and presents them in their entirety on twenty CDs. It contains just over twenty hours of music. As the old baseball announcer Phil Rizzuto would say, "Holy Cow."

The backing band consists of drummer Steve Gadd, keyboardist Chris Stainton, bassist Dave Bronze, guitarist Andy Fairweather-Low, harmonica player Roddy Lorimer, and a brass section of Tim Saunders, Roddy Lorimer, and Simon Clarke. It always adds an extra kick to Clapton's music when he performs with a brass section.

The ten shows were performed over a thirteen-day period, October 1, 1995, through October 13, 1995. As such, there is a lot of repetition, with most songs appearing at all ten performances. Interestingly, the performances are a lot more blues oriented, as most of his hit songs are missing. Songs such as "Malted Milk," "How Long Blues," "Kidman Blues," "Sinner's Prayer," "I'm Tore Down," and "Five Long Years" are representative of the set.

I would imagine getting through this set would be like being a member of the band or road crew.

The Grave Emotional and Mental Disorders—EC Compilations

This is a compilation of three charity performances recorded between 1998 and January 1, 2000. The title is taken from one of the fake group names Clapton used for his New Year's Eve charity-only performances for recovering addicts and alcoholics.

These charity concerts are small affairs and have become legendary. This is probably not the best introduction as it contains mostly material you would come to expect from Clapton, while the actual performances found him playing a more eclectic set of songs.

The allure of releases like this is that the performances not open to the general public at the time.

God's Favorite

Meanwhile, in Copenhagen, Denmark, the tape machines were running on April 17, 2004. It was almost at the point where more concerts were taped or filmed than were not. The Internet and all its outlets were in full flower, and it was easy to post and access material.

This was a two-disc set that featured the Nathan East, Chris Stainton, Steve Gadd, Doyle Bramhall II band. Billy Preston was also on hand, which is always a nice addition, as he would pass away a little over two years later.

In many ways it was a typical performance of the oft-played "I Shot the Sheriff," "Badge," "Layla," "Wonderful Tonight," "Let It Rain," "Hoochie Coochie Man," and "Bell Bottom Blues," among others.

The only interesting difference was the addition of a steel pedal guitarist on "Sunshine of Your Love" and "Got My Mojo Working."

Crossroads Guitar Festival: June 4–6, 2004

If you thought the original release contained a lot of music, it pales next to this eleven-disc, thirteen-hour-plus set. It basically contains most of the music presented at the festival, including many of the artists' complete sets. There are a lot of highlights.

- Disc one contains the complete Styx set including their take on "I Am the Walrus." There is a J. J. Cale interview, followed by his set, which includes "After Midnight" and "Cocaine."

- Disc two contains the complete fifteen-song set with Eric Clapton, Robert Cray, Buddy Guy, Robert Randolph, Hubert Sumlin, and Jimmie Vaughan. Clapton takes the lead vocal on "Five Long Years," "Going Down Slow," and "Early in the Morning."

- Disc three belongs to Neal Schoen, Steve Vai, and Sonny Landreth. It includes Schoen's performance of "The Star-Spangled Banner."

- Disc four moves in a jazz/fusion direction with sets by Larry Carlton, Pat Metheny, and John McLaughlin. The two McLaughlin songs clock in at over twenty-four minutes.

- Disc five contains the sets by Robert Cray and Jimmie Vaughan.

- I find that the listing on disc six makes it one of the most intriguing in the set and makes me regret I was not there, as the combinations and some of the musicians will not pass this way again. Jimmie Vaughan and David Johansen join Hubert Sumlin for a five-song set. Booker T. and the MG's perform a short three-song set and then sort of serve as the house band for Bo Diddley, David Hidalgo, and Joe Walsh.

- Disc seven has complete sets by Vince Gill and James Taylor. I have mentioned previously that his performances on the three official *Crossroads Festival* releases have increased my admiration for Vince Gill quite a bit.

- Disc eight gets to the heart of the blues with B. B. King's set. Eric Clapton, Buddy Guy, Jimmie Vaughan, and John Mayer support him.

- Disc nine presents the Santana set, with Clapton joining him on "Jingo."
- Disc ten is Clapton's thirteen-song set with his backing band. Jeff Beck joins him for the set, concluding with "'Cause We've Ended as Lovers."
- Disc eleven contains the eight-song ZZ Top performance. It's Texas. and ZZ top was a good addition to the roster.

Despite all the music and the overwhelming nature of the release and the festival itself, I can think of a few performances that are missing. I'm sure they are around in some form or other.

Chinese Takeaway

Eric Clapton performed at the Asia World Arena in Hong Kong on January 17, 2007, with guitarists Doyle Bramhall II and Derek Trucks in tow.

The entire sixteen-song set soon appeared in all its pristine glory, proving that China had indeed entered the modern electronic age.

Songs such as "Cocaine," "Crossroads," "Tell the Truth," "Key to the Highway," and "Wonderful Tonight" continue to be performed decades after their first appearance.

Complete Abandon: Super Friends Team Up

This is another one of those private New Year's Eve fests that have become legendary due to their not being public. This one occurred on December 31, 2007, and ended on January 1, 2008, to be precise. The performances took place at the Woking Leisure Centre, in Woking, Surrey, England.

Hats off to guitarist Andy Fairweather-Low, keyboardist/vocalist Gary Brooker, keyboardist Chris Stainton, bassist Dave Bronze, and drummer Henry Spinetti for returning year after year to support Clapton. Joe Walsh was also on hand for this performance.

There is a generous twenty-three-song set list that includes Walsh's "Rocky Mountain Way" and Brooker's "A Whiter Shade of Pale."

It is the old rock 'n' roll tracks that have always made me envious of these performances. There is nothing like Eric Clapton playing such tunes as "Sea Cruise," "Rockin' Robin," "Honey Don't," "Lucille," "In the Midnight Hour," and "Blueberry Hill."

Blind Faith in Paris Night: 2010

The title is certainly misleading, although this may be as close to a Blind Faith reunion as we will ever have.

Eric Clapton and Stevie Winwood had reconnected professionally at one of Clapton's Crossroads Guitar Festivals. This led to a series of dates together at Madison Square Garden. Everything went so well that they set out on tour together. May 25, 2010, found them at the Palais Omnisports de Bercy in Paris.

The twenty-one-song set included material from Blind Faith, the Spencer Davis Group, Traffic, Derek and the Dominos, the Yardbirds, plus solo material as well. Clapton's backing band of bassist Willie Weeks, drummer Steve Gadd, keyboardist Chris Stainton, and singers Michelle John and Sharon White are used.

It states that the concert was recorded from block P, row 23, seats 13 and 14. This may be way too much information, but you gotta love it.

EC on the Road

Speed has become essential in our society. This DVD was recorded from three concerts, February 11, 14, and 18, 2011, in Abu Dhabi, Singapore, and Hong Kong. It was shot from the audience, and its appearance was almost instantaneous as the ever-present Internet is always available for all manner of sharing.

The eighteen-song set is presented out of order, so it is more a series of live performances than a true concert. What is amazing is how fast material from three different events could be assembled and released.

As a bonus, a four-song set from the November 17, 2010, Prince's Trust Gala at the Royal Albert Hall in London is affixed to the end.

Eric Clapton: Gibson Amphitheatre, Universal City, California

I am making some final adjustments to this project, and it is now mid-March 2011. This concert was performed and recorded March 8, 2011. It purports to have been recorded by "Josephine." The concert was available on this bootleg about a week later.

Interestingly, bootlegs have now suffered from the same problems as official releases. They are quickly posted to the Internet and copied over and over again. Bootleggers, of course, have no legal recourse, which in an odd way is justice at its most basic.

37

So There I Was in Hollywood

Awards and Honors

Many artists have received numerous honors due to longevity. Other artists have sold millions of albums and been in the forefront of the music scene for decades but have little to show for it in the way of awards and honors.

Eric Clapton's career is approaching the fifty-year mark, and he has managed to stay among rock's elite for most of that time. His guitar expertise and virtuosity have been honored just about every way possible. Included in the following are some of his most important and unusual awards.

Rock and Roll Hall of Fame

The Rock and Roll Hall of Fame has become an important part of the music landscape in its short existence. Its first induction ceremony was a modest affair at the Waldorf-Astoria in New York City in January 1986. The museum itself opened its doors in Cleveland, Ohio, in 1995.

There has been criticism of their selection process at times which has centered more on who has not been included. In the Hall's defense, the obvious choices are there, and time will no doubt take care of the rest.

Eric Clapton remains the only person who has been inducted on three separate occasions. He entered first as a member of the Yardbirds, a year later for his work with Cream, and finally as a solo artist. Whether he is inducted a fourth time remains to be seen. His time with Blind Faith and Derek and the Dominos produced some of the best releases of the rock era, but his stay with both was brief. His best chance may be as a member of John Mayall's Bluesbreakers. Mayall has never been included in the Hall, and chances are, given his career, that may happen someday. The question is whether the Bluesbreakers, and how many, would be inducted with him.

Eric Clapton was first inducted in 2002 as a member of the Yardbirds. The Yardbirds had moderate commercial success but never as much as the leading British Invasion groups of the day. What they had going for them were the famous guitarists who played with the band. Eric Clapton, Jeff Beck, and Jimmy Page would all go on to superstar careers, and that enhanced the profile of the band.

The Yardbirds were in good company that evening as the Jimi Hendrix Experience, Bobby "Blue" Bland, Johnny Cash, the Isley Brothers, Sam and Dave, and Booker T. and the MG's were also inducted. Highlights included Little Richard inducting the Isleys and Phil Spector inducting Doc Pomus in the nonperforming category.

Five of the six surviving Yardbirds were on hand to accept the honor. The only one missing was Eric Clapton, who was involved with his *MTV Unplugged* project at the time, which in retrospect became one of the most important and commercially successful albums of his career. Still, he did miss one of the great honors of his life, and one wonders if he could go back in time, if he would have attended.

It was left to lead guitarists Jimmy Page and Jeff Beck to join Jim McCarty, Paul Samwell-Smith, and Chris Dreja at the ceremony and then participate in the traditional all-star jam at the end. Beck was the star of the evening, which was probably appropriate as his time with the group was the most productive commercially and for the evolution of rock guitar.

Clapton may have not been present at the 1992 ceremony, but his appearance in 1993 when Cream was inducted was historic.

Cream was part of a star-studded cast inducted into the Hall in 1993. Creedence Clearwater Revival, Etta James, Ruth Brown, the Doors, Sly and the Family Stone, Frankie Lymon and the Teenagers, and Van Morrison were honored along with Cream, but it was Eric Clapton and company who stole the show.

The all-star jam featured the first Cream reunion in a quarter of a century. It was his performance on "Sunshine of Your Love" that has always stuck in my mind when I think of Clapton, as it was so effortless.

His third induction in less than a decade was in the year 2000 when Robbie Robertson introduced him as a solo artist. He was joined by Bonnie Raitt; Earth, Wind and Fire; James Taylor; the Moonglows; and the Lovin' Spoonful. Clapton took the stage in the group performance at the conclusion of the official festivities.

What made the ceremony so special was that the first class of sidemen was also inducted. Hal Blaine, Earl Palmer, James Jamerson, King Curtis, and Scotty Moore were all made official members of the Rock and Roll Hall of Fame.

Grammy Awards

The National Academy of Recording Arts and Sciences of the United States established the Gramophone Awards in 1958, and they were first given in 1959. They quickly became known as the Grammy Awards, or Grammys, and have become a fixture in the music industry and as an award ceremony on television.

During the early days of rock 'n' roll, the popular rock stars of the day were ignored and overlooked in favor of such traditional artists as Henry Mancini, Frank Sinatra, Judy Garland,

Some countries have even issued a Clapton stamp, which is a tribute to his lasting popularity. *Author's collection*

and others of the same ilk. This was due to the age and proclivities of the voters at the time. It was not until 1967 that rock artists finally broke through, with the Beatles' *Sgt. Pepper* winning Album of the Year and "Michelle" winning Song of the Year.

George Solti is the individual with the most Grammys with thirty-one. He was nominated seventy-four times. This pales next to the Chicago Symphony Orchestra, which has won sixty. Quincy Jones has won twenty-seven awards, although he has been nominated seventy-four times. Interestingly, the modern artist with the most wins is Alison Krauss with twenty-six and only thirty-eight nominations. U2 is the leading rock band with twenty-two Grammys. Stevie Wonder also has twenty-two awards. Other notables are John Williams (twenty-one), Vince Gill (twenty), Bruce Springsteen (twenty), and Aretha Franklin (eighteen). Eric Clapton checks in with seventeen Grammys. Just for the record, the Beatles won eleven.

1970s

Discussing Eric Clapton's Grammys in the 1960s is easy because there were none. The Yardbirds, Bluesbreakers, and especially Cream not only never won a Grammy, they were never nominated. Clapton was a rock superstar at the beginning of the seventies, and his Grammy count stood at zero.

His first nomination and award came as a result of his participation in *The Concert for Bangladesh*. It won the award for Album of the Year. All the participants received statues. There was a lot of star power including

George Harrison, Ringo Starr, Bob Dylan, Leon Russell, Ravi Shankar, Billy Preston, and Eric Clapton.

It was somewhat that ironic after providing some of the best and most creative guitar work of his era, Clapton would win an award for a live album he just managed to get through and for the most part remained an invisible presence in the band.

1980s

Clapton waited sixteen years for his next nomination. It finally came in 1986 in the category of Best Album or Original Score Written for a Motion Picture or Television Special. He shared the nomination with Johnny Colla, Chris Hayes, and Huey Lewis for his contributions to the film *Back to the Future*.

He did not win the award, as the soundtrack to the film *Beverly Hills Cop* got the honor.

There is some controversy about whether he actually received an award for Best Performance Music Video in 1988. He took part in the Prince's Trust All-Star Concert, which was released as a video. Anthony Eaton was honored as the producer, but all the performers in the film shared the award.

He finished the decade with one final Grammy nomination. There is an old saying that everything comes to those who wait, and so it was with an old Eric Clapton staple.

"After Midnight" was recycled as part of his *Crossroads* set, and it was among the nominated songs at the 1989 ceremony.

Unfortunately, Robert Palmer's "Simply Irresistible" won for Best Rock Vocal Performance—Male.

1990s

Clapton's Grammy nominations at the beginning of the nineties may have been few and far between, but by the end of the decade that fact changed dramatically.

One of his most obscure Grammy wins occurred at the 1991 ceremony, when he won for Best Rock Vocal Performance—Male. "Bad Love" was a huge radio hit, reaching #1 on the *Billboard* Album Rock Tracks chart for three weeks.

The categories changed a bit at the 1992 ceremony, as he found himself nominated for Best Rock Vocal Performance—Solo for *24 Hours*. He lost as Bonnie Raitt's *Luck of the Draw* swept to victory.

It was at the 1993 ceremony that he became a Grammy superstar. He received nine nominations and took home six statues.

The year 1992 was a big one for Eric Clapton. He had been inducted into the Rock and Roll Hall of Fame with the Yardbirds, and his *Unplugged* album became the most successful of his career.

He did not win in three categories. His "It's Probably Me" from the film *Lethal Weapon 3* and "Tears in Heaven" for the film *Rush* were both nominated for Best Song Written for a Motion Picture, Television or Other Visual Media. The song "Beauty and the Best" by Peabo Bryson and Celine Dion won the category. He was also nominated for Best Instrumental Composition Written for a Motion Picture or for Television for his *Rush* soundtrack. This time he lost to "Harlem Renaissance Suite," which was composed by Benny Carter.

The big awards of the night were all his to bring home.

1. Album of the Year for *Unplugged.*
2. Song of the Year for "Tears in Heaven." He shared the award with Will Jennings.
3. Best Pop Vocal Performance—Male for "Tears in Heaven."
4. Record of the Year for "Tears in Heaven."
5. Best Rock Vocal Performance–Male for *Unplugged.*
6. Best Rock Song for "Layla." This award was shared with Jim Gordon.

The awards flowed in but Clapton continued to tour.

Author's collection

In 1994, he was up for another Grammy for his part in the all-star jam at the tribute concert for Bob Dylan. Clapton, Dylan, Roger McGuinn, George Harrison, Tom Petty, and Neil Young were all onstage for a performance of "My Back Pages." They were nominated in the Best Rock Vocal Performance by a Group or Duo. They lost to "Livin' on the Edge" by Aerosmith.

Clapton received two more nominations for his *From the Cradle*, issued in 1994. He lost Best Album of the Year honors to Tony Bennett's *MTV Unplugged*, which I still can't figure out and will probably always remain a mystery. He did win the Grammy for Best Traditional Blues Album at the 1995 ceremony. Sheryl Crow won the prestigious Best New Artist Award at the same ceremony.

The 1997 Grammys were another big year for Clapton. He received four nominations and took home three awards. His only loss was in the Best Rock Vocal Performance—Male category, where his "Ain't Gone 'N Give Up on Your Love" lost to "Where's It's At" by Beck.

It was still a good evening as he won in the following categories:

1. Best Rock Instrumental Performance for "SRV Shuffle" with Bonnie Raitt, Jimmie Vaughan, B. B. King, Buddy Guy, and Art Neville
2. Record of the Year for "Change the World"
3. Song of the Year for "Change the World"

After skipping a year, he was back on the nomination list at the 1999 ceremony.

He was nominated in the Best Pop Album category, where his *Pilgrim* lost to *Ray of Light* by Madonna. He did wing Best Male Pop Vocal Performance for "My Father's Eyes." The ceremony belonged to Lauren Hill, who won five awards, and to Celine Dion's "My Heart Will Go On," which won three including record and song of the year.

2000s

The 2000 Grammys took place on February 23 and were Carlos Santana's night. He won eight individual awards plus a ninth for his album *Supernatural*.

Clapton shared in the glory a bit as their duet on "The Calling" from the album won Best Instrumental Performance.

Clapton was nominated for two Grammys himself at the 2002 ceremony. His "Superman Inside" lost the Best Rock Vocal Performance—Male category to "Dig In" by Lenny Kravitz.

He did garner one statue for Best Pop Instrumental Performance for the song "Reptile." Another old Yardbird guitarist did well, as Jeff Beck won Best Rock Instrumental for *Dirty Mind*.

In 2005, the Grammys returned to their usual stomping ground, the Staples Center in Los Angeles, and he received two more nominations.

His *Me and Mr. Johnson* lost the Traditional Blues Album category to Etta James's *Blues to the Bone*. While it was not my favorite Eric Clapton album, it would have been nice to have seen Robert Johnson honored, if indirectly.

He was also nominated in the Best Pop Collaboration with Vocals category for his and Paul McCartney's version of "Something." But they lost to the Norah Jones juggernaut that evening.

In 2006, the Grammys were held at the Staples Center on February 8th to honor the best of 2005's music, and Eric Clapton was along for the ride again. He was nominated in the Best Rock Solo Vocal Performance category for the song "Revolution," which appeared on his *Back Home* album. It was an odd choice, but in the end it was a moot point as "Devils & Dust" by Bruce Springsteen won the category.

Clapton returned to the winner's circle in 2008 when his duet album with J. J. Cale, *The Road to Escondido,* took home honors in the Best Contemporary Blues Album category.

Clapton and Stevie Winwood were nominated for two Grammys in 2010. I was rooting for them as it would have been a nice way to honor their ongoing successful collaboration, but they lost both times.

They were nominated for Best Rock Album for their *Live at Madison Square Garden,* but Green Day's *21st Century Breakdown* took the honor. They were also honored for Best Rock Performance by a Duo or Group with Vocals for "Can't Find My Way Home," but they lost once again, to "Use Somebody" by the Kings of Leon.

The 2011 Grammys was held February 13th in Los Angeles. The nominations were announced on television as part of the Grammy Nominations Concert Live. The eligibility period was September 1, 2009, to September 20, 2010. Eminem led the parade with ten nominations.

Clapton was nominated for Best Solo Rock Vocal Performance for "Run Back to Your Side" from *Clapton*. His competition was "Crossroads" by John Mayer, "Helter Skelter" by Paul McCartney, "Silver Rider" by Robert Plant, and "Angry World" by Neil Young.

Stay tuned for further *Grammy* developments from Eric Clapton.

P.S. He didn't win as Sir Paul McCartney took home the statue. The 2012, and it looks like the 2013 Grammy Awards will be Clapton-less.

Other Awards

- 1969: *Melody Maker* Pop Poll Winner for Best International Musician
- 1983: Silver Clef Award for Outstanding Achievement in the World of British Music
- 1986: NAFTA TV Award for Best Original Television Music for *Edge of Darkness*
- 1987: Lifetime Achievement Award from the British Phonographic Institute
- 1988: Received a Silver Stratocaster from Prince Charles to commemorate his 25th anniversary in the music industry
- 1988: BMI Film Music Award for *Lethal Weapon*
- 1989: Received award for Best Guitarist at the 1st Elvis Awards
- 1990: Received Living Legend Award at the 2nd Elvis Awards
- 1990: Named Top Rock Artist at the 1990 Billboard Music Awards
- 1990: BMI Film Music Award for *Lethal Weapon 2*
- 1992: MTV Video Music Award for Best Male Video for "Tears in Heaven"
- 1992: MTV Video Nomination for Best Video from a Film for "Tears in Heaven"
- 1992: MTV Movie Award Nomination for Best Movie Song for "Tears in Heaven" from the film *Rush*
- 1993: MTV Movie Award Nomination for Best Movie Song for "It's Probably Me" from the film *Lethal Weapon 3*
- 1993: World Music Award for Best Selling British Artist of the Year
- 1993: BMI Film Music Award for *Lethal Weapon 3*
- 1993: American Music Award for Favorite Pop/Rock Artist
- 1994: American Music Award for Favorite Pop/Rock Artist
- 1994: World Music Award for World's Best Selling Rock Artist of the Year
- 1997: American Music Award for Favorite Pop/Rock Artist
- 1997: MTV Movie Award Nomination for Best Movie Song for "Change the World" from the film *Phenomenon*
- 1999: Stevie Ray Vaughan Award from the Music Assistance Program. He was recognized for his efforts to give back to the community for his fund-raising efforts to establish the Crossroads Centre
- 1999: BMI Honors "My Father's Eyes" as the most played song of the year

- 1999: GQ Man of the Year Award for Music
- 2001: Inducted into the Songwriters Hall of Fame
- 2001: W. C. Handy Award for Contemporary Album of the Year for *Riding with the King* with B. B. King
- 2008: BMI Honors "Layla" for seven million plays on U.S. television and radio
- 2009: Honored for 150th Performance at the Royal Albert Hall

38

How Many Times Must We Tell the Tale

Coming to a City Near You

I found a website that listed over 2,500 Clapton concerts, 100-plus tours, assorted charity and guest appearances, and they stopped keeping track almost four years ago. Any way you look at it, that's a lot of live appearances. It probably adds up to close to fifty thousand songs performed before in the tens of millions of people.

I have assembled some of the more interesting or important ones during the course of his career. These are the tip of the iceberg, and there are thousands more to be explored, so enjoy.

The Roosters—1963

Eric Clapton had performed on street corners and played informally in pubs, but this was just a matter of showing up.

When he joined the Roosters, it marked the first time he was in a formal band that intended to make money. The only way to accomplish that was to either sell records or perform live. The Roosters did not have a recording track, so that left live gigs.

The first task the group accomplished was to shorten their name from Rhode Island Red and the Roosters to just the Roosters. How an English band could name itself after an American chicken that is the state bird of Rhode Island is beyond me.

By the time the band was ready to play live, founding members Brian Jones (Rolling Stones) and Paul Jones (Manfred Mann) were long gone.

The Roosters played less than twenty concerts, or more appropriately gigs, with Eric Clapton. They mostly took place in London and the surrounding area.

Their first performance was at St. Johns Ambulance Hall in Reading, Berkshire, England. Their second was as the opening act for the Mann-Hugg

Blues Brothers at London's Marquee Club. Mann and Hugg would evolve into Manfred Mann.

Their most regular gig was three consecutive Wednesdays at the Cellar Club in Kingston. They even played at Uncle Bonnie's Chinese Restaurant in Brighton. The thought of a British Blues Band led by Eric Clapton performing at a Chinese Restaurant named Bonnie's is almost beyond comprehension.

Eric Clapton has always been a road warrior, with his live performances with the Yardbirds, John Mayall, Cream, Blind Faith, Derek & the Dominos, less successful groups, as a guest, and, ultimately, as a solo artist now number in the thousands.   *Courtesy of Robert Rodriguez*

They were a basic blues cover band. Songs in their short sets included "Boom Boom," "Hideaway," "I Love the Woman," and "Hoochie Coochie Man."

He remained with the Roosters from January to August 1963, and they gave him his early training in a group setting and onstage. It is doubtful he realized at the time that these primitive live performances would be the first of thousands.

December 7–8, 1963

Eric Clapton's first gig with the Yardbirds probably occurred on October 20, 1963, at Studio 51 in London.

The Yardbirds were typical of hundreds of struggling bands at the time whose repertoire was comprised of rock and blues covers with little or no original material. They were also atypical in that they were more talented than most of the groups performing on the club and pub circuits.

They began working regularly, and between October 20 and the end of the year they performed thirty-three times. Their concerts at the Star Club in London were typical of their live act. They played a short set of cover songs but left room for Clapton to step forward and improvise. "Smokestack Lightning," "Let It Rock," "Honey in Your Hips," "I Wish You Would," "You Can't Judge a Book by Its Cover," and "Who Do You Love" would appear with regularity during Clapton's time with the band.

After their December 7th appearance at the Star Club, they moved to the Crawdaddy Club in London to back Sonny Boy Williamson, one of dozens of American bluesmen who were brought to England to cash in on the emerging blues boom. It was too costly to bring their bands, so backing musicians had to be supplied. The up-and-coming Yardbirds were chosen as one of those backing bands.

Keith Relf is not listed as a part of the actual concert as he was a vocalist/ harp player and so was star Williamson; thus he was not needed.

The show featured Williamson staples such as "Bye Bye Bird," "Mr. Downchild," "Pontiac Blues," "Take It Easy Baby," "Honey in Your Hips," and "Western Arizona."

Clapton's knowledge of the blues was already extensive, and he had no problem playing the lead on the eleven songs that would eventually comprise the album *Sonny Boy Williamson & the Yardbirds*.

While Williamson was the recognized star and master, within a year the roles would be reversed.

December 7, 1964

The Yardbirds played just over 160 concerts in 1964. They had become well known enough to be part of what were known as package tours. A number of groups who had developed a reputation were packaged together to perform in bigger halls. Each group would perform a few songs and then make way for the next in a rapid-fire presentation. The second half of 1964 found the Yardbirds in two of these tours. They were joined by Billy J. Kramer and the Dakotas, the Nashville Teens, and Jerry Lee Lewis.

The stop that stands out was the December 7th one in the Royal Albert Hall in London. Over two decades later, he made this venue his concert home with a yearly series of concerts. This first appearance was "Good Morning Little School" plus a couple of other songs, and then they were off.

December 24, 1964–January 16, 1965

The Beatles are remembered today as a band that did not tour much, which was true during the second half of their career. They confined themselves to the studio and recorded some of the best and most complex music that has ever been created. It was not always so, however.

The Beatles embarked on an ambitious series of concerts between Christmas Eve, 1964, and January 16, 1965, performing thirty-eight times at the Hammersmith Odeon in London. That's a lot of concerts no matter how you look at it. All the shows quickly sold out.

They had a variety of opening acts, which included Elkie Brooks, Freddie and the Dreamers, Jimmy Saville, Sounds Incorporated, and the Yardbirds.

The Yardbirds are listed as performing on twenty-one different days, although the opening acts differed from concert to concert. What was amazing about the Yardbirds is that they performed at the Crawdaddy Club on their off days.

They were a somewhat odd choice for an opening act as they were still rooted in the blues at the time. When you compare them to the other opening acts, and even to the Beatles themselves, you have a far different sound.

Still, you have Eric Clapton being exposed to the Beatles, continually, for over three weeks. Even at this point in his life and career, he was still a guitarist of note, and John, Paul, George, and Ringo must have noticed.

February 28, 1964

The Yardbirds' manager Giorgio Gomelsky had the idea of producing the 1st British Rhythm and Blues Festival. Given what music festivals would quickly become, it was a modest affair.

The highlight of the one-day festival at the Town Hall in Birmingham was Sonny Boy Williamson backed by the Yardbirds. Their set included "Highway 69," "My Little Cabin," "Slow Walk," and "Bye Bye Bird."

There were three warm-up acts: Spencer Davis R&B Quartet with Muff and fifteen-year-old Stevie Winwood, the Liverpool Roadrunners, and Long John Baldry. The evening ended with a jam of "You Got My Mojo Working" with Clapton on lead guitar. Baldry, Winwood, and Rod Stewart joined him among others.

All five of Clapton's tracks were issued on the *The Steampacket: The First British R&B Festival (Live 1964)* bootleg. Be aware that the sound quality is poor.

August 9, 1964

The Yardbirds ended up at a more organized festival in the summer of 1964. The 4th National Jazz and Blues Festival at Richmond Upon Thames was a three-day affair featuring the Rolling Stones, Long John Baldry, Manfred Mann, Jimmy Witherspoon, Mose Allison, and Georgie Fame.

The Yardbirds closed the festival on Sunday evening but just barely. Keith Relf was ill and could not appear with the rest of the group, but Mick O'Neill filled in on vocals at the last minute.

The festival ended with a jam that was notable for Clapton's future. Ginger Baker and Jack Bruce were among the participants who joined him onstage, making it the first time the future bandmates would share the stage.

April 26, 1965

The Yardbirds were in Eric Clapton's rearview mirror. He had left and quickly joined John Mayall's band. His first show with Mayall was April 6, 1975.

At the end of April, they appeared at the BBC Studios in London. Many of the leading British groups of the day would record songs live to be broadcast on the BBC. Clapton in his Cream days was a regular in their studio.

On this trip, five tracks were recorded for broadcast. "Crawling up a Hill," "Heartache," "Hideaway," "Crocodile Rock," and "Bye Bye Bird" formed their just over thirteen-minute set. Mayall and Clapton were accompanied by drummer Hughie Flint and bassist John McVie. The show was broadcast on BBC Radio May 1, 1965.

The upside of the BBC was that it provided massive publicity for the artists involved, as there were fewer channel options than in the United States. The downside was that the performances were almost always bootlegged.

November 7, 1965

Eric Clapton had returned from his grand adventure in Greece, and John Mayall was waiting with open arms. Clapton officially rejoined Mayall November 6th, and the next night he was onstage. Clapton's first appearance during his second stint with Mayall was at the Flamingo Club in London.

What made this concert unique was the fact that Peter Green was also onstage. Mayall would subsequently fire Green, as he did not want to carry two guitarists. When Clapton left again, the silver-tongued Mayall convinced Green to return. The next time Green left, it was on his own terms, and he eventually took fellow Bluesbreaker John McVie with him to form Fleetwood Mac.

November 28, 1965

The Bluesbreakers returned to the Flamingo Club on November 28, 1965. The tape machine was running that night, and "Maudie," "Stormy Monday," "Hoochie Coochie Man," "It Hurts to Be in Love," "Have You Ever Loved a Woman," and "Bye Bye Bird" have all appeared on a number of John Mayall and Eric Clapton albums over the years. Five of them appeared on *Primal Solos* by John Mayall and the Bluesbreakers.

The concert was notable for being Jack Bruce's last with the group. He had a better offer from Manfred Man and so moved on. It ended his tenure with Eric Clapton at twenty-two days, but there would be a lot more performances to come.

March 14, 1966

To kick off the second half of their U.K. club tour, Mayall and group stopped off at the BBC Studios again. It would be Clapton's last tour with the band. Over the next three months, he played thirty-two concerts with the Bluesbreakers to bring that part of his career to a close.

They recorded five songs for broadcast on March 19th. "Burned My Fingers," "All Your Love," "Steppin' Out," " Sittin' on Top of the World," and "Key to Love" were almost immediately bootlegged.

Clapton's last performance with Mayall was at the Ricky Tick at the Stock Hotel in London on July 15, 1966. He had already begun rehearsing with Jack Bruce and Ginger Baker for his new band.

Clapton may have had Baker and Bruce waiting in the wings, but Mayall had Green, who would be onstage with him a mere two nights later.

July 31, 1966

The 6th National Jazz and Blues Festival at the Royal Windsor Race Course was scheduled for July 30–31. The Who were the headliners on the 30th, and how they fit in with the jazz and blues theme was not explained.

Georgie Fame was scheduled to be the headliner the second evening but was informed he was being pushed to the second spot. The reason was that Cream had decided to use the festival for their official debut.

Cream definitely fit in with the blues theme as "Spoonful," "Traintime," and "Toad" were included in their set. Clapton was at his improvisational best as Cream began a career that would reverberate through music history.

November 13, 1966

Cream's early concerts and tours were modest affairs as they were confined to the club circuit in England.

Their debut album had not been released when they pulled into the Redcar Jazz Club in Redcar and Cleveland, England. They were well known but not the stars they would soon become. It was a basic set of "Steppin' Out," "Spoonful," "Traintime," "Toad," "I'm So Glad " and "N.S.U." Their early live shows would be a lot bluesier than their first release.

Their concerts were primitive when compared to today, with a bar-like feel. Clapton and Bruce traveled with one guitar and so used it throughout the performance. Baker and Bruce each had they own amplifiers and microphones Interestingly, Baker's drums were not amplified, so his sound had to reach the vocalists' microphones. The lighting was basic and stayed on throughout the show, while the rest of the hall or club remained dark.

January 15, 1967

Cream's first album had been released the month before, but they were still playing the club circuit when they returned to the Ricky Tick in London.

Three songs from their debut were included in their seven-song set. "Sweet Wine," a very different take of "Toad," and "Rollin' and Tumblin'" were a part of their live act, although "Toad" had been played regularly before the album's release.

"Sunshine of Your Love" had not been released by the band but was now being played live. "Spoonful" remained one of their core songs throughout their career, and "Lawdy Mama" and "Sitting on Top of the World" would be released on their *Wheels of Fire* album.

March 6, 1967

Cream was in Denmark for an evening show on March 6, 1967. They performed at Falkoner Contret before an audience of two thousand. The concert was recorded for Danish radio and broadcast March 21st. The set consisted of "I Feel Free," "Steppin' Out," and "Toad." The radio broadcast of their show lasted just over twenty-five minutes.

I am always amazed at the variety of acts that opened for Cream and other major artists at the time. Many quickly disappeared from the music scene. Sharing the stage with Cream that night were the Defenders, the Hitmakers, the Lollipop. Peter Belli and the Seven Sounds, and my personal favorite, Sir Hendry and His Butlers. That's a lot of people who for the rest of their lives could say they shared the stage with Eric Clapton and Cream.

March 25–April 2, 1967

I touched on one of my all-time favorite series of Cream performances in an earlier chapter. If there was one type of concert Cream did not fit, it was the ones put on by Murray the K.

Murray the K was a noted radio personality during the fifties and sixties. He also organized concerts that featured a number of artists playing a few songs, similar to the package tours in England. He hired Cream to participate in his Music Is the Fifth Dimension at the RKO Theatre in New York City. It was nine days of five shows per day. Each show lasted about an hour and fifteen minutes. It was like a movie theater. As soon as one performance ended, the audience would leave and another would take its place.

Mitch Ryder, Wilson Pickett, the Who, and the Blues Project were some of the artists who shared the stage with the Who.

The problem was that Cream playing three songs could last thirty to forty minutes. They were told to cut back to two songs, and then one, or to choose shorter songs. They rotated "I Feel Free," "I'm So Glad," "Traintime," "Crossroads," and "Spoonful." The last three were known for Cream extending them through their improvisational skills and were not a good fit for this type of live performance.

May 7, 1967

Cream was in the middle of a European/U.K. tour when they decided to take part in the *New Musical Express* Poll-Winners concert held at the Empire Pool, Wembley, England on May 7, 1967.

They played two songs, "N.S.U." and "I'm So Glad," as part of an all-star lineup of artists. Their song choice seems a little unusual for this point in their career.

Other artists who appeared were the Beach Boys, the Spencer Davis Group, Georgie Fame, Cliff Richard, the Small Faces, Dusty Springfield, Cat Stevens, the Tremeloes, the Troggs, Stevie Winwood, and a number of supporting acts including Dave Dee, Dozy, Beaky, Mich, and Tich. I've always made fun of Dave Dee's group's name, although in fairness they did produce a number of hits during their time together.

As I look back on the people listed, it was a show I would have loved to see, but since I was finishing my junior year of high school thousands of miles away, it was not to be.

September 3, 1967

Cream's 1967 U.S. tour began August 22 at the Fillmore Auditorium in San Francisco, when they played twelve shows in thirteen days. When the tour ended in mid-October, they had played close to fifty shows including twelve at the Café Au Go Go in New York City and seven at the Psychedelic Supermarket in Boston.

Their last show at the Fillmore on September 3 found a far different Cream than just a few months before. They were now stars, and the set list reflected their new confidence. "Spoonful," "Sunshine of Your Love," "Sweet Wine," "N.S.U." "Lawdy Mama," Sleepy Time Time," and "Steppin'

Out" were now part of their elongated performances. They engaged in long improvisational excursions that quickly became their concert trademark.

March 29, 1968

It was the *Disraeli Gears* tour that signaled the beginning of the end for Cream. They were living the rock star life, having just produced one of the classic albums in rock history. Women and drugs were constantly present, and they performed sixty-five concerts between February 23 and June 16, 1968, which not only were exhausting, but the continual close contact of the group members caused the tension to reach almost unbearable levels. This was especially true between Bruce and Baker.

Their show at Hunter College was typical, as five songs were extended to about seventy-five minutes. "Sunshine of Your Love," "Steppin' Out," "Traintime," "Toad," and "N.S.U." formed their show the night of March 29, 1968.

May 17, 1968

The Smother Brothers Comedy Show was one of the more popular shows on American television at the time. It was different, irreverent, and cutting-edge. Their astute and critical political commentary would ultimately lead to the show's cancellation despite strong ratings.

Cream were their musical guests for the May 19th broadcast, which was recorded two days prior.

They performed two songs on the show, which were as different as performances can be. They mimed "Anyone for Tennis." It was one of the oddest songs in the Cream catalog, and why they chose it for national expose is beyond me. They were also one of the premier live bands in the world at the time, but they did not perform it live. It may have been amusing within the context of the show, but it certainly turned away from their strengths.

On the positive side, they were at their incendiary best with "Sunshine of Your Love." This performance finds Cream at the top of their game, and it can be heard on the Polydor album *Those Were the Days*.

October 25, 1968

The *Wheels of Fire* tour turned out to be Cream's farewell. Tensions trimmed the tour to nineteen shows between October 4 and November 4. Few groups have called it quits after so short a career when sitting on top of the rock world.

They were about two-thirds through their tour when they pulled into the Memorial Auditorium in Dallas, Texas. Their set had remained similar to their previous tour, with a few additions. They began with their two big hits, "White Room," and "Sunshine of Your Love," before going into "I'm So Glad," "Sitting on Top of the World," and old faithfuls, "Crossroads," "Traintime," "Toad," and "Spoonful."

November 26, 1968

Cream flew home from America after their last show in Providence, Rhode Island, on November 4th.

They played two shows at the Royal Albert Hall that were vastly different from Clapton's first appearances at the venue a few years earlier when he was a member of the Yardbirds.

The cameras were rolling, the recording equipment was turned on, and many celebrities were in the audience for Cream's swan song.

The sets for the two shows were identical: "White Room," "Politician," "I'm So Glad," "Sitting on Top of the World," "Crossroads," "Toad," "Spoonful," "Sunshine of Your Love," and "Steppin' Out."

When the concert ended, Clapton could now move on to the next phase of his career.

December 10, 1968

Freed from the constraints of Cream and the pressures of the rock star life, he accepted the Rolling Stones' offer to participate in their Rock and Roll Circus.

It was quite a production, with a cast of Jethro Tull, Taj Mahal, Jesse Ed Davis, the Who, the Lennons, Mitch Mitchell, Marianne Faithful, and Eric Clapton. Jimmy Miller produced the album, and Glynn Johns was the engineer.

The big problem with the production was the Rolling Stones themselves. Mick Jagger was so dissatisfied with their performance, he refused to release the film.

December 10 was actually an official rehearsal, but the highlight was the set comprised of lead guitarist Eric Clapton, rhythm guitarist and vocalist John Lennon, bassist Keith Richards, drummer Mitch Mitchell, and vocalist Mick Jagger. The set included "It's Now or Never," "Peggy Sue," "Hound Dog," "Lucille," "Sweet Little Sixteen," and "Yer Blues."

March 18, 1969

Some ideas work well, and some others not so well.

The idea was to gather a number of musicians in the studio together in different configurations and just let them jam and see what happens. The cameras would be rolling and capture the history being made. The sessions of March 18, 1969, contained two jams, both with Eric Clapton.

"Slate 27" featured Clapton, Jack Bruce, upright bassist Vernon Martin, organist Ron Burton, drummer Jon Hiseman, and sax players Dick Heckstall-Smith and Roland Kirk.

The second jam, "Everything's Gonna Be Alright," is the more interesting of the two. Buddy Guy is on hand as a second guitarist. Stephen Stills was the bassist, while Buddy Miles and Dallas Taylor handled the drum duties. Harpist Duster Bennett, saxophonist Chris Mercer, and Jack Bruce on organ completed the lineup.

Somehow the show was lost for fifteen years but was finally released on video in 1986.

June 7, 1969

It is difficult to make your debut in front of over one hundred thousand people, but so it was for Eric Clapton and Blind Faith.

The Rolling Stones were headlining a free concert in Hyde Park. Acts such as Long John Baldry, Lulu, and Richie Havens were in support. The emphasis was on free, and anytime you combine that with a highly anticipated new group with Eric Clapton and Stevie Winwood, people will come.

Blind Faith's set included "Well All Right," "Sea of Joy," "Sleeping on the Ground," "Under My Thumb," "Can't Find My Way Home," "Means to the End," and "Had to Cry Today."

Clapton was not happy about the performance, and worse for him, the band was cheered even when they played poorly. He realized he was back in a Cream situation, which seems obvious in retrospect.

June 12, 1969

Five days after their less-than-stellar debut, Blind Faith found itself in a similar situation in Helsinki, Finland, for two sold-out shows on June 12, 1969.

Their set was similar to their Hyde Park concert. "Means to the End" was eliminated and replaced by "Do What You Like" and "Presence of the Lord." The second song would become a part of Clapton's live show for decades, so not all was lost.

July 11, 1969

Blind Faith was scheduled to play at the Fort Adams State Park Concert Arena in Newport, Rhode Island, on July 11, 1969, but the city cancelled their appearance.

The Newport Folk Festival, at the time, was one of the most respected in the country and had been instrumental in introducing such artists as Bob Dylan and Joan Baez to the world. It also had reintroduced many of the legendary blues artists of the past. It was a nice little laid-back festival.

All that changed when they booked Led Zeppelin and Sly and the Family Stone, who were not little or laid back. The damage from fans ran in the hundreds of thousands of dollars, and there was no more folk festivals or concerts for years.

I was living and attending college in Rhode Island at the time and remember it well. I was considering seeing Blind Faith but never got the chance. Let me also go on record as saying I was not at the Zeppelin or Sly shows, so it was not my fault.

September 13, 1969

Eric Clapton was relaxing in London after finishing a North American tour with Blind Faith when John Lennon called, asking him to fly to Toronto the next day.

Lennon had agreed to appear at the Toronto Rock and Roll Revival more as a personality than anything else. At the last minute, he got the itch to perform but had no band, hence the call to Clapton.

It must have been quite a day because for the price of $6.00 you were able to see the Doors, Little Richard, Jerry Lee Lewis, Gene Vincent, Bo Diddley, Alice Cooper, Doug Kershaw, Tony Joe White, Screaming Lord Sutch, the Chicago Transit Authority, Cat Mother and the All Night News Boys, and several supporting acts. The highlight of the day turned out to be the hastily assembled Plastic Ono Band.

The album became a hit, but the film of the concert was not released for almost two decades. It was the only time the Plastic Ono band was filmed, unless there is something lurking in the vaults somewhere.

December 7, 1969

The hitherto obscure rock and white soul group Delaney and Bonnie and Friends pulled into Fairfield Hall in London for the last stop on their U.K. tour. What made the tour so different was that George Harrison and Eric

Clapton was along for the ride. They had raised the Delaney and Bonnie profile to near the top of the rock pantheon.

This December 7 concert would be immortalized on the album *On Tour with Eric Clapton*. The tour began with four dates in Germany; seven dates in Britain, including a stop at the Royal Albert Hall; and five more performances in Europe. Their tour lasted from November 26 to December 12 with only one day off. They then took some time off before embarking on a sixteen-date U.S. tour February 2–March 3.

The Fairfield Hall show was a much tighter set than usual, as many of their concerts stretched out to twelve to eighteen songs. Some of their regulars missing were "Oh Lord," "Tutti Frutti," "Someone," "I Don't Know Why," "Special Life," and "Those Who Will."

December 10, 1969

Clapton was back in Denmark on December 10, 1969, for a recording session for Danish television. I have found it interesting and a little frustrating after the fact that European television and radio were a lot friendlier to broadcasting complete concerts than their American counterparts.

The full band was present, including Clapton, Harrison, Mason, Whitlock, Gordon, Radle, and the rest. They performed an eight-song set that lasted forty-five minutes. While it was not broadcast until February 20, 1970, it remains a nice look at the band during the Clapton era. Seeing and hearing them end the show with Little Richard's "Tutti Frutti" is priceless.

December 15, 1969

Three days after finishing the Delaney and Bonnie European leg of their tour, Eric Clapton found himself onstage with John Lennon again. George Harrison was also on hand, making it the first time two former Beatles were onstage together since their breakup.

It was a more structured gig than the Toronto show. The Bramletts, drummers Jim Gordon and Alan White, perennial solo Beatles bassist Klaus Voormann, keyboardist Billy Preston, and a brass section plus Keith Moon were also on hand.

The Peace for Christmas Show was for charity. Clapton played on two songs, "Cold Turkey" and "Don't Worry Kyoko."

February 5, 1970

Delaney and Bonnie appeared on *The Dick Cavett Show* February 5, 1970 with their band in tow. They played three songs, their single "Coming Home," "Where There's a Will," and an acoustic "Poor Elijah/Tribute to Robert Johnson."

Dick Cavett had to ask which musician was Eric Clapton. He didn't realize that he had all the basic members of Derek and the Dominos onstage that night. Clapton was just a member of the band and did nothing to stand out. Just for the record, he played his famous Brownie guitar.

The highlight of the affair was a story told by Bonnie Bramlett. She stated they were booed in Germany because fans expected three bands at their performance; Delaney, Bonnie, and Friends starring Eric Clapton.

June 14, 1970

Derek and the Dominos made their debut at a charity show concert to benefit Dr. Spock's Civil Liberties Defense Fund. The concert was held at the Lyceum Ballroom in London.

It is often forgotten that Dave Mason was an early member of the band but only stayed for a very short time. Maybe he sensed that something was amiss. He would be missed as it took the second guitar out of the concert mix. Duane Allman provided that missing element in the studio, but he was only available for a couple of appearances as his allegiance was to the Allman Brothers Band. Many of the Dominos songs were better with a second guitar present, and "Layla" could not be performed without one. Dave Mason would have been excellent in fulfilling that role.

Their first concert consisted of some Derek songs and filling in the rest of the set with whatever came to mind. Some of the songs performed were an acoustic "Easy Now," "Layla." "Bottle of Red Wine," "Blues Power," "Crossroads," and "Feelin' Alright" with Mason providing the lead vocal.

October 24, 1970

Derek and the Dominos toured the United States, October 15–December 6, 1970, playing thirty-one dates. It was the basic band of Clapton, Whitlock, Radle, and Gordon.

October 23 and 24 found them at the famous Fillmore East for two shows each day. These concerts would later comprise their famous live album.

Many of their most famous songs were in place for the recording session. "Blues Power," "Have You Ever Loved a Woman," "Key to the Highway," "Tell the Truth," "Let It Rain," "Presence of the Lord," "Roll It Over," and "Little Wing" were all part of the twelve-song set. There was no "Layla," which brings up the problem of no second guitarist again.

November 5, 1970

Johnny Cash had a period of years when he had one of the most popular television programs in the United States. "Hello, I'm Johnny Cash" was heard in millions of homes each week.

Derek and the Dominos were guests in early November 1970. They recorded "It's Too Late," "Got to Get Better in a Little While," "Blues Power," and the classic rockabilly song "Matchbox. The two songs that made it onto the broadcast were "It's too Late" and their third take of "Matchbox." Both Johnny Cash and Carl Perkins joined in on "Matchbox."

December 6, 1970

Suffolk Community College in Selden, New York, was founded in 1959 and today has three campuses. It has just over twenty-five thousand part- and full-time students.

On December 6, 1970, it was just over ten years old, and it was about to enter music history as the location for the last concert by Derek and the Dominos.

Clapton may have been in his mid-twenties at the time, but the years of being the focal point of several high-profile rock bands plus his growing drug addiction had caused extreme burnout. He was ready to bring Derek and the Dominos to a close. At the conclusion of the concert, he virtually became a drug-laden recluse for the next few years.

August 1, 1971

Clapton's increasing drug problems during the late sixties became over-whelming in the early seventies. It got so bad that he rarely ventured outside his house. Jimi Hendrix's death in September 1970 and Duane Allman's in October 1971 only deepened his depression.

It was under those conditions that he agreed to play a concert with old friend George Harrison in New York City to benefit the people of Bangladesh.

It was an ill Clapton who finally arrived in New York City. He was unable to participate in any of the rehearsals. Harrison and the concert producers were worried enough to bring in Jesse Ed Davis as another guitarist. It did not help that Clapton shot up before the concert.

He managed to make it through the day and play competently, if not spectacularly. His main contribution was his famous guitar part on "While My Guitar Gently Sleeps." The rest of the time he was content to just fade into the background with the rest of the backing band.

His only other performance of the year was a ten-minute stint with Leon Russell at London's Rainbow Theatre on December 4th. He did not make a live appearance in 1972.

January 13, 1973

Pete Townshend of the Who was so concerned for Clapton's health and well-being that he organized a unique intervention. He coaxed Clapton onstage on January 13, 1973, at the Rainbow Theatre. Clapton was surrounded by Ronnie Wood, Jim Capaldi, Ric Grech, Steve Winwood, and some supporting musicians.

The sets for the two shows were centered on his recent material. "Layla" in all its glory was presented with Clapton, Wood, and Townshend playing the various guitar parts and was a highlight of the shows. "Badge," "Blues Power," "Little Wing," "Crossroads," "Tell the Truth," and "Presence of the Lord" were performed at both shows.

Some of the material was released as a famous and successful album. While it remains a grand gesture by Townshend, it would not be a cure for Clapton's problems, as it would be his only live performance of the year.

July 28, 1974

Eric Clapton returned to full-time touring in June 1974 with the release of the *461 Ocean Boulevard* album. In many ways it signaled the second half of his career, as he would never again be a part of a full-time band. From this point on, he would always be the star and would perform and record with a backing band.

The first leg of his U.S. tour was comprised of twenty-eight stops. He went on to a shorter second leg and then headed for Europe and Japan to conclude a very ambitious year.

His drug of choice was switching over to alcohol, and while his addiction became severe, he would never be off the road for very long during the rest of his career.

If you had traveled to Hawaii in 1975, you could have seen Clapton for under $6.00.

Courtesy of Robert Rodriguez

June 28, 1974

His stop at the Yale Bowl in New Haven was typical of his concerts of the day. I chose this appearance because it was one of the mid-seventies Clapton concerts that I actually attended.

It was an overcast day, and there was some rain here and there, but the weather report did not stop seventy thousand people from attending the event. They proved that Clapton could fill a stadium on his own. He has retained the drawing power to fill just about any venue he has chosen to appear at, no matter what the size, for the last four decades.

The opening act was Legs Larry Smith, who was the drummer of the Bonzo Dog Doo-Dah Band and was just as strange as his band. He performed dressed as a Roman soldier, which was better than the times he performed onstage wearing a tutu. He was also a drinking buddy of Clapton's.

Clapton's set covered much of his career. "Let It Rain," "Driftin' Blues," "Badge," "Blues Power," "Have You Ever Loved a Woman," "Little Queenie," "Willie and the Hand Jive," "Get Ready," "Little Wing," "Mainline, Florida," "Key to the Highway," "Layla," "Can't Find My Way Home," "Matchbox," "Presence of the Lord," and "Crossroads" were part of his extended sets. This was the period when he depended on second guitarist, George Terry, quite a bit.

June 22, 1975

Both Eric Clapton and the Rolling Stones were on tour in the United States in mid-1975, and their paths crossed in late June.

Clapton joined them onstage for their encore, providing guitar work for "Sympathy for the Devil."

June 25, 1975

The other mid-seventies Clapton concert that I attended was at the Providence Civic Center in Providence, Rhode Island, on June 25, 1975. It was probably a representative stop on his *One in Every Crowd* tour.

The highlight was the encore when Carlos Santana joined him onstage for "Eyesight to the Blind" and "Why Does Love Have to Be So Sad."

"Eyesight" developed into a twenty-four-minute guitar extravaganza. It appears on *Crossroads 2: Live in the Seventies,* as do three other tracks from the concert.

The other dynamic was that Clapton was still relying on George Terry to fill in on a lot of the lead guitar work.

"Layla," "I Shot the Sheriff," "Sunshine of Your Love," "Bell Bottom Blues," "Knockin' on Heaven's Door," and "Badge" were all a part of the seventeen-song set.

May 15, 1976

The Rolling Stones and Eric Clapton crossed paths again in May 1976, but this was more of a planned event.

He joined them onstage at Granby Hall, in Leicester, Leicestershire, England, on May 15, 1976. This time he participated on four songs, including his own "Key to the Highway," plus the Stones classics, "Brown Sugar," "Jumpin' Jack Flash," and "Street Fighting Man."

November 26, 1976

The years 1977 and 1978 were both spent on the road. In the middle of his touring, Clapton took some time off to support the Band at their farewell concert. The Last Waltz concert took place in San Francisco on November 26, 1976.

Clapton's performances were limited by the concert structure as artists meandered on and off the stage in rapid fashion. He performed "All Our Times Past" and "Further on up the Road."

He then participated in the two group efforts with some of music's elite. He was joined on "I Shall Be Released" by the likes of Bob Dylan, Ringo Starr, Neil Young, Joni Mitchell, Dr. John, Neil Diamond, Ronnie Hawkins, Paul Butterfield, Bobby Charles, and Van Morrison. His final contribution was an "Instrumental Jam" with Young, Butterfield, Starr, Dr. John, Carl Radle, and Ronnie Wood.

It is an example of Clapton's stature that he appears at so many of the important and memorable concerts and events of the rock era.

February 14, 1977

Throughout his career, Eric Clapton has performed at numerous charity shows, both under his own name and under fake names as well. His New Year's Eve shows are a prime example of his generosity in this area.

Eddie and the Earth Tremors with special guests were advertised as performing at the Cranleigh Village Hall, Cranleigh, Surrey, England, on Valentine's Day, 1977.

I don't know what people were expecting, and maybe word leaked out, but those who attended saw Ronnie Lane and his band with special guest Eric Clapton. They played "How Come," "Willie and the Hand Jive," "Oh-La La," "Goodnight Irene," and "Alberta."

April 19, 1978

Alexis Korner was one of the early fathers of the British Blues. He never attained the consistent commercial success of many of the musicians who would follow him, yet most of those artists recognized his influence. He threw himself a fiftieth birthday bash, April 19, 1978, at the Gatsby Room, Pinewood Studios, Buckinghamshire, England.

It was an eclectic cast of characters that ended up onstage. Zoot Money, Dick Heckstall-Smith, Chris Farlowe, John Paul Jones, and close to a dozen others provided Korner with a rocking birthday.

Clapton was by far the biggest star to turn out that evening, as he always recognized those artists who had gone before him. He plays on "Hey Pretty Mama," "Can't Get You Out of My Mind," "Hi-Heel Sneakers," and "Stormy Monday Blues."

The concert was immortalized as *The Party Album,* released later in the year. Korner died in 1984 at the age of fifty-five.

July 15, 1978

Eric Clapton found himself sharing the stage with Bob Dylan at three festivals during 1978. The last of these occurred at the Blackbushe Aerodrome in Surrey, England.

Clapton was still with his late 1970s band consisting of George Terry, Carl Radle, Dick Sims, Jamie Oldaker, and Marcy Levy. His fourteen-song set lasted about ninety minutes and was representative of this part of his career. Well-known songs such as "Wonderful Tonight," "Lay Down Sally," "Cocaine," "Badge," "Layla," and "Key to the Highway" are joined by lesser-known compositions, "Rodeo Man," Fool's Paradise," and "Double Trouble."

He then joined Dylan's band for renditions of "Forever Young," "The Times They Are a Changin'" and "Changing of the Guard."

March 13, 1981

The year 1981 proved to be a bad one for Eric Clapton. He was eight days into his *Another Ticket* tour when he collapsed and was rushed to the hospital in St. Paul, Minnesota. The remaining forty-nine concert dates were cancelled.

His last performance was at the Dane County Exposition Center in Madison, Wisconsin. The set was representative of his music at the time. Hits such as "Tulsa Time," "Lay Down Sally," "Wonderful Tonight," "Cocaine," and "Layla" were combined with blues songs such as "Have You Ever Loved a Woman," "All Our Times Past," and "Leave the Cradle." He did not perform again for close to six months.

September 9, 1981

Clapton returned to performing at the four concerts that comprised the Secret Policeman's Other Ball for Amnesty International. The concerts took place September 9–12, 1981. It was a combination of charity and music. Sting, Jeff Beck, Bob Geldof, and an array of comedians shared the stage for the event, organized by John Cleese of Monty Python fame.

Clapton performed two songs at the September 9 show: "Crossroads" and "'Cause We Ended as Lovers." He also participated in the usual jam finale, this time on "I Shall Be Released."

November 13, 1984

Eric Clapton found himself Down Under at the Modern Pavilion in Sydney, Australia, on November 13, 1984.

He was touring with two keyboardists, Chris Stainton and Peter Robinson, a great bassist in Donald "Duck" Dunn, drummer Jamie Oldaker, and backing singers Marcy Levy and Shaun Murphy. The big differences was there was no second guitarist, which meant Clapton had to step forward more than on recent tours. While he could hide in the dual keyboards and especially Robinson's synthesizer sound (after all it was the mid-1980s), he provided excellent guitar work.

The set list was changing a bit as "Tulsa Time," "Knock on Wood," and old favorite "I Shot the Sheriff" were joining live perennials, "Cocaine," "Layla," and "Wonderful Tonight." Blues favorites such as "Motherless Children," "Have You Ever Loved a Woman," and "Same Old Blues" were interspersed throughout the nineteen-song set.

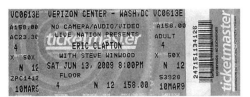

Clapton has maintained a heavy touring schedule for half a century.

Courtesy of Robert Rodriguez

May 8, 1985

One of his most unusual live performances took place on the Dave Letterman Show May 8, 1985, when he was a part of the studio band.

Letterman was the "IN Guy" at the time and would invite musicians to play in Paul Shaffer's house band. I remember Jerry Garcia making a similar appearance.

There was no interview, although Clapton was acknowledged. He melded into the studio band as they played a number of his songs including "Layla," "White Room," "Forever Man," "Lay Down Sally," and "Further up the Road." The band kept playing during commercials, so what happened during that time remains a mystery.

"White Room" had not been a part of his concert act up until that time, but from this point on, it would begin to makes appearances.

July 13, 1985

Bob Geldof, formerly of the Boomtown Rats, organized one of the biggest charity concerts of all time. The proceeds went to support famine relief in Ethiopia. Dual concerts were held in London's Webley Stadium before seventy thousand and JFK in Philadelphia with one hundred thousand people in attendance. In addition, it was broadcast live to an estimated 1.5 billion people around the globe.

Clapton was in the United States at the time and so took part in the JFK concert. Phil Collins performed in London, hopped a jet, and made it to JFK in order to perform there as well.

Joan Baez; the Beach Boys; Black Sabbath; the Pretenders; Santana; Madonna; Tom Petty; the Cars; Neil Young; a Led Zeppelin reunion; Crosby, Stills, Nash and Young; and Bob Dylan were only the tip of the performing iceberg.

Clapton performed about two-thirds of the way through the show. He was preceded by the Thompson Twins and was followed by a Phil Collins solo set. Collins had sat in with Clapton and then stuck around to perform with Led Zeppelin, which brought his long day to a resounded close.

Clapton played a three-song set consisting of "White Room," "She's Waiting," and "Layla." He also participated in the grand finale of "We Are the World."

February 23, 1986

Ian Stewart was one of the cofounders of the Rolling Stones, who took one for the team when their manager at the time didn't think he fit the image of the group, and so he stepped aside. He remained an unofficial sixth Stone. He was one of the few people in the world that Keith Richards and Mick Jagger would actually listen to. He was their de facto road manager and severest critic at times. In his 2010 autobiography, Keith Richards wrote, "I'm still working for him." He was one of eight Rolling Stones inducted into the Rock and Roll Hall of Fame in 1989.

The Rolling Stones hosted the Ian Stewart Memorial Jam Session at the 100 Club in London on February 23, 1986. It took them a while as he died on July 18, 1985, at the age of forty-seven. In addition to the Rolling Stones, Eric Clapton, Pete Townshend, Jeff Beck, Jack Bruce, drummer Simon Kirke, and bassist Collin Golding were on hand for the primarily blues set before a crowd of about 350.

Clapton played on about half of the songs, including "Down the Road a Piece," "Hoochie Coochie Man," "Key to the Highway," "Bye Bye Johnny," "Down in the Bottom," and "Little Queen." He and Beck were together onstage for "Down in the Bottom" and "Little Queenie."

October 16, 1986

October 16, 1986, found Clapton in St. Louis, Missouri, for Chuck Berry's sixtieth birthday party. His contributions were limited to three and two songs at the two shows. He provided guitar and vocals on "Wee Wee Hours" and guitar on "Havana Moon" and "One of These Days" at the first show. He repeated "Wee Wee Hours" and then joined Joe Walsh on "School Days" at the second performance.

I think the show was broadcast on PBS at the time. It has since been released on CD and DVD.

The highlights were not Clapton but Linda Ronstadt singing "Back in the USA" and Etta James wailing away on "Rock 'N' Roll Music" and "Hoochie Coochie Man," proving that both of those ladies can just plain sing.

One of my fondest recollections is Keith Richards's unhappiness with Berry. Richards was the music director for the show and was constantly irritated by Berry's lack of preparedness and poor work ethic, which continues to amuse me.

While Clapton was not a standout, yet it was another instance of his taking the time to honor the generation of performers that had preceded him.

September 14, 1988

Eric Clapton pulled into the Greatwoods Center for the Performing Arts in Mansfield, Massachusetts, on September 14, 1988, as part of his North American tour.

I have attended concerts at this facility, and it is excellent. Unfortunately, I did not attend this concert, as Mark Knopfler was on hand as his second guitarist. Knopfler is one of the few guitarists who can approach Clapton for wringing a perfect sound and tone from his instrument.

The set may have been a tad shorter than usual, but there were more classics presented, which may have been due to Knopfler's presence. There was also no keyboardist, which made the guitarists stand out. They were backed by a rhythm section of just bass and percussion plus two background singers.

The set included "Crossroads," "White Room," "I Shot the Sheriff," "After Midnight," "Cocaine," "Layla," and "Sunshine of Your Love," among others. They even gave the Dire Straits hit "Money for Nothing" a workout.

I can't help but think I was living in the area.

October 11, 1988

Clapton is notable for always looking for people to join onstage for formal and informal jam sessions.

Old Cream cohort Jack Bruce was performing at the Bottom Line club in New York City on October 11, 1988. Clapton joined him for a performance of "Sunshine of Your Love" and a jam on the old Cream favorite "Spoonful."

Two-thirds of Cream is better than none.

May 9, 1989

This is another of those shows I am regretful at not having been present.

Carl Perkins was performing at the Bottom Line in May 1989 for two nights. Eric Clapton joined him onstage for both shows as a second guitarist.

It's always nice when Clapton supports an artist of Perkins's stature as he plays on material that he would otherwise not perform. In this case, he and Perkins ran through a set of classic rock 'n' roll. "Mean Woman Blues," Matchbox," "Roll Over Beethoven," Maybelline," "Long Tall Sally," "Whole Lotta Shakin' Goin' On," "Blue Suede Shoes," and others were always a treat to hear by Perkins, but when you add Clapton as the second guitarist, you have memorable performances.

June 30, 1990

One of the largest crowds Eric Clapton ever played before—125,000 fans—was for the Nordorff-Robbins Music Therapy Organization in Knobworth, Hertfordshire, England. The center provided music therapy for all types of handicapped children.

Clapton and his touring band were onstage for an eleven-song set. Mark Knopfler joined him for "Solid Rock," "Money for Nothing," and "I Think I Love You Too Much." Elton John was present for "Sacrifice," "Sad Songs," and "Saturday Night's All Right for Fighting." Clapton played his own "Pretending," "Before You Accuse Me," "Old Love Tearing Us Apart," before ending with "Sunshine of Your Love."

Also appearing at the affair were Tears for Fears, Status Quo, Cliff Richards and the Shadows, Robert Plant and Jimmy Page, Pink Floyd, Paul McCartney, and a Genesis reunion of Phil Collins, Mike Rutherford, and Tony Banks.

October 16, 1992

Bob Dylan celebrated his thirtieth recording anniversary October 16, 1992, at Madison Square Garden in New York City in front of eighteen thousand fans and admirers.

The several dozen musicians who joined him onstage played only his compositions. The house band for the event was Booker T. & the MG's, with Anton Figg replacing the deceased Al Jackson.

John Cougar Mellencamp, with Al Kooper on organ, ripped through "Like a Rolling Stone." Kooper had been the organist on the original recording. Stevie Wonder had a hit single in 1966 with "Blowin' in the Wind," and he performed the song live at this event. Other performances of note were Johnny Cash and June Carter on "It Ain't Me Babe," Johnny Winter on "Highway 51 Revisited," Neil Young on "Just Like Tom Thumb's Blues"/"All Along the Watchtower," Chrissie Hyde on "I Shall Be Released," the Band with "When I Paint My Masterpiece," and George Harrison on "If Not for You"/"Absolutely Sweet Marie." Clapton played "Love Minus Zero" and "No Limit." Steve Cropper of Booker T. fame was his second guitarist that night.

Clapton naturally stuck around for the all-star finale, joining Dylan, Roger McGuinn, Tom Petty, Neil Young, George Harrison, Al Kooper, Jim Keltner, and several others for "My Back Pages" and "Knockin' on Heaven's Door."

December 31, 1993

New Year's Eve 1993 found Eric Clapton at the Woking Leisure Centre, Woking, Surrey, England, for a two-set show. He would appear at the center on many New Years to come. These were private, by-invite-only affairs for fellow Alcoholics Anonymous members.

Clapton would always make up a fake group name for each appearance. The Resentments (1993), the Traditions (1995), Men Without Legs (1997), the Grave Emotional and Mental Disorders (1999), the Conscious Contact (2000), the Usual Band (2001), and Doctor Bob's Swing (2003) have all gone down as footnotes in rock history.

The sets have been comprised of many famous Clapton songs, but over the years there have been some additions that would make any of his fans drool. "Stone Free," "In the Midnight Hour," "He Ain't Heavy, He's My Brother," "You'll Never Walk Alone," "Gin House," "Rock 'N Roll Music," "Peter Gunn," "Hold On I'm Coming," "Good Golly Miss Molly," "Hi-Heel Sneakers," and "Whole Lotta Shakin'" were some of the songs that made appearances over the years.

Chris Stainton, Steve Gadd, Simon Climie, Andy Fairweather-Low, Henry Spinetti, and Gary Brooker are some of the musicians who have given of their time and put in multiple appearances.

May 11, 1995

Jimmie Vaughan organized a tribute concert for his brother Stevie Ray five years after his death. He gathered together the musicians who had played at his brother's last concert in Alpine Valley, Wisconsin. The concert was not open to the public but was by invite only.

In addition to Jimmie and his backing band, Bonnie Raitt, B. B. King, Buddy Guy, Robert Cray, Dr. John, Art Neville, and of course Eric Clapton all accepted invitations.

Clapton was a member of the basic backing band throughout, but he stepped forward to play "Empty Arms" and "Ain't Gone 'N Give Up on Your Love."

July 3, 1997

The Montreux Jazz Festival is one of the most respected in the world, although the use of jazz in the title does not aptly describe the variety of artists. The thirty-first festival was scheduled for July 4–19, 1997.

Eric Clapton, bassist Marcus Miller, saxophonist David Sanborn, keyboardist Joe Sample, and drummer Steve Gadd were scheduled to rehearse on July 3rd, and they opened it up for staff, friends, sponsors, and anyone else who may have been lurking about. In the end, about three thousand people were in the audience.

It was scheduled to be a instrumental performance, but five songs into the rehearsal Clapton provided the vocal for "Going Down Slow." Songs such as "Full House," "Snakes," "1st Degree Tango," and "Marcus #1" may have been more in the area of David Sanborn and Joe Sample instrumental material, but songs such as "Layla" and "Everyday I Have the Blues" gave it all an Eric Clapton concert feel.

September 15, 1997

He remained in a charity mode when he joined some of the cream of English rock and a few Americans to raise over a million dollars for the benefit of the island of Montserrat, which had been ravaged by a volcanic eruption. Sting, Paul McCartney, Carl Perkins, Jimmy Buffet, Elton John, Phil Collins, and others gave of their time and talent for the pay-per-view concert that was broadcast in forty countries on September 20.

The concert was organized by former Beatles producer George Martin and took place at the Royal Albert Hall.

Clapton was introduced by Carl Perkins and began with an acoustic version of "Broken Hearted Me." He then moved on to "Layla," and "Same Old Blues" with Mark Knopfler, keyboardist Jools Holland, drummer Phil Collins, percussionist Ray Cooper, and keyboardist Chris Stainton.

He was back onstage for the concert-ending "Hey Jude" and "Kansas City" with Elton John, Paul McCartney, Sting, Midge Ure, Knopfler, and Perkins. It was all a bargain at $19.99.

December 17, 1998

Whoopi Goldberg hosted two hundred friends of Bill Clinton at the White House on December 17, 1998, to celebrate the thirtieth anniversary of the Special Olympics. This Christmas celebration was taped and broadcast five days later.

Clapton performed "Merry Christmas Baby" with Sheryl Crow, "Christmas Without You" with John Popper, and "Gimme One Reason" with Tracy Chapman. He also performed "Christmas Tears" solo before returning for a group "Santa Claus Is Coming to Town."

His original concert posters are highly collectable. They have been reissued by the thousands. *Author's collection*

Jon Bon Jovi, Vanessa Williams, and Run-D.M.C. were also on the bill for the rocking Clintons. Seeing Run-D.M.C. perform "An Undecipherable Mess" at the White House would have been worth the price of admission alone. When you are the President of the United States finishing your second term of office, you can basically party as you want.

September 14, 1999

Sheryl Crow gave a free concert at New York City's Central Park on September 14, 1999. She and Clapton had been romantically involved, and he was there to lend a hand. Mostly performing live for the first half of the concert, she was joined by her guests during the second half. The Dixie

Chicks, Stevie Nicks, Chrissie Hynde, Keith Richards, Sarah McLachlan, and finally Clapton joined her onstage.

She and E. C. performed "White Room" and "Little Wing." He also joined the first encore for a performance of "Tombstone Blues."

The concert was broadcast live on Fox Television. It was also released as a live album on December 7 and was a steady, if not spectacular seller for Crow, finally passing the half million units sold level.

April 25, 2000

Bobby Whitlock was preparing for a performance on Jools Holland's BBC Television program, and who should show up but old Derek and the Dominos bandmate Eric Clapton with his black Stratocaster.

It would be the first time in twenty-nine years that Clapton and Whitlock would play together. Whitlock on piano and vocals and Clapton on guitar were joined by host Holland on the organ. They played "Wing and a Prayer," "Bell Bottom Blues," and "Southern Gentlemen," which featured a number of improvisational solos by Clapton.

The show was broadcast on April 29, 2000. Whitlock was one of Clapton's better bandmates, and it was nice that Clapton finally made the gesture to heal the break caused by the Dominos' disintegration. Given Jim Gordon's continuing institutionalization, they are the last members standing from Derek and the Dominos.

October 20, 2001

October 20, 2001, was the date of the concert in Madison Square Garden to benefit the families of the September 11 terrorist attacks. Tickets ranged from $250 to $10,000 and raised $14,000,000 on their own. Donations were also taken by phone that numbered in the tens of millions. Many of America's leading celebrities manned the phones while the concert was in session.

When I look at the lineup, I am amazed at the number of British artists who turned out. David Bowie, the Who, Mick Jagger, Keith Richards, Elton John, and Paul McCartney were joined by Bon Jovi, Billy Joel, Destiny's Child, James Taylor, John Mellencamp, and a host of others to create a star-studded affair.

Harrison Ford introduced Clapton, who had flown in from Mexico City for the concert. He brought along Buddy Guy as his second guitarist, and they played "Hoochie Coochie Man" and "Everything's Gonna Be

Alright." As usual, he stuck around for the all-star finale of "Let It Be" and "Freedom." The concert was broadcast live and on the Internet.

June 3, 2002

I can envision Bill Clinton hosting a rock 'n' roll show, but the Queen of England grooving to the tunes of Eric Clapton and other rock artists is a stretch for the mind and soul.

Queen Elizabeth celebrated the Golden Jubilee of her coronation during June 2002. She held a series of open-air concerts in the gardens at Buckingham Palace. Ten thousand people, mostly chosen by lottery, were invited.

Some of the musicians who performed were Shirley Bassey, Joe Cocker, Phil Collins, Elton John, Tom Jones, Annie Lennox, Paul McCartney, Queen, Cliff Richard, Rod Stewart, and of course Mr. Clapton. Even a few American artists such as Brian Wilson, Tony Bennett, and Aretha Franklin were also included on the bill.

Clapton first hit the stage to support Brian Wilson for a performance of "The Warmth of the Sun." He returned for an electric version of "Layla." He appeared for a third time with McCartney to play his famous solo on "While My Guitar Gently Weeps." His final appearance was in the all-star finale for a rendition of "All You Need Is Love."

His appearance at the show ended on an amusing note when the Queen asked if he had been performing long.

October 6, 2002

October 6, 2002, found Clapton in Los Angeles, California, for another charity event, this time for the Carl Wilson Foundation.

Brian Wilson was the headliner, and Clapton used his backing band for his two-song set consisting of "Stormy Monday" and "Layla." He then joined in on such Beach Boys classics as "The Warmth of the Sun," Good Vibrations," "Barbara Ann," and "Surfin' USA." He and Wilson shared a vocal duet on "The Warmth of the Sun."

July 19, 2003

The decades quickly passed for John Mayall, and he found himself turning seventy. What better way to celebrate than onstage with some friends?

Mick Taylor and Clapton joined him for a performance July 19 in Liverpool for his seventieth birthday party. It marked the first time in almost forty years that Mayall and Clapton had been onstage together.

Clapton played guitar on nine of the seventeen songs. It was basically a blues concert, with such nuggets as "No Big Hurry," "Please Mr. Lofton," "Hideaway," "All Your Love," "Have You Heard," "Hoochie Coochie Man," "I'm Tore Down," and "It Ain't Right" being resurrected for the show.

May 6, 2005

Cream's induction into the Rock and Roll Hall of Fame and subsequent reunion at the induction ceremony evolved into a series of full-blown concerts. The first was May 2–6, 2005, at the Royal Albert Hall in England and three more at Madison Square Garden October 24–26. Old tensions quickly resurfaced in New York, which took the bloom off the rose. If they had called it quits after the English concerts, they would have left the stage with a better feeling.

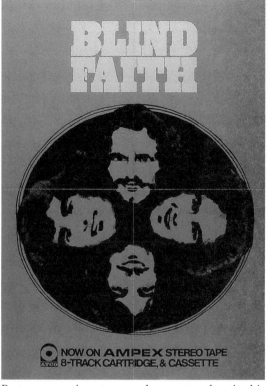

Posters were given to record stores to advertise his new releases.   *Author's collection*

The four May concerts all included the same set list. The songs were no longer extended out with long improvisational solos but rather were performed similar to their studio versions. An example would be the six-minute "Toad."

October 27, 2006

Many of Clapton's concerts over the last four years or so have settled into a comfortable sameness. His stop at the American Airlines Arena in Miami is representative of his approach.

He bookended his electric material around an acoustic set in the middle. Acoustic versions of "Key to the Highway," "San Francisco Bay Blues," "Nobody Knows You When You're Down and Out," and "Running on Faith" joined such electric perennial classics as "Pretending," "I Shot the Sheriff," "After Midnight," "Wonderful Tonight," "Layla," "Cocaine," and "Crossroads."

February 25, 2008

Steve Winwood and Eric Clapton teamed up for four concerts at Madison Square Garden February 25–28, 2008.

The old bandmates performed material from their Blind Faith days, plus reached back to Traffic, Derek and the Dominos, solo material, and even a little Jimi Hendrix to form their concert sets.

Everything went so well that they toured together in 2009 and 2010, which returned Clapton to more of a group concept.

39

All Along, We Had to Talk About It

Books

ric Clapton has had literally millions of pages written about him. Books, magazine articles, and websites have reviewed, examined, and chronicled just about every note he has played, every word he has spoken, and most everything he has done during the course of his life. The last fifty years of his life is an open book, to use a bad pun.

Books have been well researched and otherwise. They have been based on fact and rumor. They have provided enjoyable, interesting, and sometimes boring reads. They have sold well, and many have quickly disappeared. No matter how many books have been written, there will always be more on the way.

Eric Clapton is one of a very few musicians who has maintained a high level of popularity for nearly half a century. He has, for better or worse, kept himself in the public eye, and yes, some of it was unintentional. He has accomplished a lot, produced an extensive catalog of music, and lived a life of brilliance and sometimes excess. He has proven himself to be a music god on one hand and a very normal and often vulnerable human being on the other. Through it all he has been fascinating for his huge fan base.

The following books are both helpful and at times essential in understanding Eric Clapton as both a person and musician.

Eric: The Autobiography

The first book anyone should turn to when exploring, or trying to understand, someone of note is his autobiography, if available.

Clapton published his autobiography in May 2008, and it remains the definitive book about his life for obvious reasons.

Like all autobiographies, it only contains what the author wants his readers to know. Everyone has secrets, and if the author wants to keep something private, whether thoughts or actions, then so be it.

Any autobiography is life as the author or principal participant sees it. Examining oneself is not always easy. There must be an ability to look inside with insightfulness and clarity, which is not an ability all people can do.

Eric Clapton, to his credit, managed to produce a very personal book. His childhood and formative years find him at his most vulnerable.

His relationships with women are probably the area of least depth, especially concerning some who were not as well known as Patti Harrison Clapton Boyd.

As with many books of this type, the response was both critical and worshipful, which is probably as it should be. Yes, the book is self-centered in places, but that is the nature of the autobiographical beast. If you consider yourself important enough to write about, especially hundreds of pages, then some self-centeredness is needed.

Clapton has been one of the best guitarists in the world for close to fifty years; his fans have known it, and he has known it as well. He has very few living equals. "Clapton is god" rings true for his fans and for him.

He did not really need to write this book, as his fame and fortune are secure. It for some reason helped him on his journey through life. Whatever the hesitations may have been, understanding Eric Clapton as a person starts here.

Wonderful Tonight: George Harrison, Eric Clapton, and Me by Patti Boyd

Except for the musicians themselves, very few people have been as much a part of the inside story of the 1960s and 1970s music scene as has Patti Boyd.

She has received a lot of criticism along the way, and such was the case when this book was published. There are a lot more Clapton fans in this world than there are Boyd fans. She is telling her side of the story concerning her relationships with George Harrison and Eric Clapton. They were and always will be two of the more iconic figures in music history, and there is no way she could have completely pleased their huge fan base.

Still, for anyone even remotely interested in the life of Eric Clapton, it is an essential read, for better or worse.

In the final analysis, I found it more fascinating than good.

Cream: Eric Clapton, Jack Bruce, and Ginger Baker— The Legendary Supergroup by Chris Welch

Chris Welch was a writer for the British magazine *Melody Maker.*
His book is a nice overview of the band that includes interviews with most of the principal characters.

Welch takes the time and energy to probe beneath the surface a bit, and his examination of the group's label at the time puts a different spin on the book, which is welcome.

The extensive concert dates and recording sessions may be more than casual fans would want, but they will be of interest to Clapton aficionados.

This book is an overview of Eric Clapton at a certain period of his life and should be approached as such.

Crossroads: The Life and Music of Eric Clapton by Michael Schumacher

While the book was published in 1999, which makes it a little antiquated, until the Boyd/Clapton autobiographies, it was one of the better examinations of Clapton's life. It remains an interesting read.

It's nice to compare many of the stories and situations to the versions in the aforementioned autobiographies.

Crossroads is a very smooth journey through the life and music of Eric Clapton from a somewhat unbiased viewpoint. It is well written and has a flow to it, which not only increases one's knowledge of E. C. but does so in an entertaining way.

It is time well spent for any Eric Clapton fan.

Eric Clapton: The Complete Recording Sessions: 1963-1992 by Marc Roberty

Marc Roberty is one of the foremost Clapton experts on the planet. Just google his name or plug it into the Amazon book section, and you will find a multitude of books written by him that deal with our favorite subject. He recently joined Bobby Whitlock on his autobiography, and they have produced one of the better looks at the rock music scene of the last forty years that you will ever find. Any of his books concerning Eric Clapton are highly recommended.

The original publication date was 1993, which makes it another somewhat out-of-date book, as 20 more years of Clapton's recording career have come and gone. However, what is there is well researched, comprehensive, and exhausting in a good way.

Roberty does not miss much, as bands, personnel, songs, guitars are present.

It remains a fine reference for anyone even remotely interested in the career and history of Eric Clapton.

Strange Brew: Eric Clapton and the British Blues Boom 1965–1970 by Christopher Hjort and John Mayall

Everything you ever want to know about the British blues and then some.

The book is basically a document of the day-to-day, and sometimes hour-to-hour, lives of Eric Clapton, John Mayall, Peter Green, Mick Taylor, and others who have entered Mayall's musical orbit through the years. The book then moves outward from its base to the likes of Jimi Hendrix, Free, Jeff Beck, and others.

The nature of the book takes it beyond just Eric Clapton, but in doing so it provides a solid introduction to many of the characters who have shared the musical stage with him.

Clapton's career is covered from his time with the Yardbirds through his Derek and the Dominos period.

The sheer amount of research that was needed for its publication is overwhelming.

It is a good read for anyone interested in the period and music. It may seem all-inclusive, but it is not and does not try to be. It covers a period of British music now frozen in time and does so very well.

Clapton, The Authorized Biography by Ray Coleman

If you want to go way back in time, and I shudder at the thought that 1988 is now a part of history and that there are now Clapton fans who were not born in that year, then Ray Coleman's book is a nice introduction. The best part is you can pick up a used copy on Amazon for about $1.00.

The book is extremely dated twenty-five years after the fact and has a cheerleader aspect to it, but it is a nice overview of the now first part of his career.

It doesn't really dig beneath the surface and should be used as a primer before moving on to the more substantial reads that are out there.

It you go to the book sections in Amazon and Ebay and do a search for Eric Clapton, hundreds of titles will surface. No doubt many more will be added in the ensuing years. They are all available for exploration, relaxation, knowledge, and criticism. Have at it!

40

Guess There's Nothing Left for Me to Explain

Legacy

I am continually amazed at how popular Eric Clapton has become. I am even more amazed at how many people know who he is and what he does for a living. The music has now affected three generations as grandparents, their children, and the grand-children have now been exposed to and come to appreciate his music.

Eric Clapton did not invent the guitar, or the electric blues, or the British blues for that matter. There have also been guitarists as creative as him. My first thought in that regard is that Jeff Beck was more creative as a member of the Yardbirds than Clapton. Clapton's creative peak may have been his tenure with Cream.

What he has done is popular-ize the modern blues sound. He has helped take it from obscu-rity and bring it into the main-stream. He also showed that the blues and rock could be fused

Looking back on the career of Eric Clapton, this was one of his most affecting performances. *Author's collection*

Clapton will continue to tour and remain popular as long as his
desire and health lasts.   *Author's collection*

together with stunning results. It may be that his popularization of this
musical form will be his lasting legacy.

He has also popularized the guitar as an instrument. His virtuosity
for the past almost five decades has kept it in the forefront of the public
consciousness. His obituary will no doubt focus on his guitar ability, and he
remains one of the best living guitarists. The tone he is able to coax from
his instruments is second to none. Other artists can play the same guitar
but not come close to the sound he can produce.

He has never been the flashiest of guitarists. He is above all a stylist who astonishes with his precision and technique. He has the ability to make each note crystal clear.

Of all the musicians active today, his is one of the most secure reputations and legacies. His large body of work will continue selling long after he is gone.

The last legacy he will leave is his faithful service to his Crossroads Centre. While it may not be as well known as his music, it has directly affected the lives of hundreds and possibly thousands of persons in need. That is indeed a good legacy to leave behind.

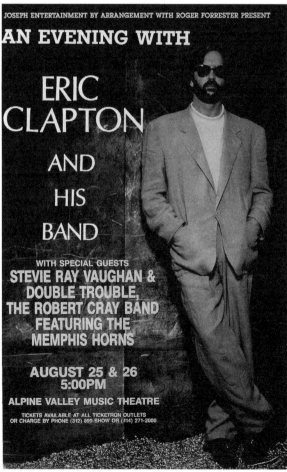

How many evenings have people spent with Eric Clapton?

Author's collection

41

Then I Can Change the World

What Will Happen To

E ric Clapton released his twentieth solo album on September 27, 2010. It was a huge commercial success, reaching #6 on the U.S. album charts and #7 in Britain. It is another testament to his lasting appeal.

ERIC CLAPTON
FIVE DECADES... ONE CONSTANT.
ERNIE BALL STRINGS

THANK YOU ERIC,
FOR TAKING US ALONG FOR THE RIDE.

Enough Said!   *Author's collection*

There is little doubt that he will continue to tour and record until mortality or deterioration prevents him doing so. He is one of those artists who has never tired of touring and has always stated he will continue to do so. His popularity is enduring, and he will have little problem filling concert halls as long as he cares to do so. His music is who he is and what he does.

Many guitarists have maintained their virtuosity well into old age. B. B. King and Chuck Berry come immediately to mind. Now in his mid-sixties, Clapton shows no signs of slowing down as a guitar technician.

What is interesting are his three young daughters. He will continue to be a father to them and his older daughter Ruth. One wonders if any of the three will inherit his guitar gene, but only time will tell that story.

Life goes on, and so will Eric Clapton's story and music.

Selected Bibliography

The material consulted for this book consists of recordings, books, magazines, and websites. The following is a breakdown of what was used.

Books

Bacon, Tony. *The Ultimate Guitar Book*. New York: Alfred A. Knopf, 1991.

Baker, Ginger. *Ginger Baker: Hellraiser: The Autobiography of the World's Greatest Drummer*. London: John Blake Publishing, 2010.

Boyd, Pattie, and Penny Junor. *Wonderful Tonight: George Harrison, Eric Clapton, and Me*. London: Three Rivers Press, 2008.

Boyd, Pattie, and Penny Junor. *Wonderful Today: The Autobiography*. London: Headline Review, 2007.

Burrows, Terry. *The Complete Encyclopedia of the Guitar: The Definitive Guide to the World's Most Popular Instrument*. New York: Schirmer Books, 1998.

Clapton, Eric. *Clapton: The Autobiography*. London: Three Rivers Press, 2008.

Cohn, Lawrence. *Nothing but the Blues: The Music and The Musicians*. New York: Abbeville Press, 1999.

Coleman, Ray. *Clapton, The Authorized Biography*. New York: Warner Books, 1986.

Duchossoir, A. R. *The Fender Stratocaster*. Milwaukee, WI: Hal Leonard Publishing, 1995.

Guralnick, Peter. *Searching for Robert Johnson: The Life and Legend of the King of the Delta Blues Singers*. New York: Plume Publishing, 1998.

Heckstall-Smith, Dick, and Pete Grant. *Blowing the Blues: Fifty Years Playing the British Blues*. Clear Books, 2004.

Hjort, Christopher, and John Mayall. *Strange Brew: Eric Clapton and the British Blues Boom 1965–1970*. Jawbone Press, 2007.

Myers, Paul. *It Ain't Easy: Long John Baldry and the Birth of the British Blues*. Greystone Books, 2007.

Palmer, Robert. *Deep Blues: A Musical and Cultural History of the Mississippi Delta*. Penguin, 1982.

Rees, Dafydd, and Luke Crampton. *Encyclopedia of Rock Stars*. New York: DK Publishing, 1996.

Roberty, Marc. *Eric Clapton: The Complete Recording Sessions, 1963–1992.* Blandford Press Press, 1993.

Roberty, Marc. *Slowhand: The Life and Music of Eric Clapton.* New York: Crown, 1993.

Roberty, Marc. *The Eric Clapton Album: Thirty Years of Music and Memorabilia.* Studio Publishers, 1994.

Rowe, Mike. *Chicago Blues: The City & the Music.* New York: Da Capo Press, 1981.

Russo, Greg. *Yardbirds: The Ultimate Rave-Up.* Crossroads Publications, 2001.

Schumacher, Michael. *Crossroads, The Life and Music of Eric Clapton.* Hyperion, 1985.

Strong, M. C. *The Great Rock Discography.* Edinburgh: Omnibus Press, 1996.

Ward, Ed, Geoffrey Stokes, and Ken Tucker. *Rock of Ages: The Rolling Stone History of Rock & Roll.* New York: Rolling Stone Press/Summit Books, 1986.

Welch, Chris. *Cream: Eric Clapton, Jack Bruce, and Ginger Baker—The Legendary 60's Supergroup.* New York: Backbeat Books, 2000.

Wheeler, Tom. *The Stratocaster Chronicles: Celebrating 50 Years of the Fender Strat,* Milwaukee, WI: Hal Leonard Publishing, 2004.

Whitburn, Joel. *The Billboard Book of Top 40 Albums,* Billboard Books, New York, 1995.

Whitburn, Joel. *Top Pop Singles 1955–1996.* Menomonee, WI: Record Research, 1997.

Wild, David, and Quincy Jones. *And the Grammy Goes To . . . : The Official Story of Music's Most Coveted Award.* State Street Press, 2007.

Magazines

Magazines have always been an important part of the story for many artists and personalities. The following, in list form, are the ones that contributed to my research.

Billboard (1963–Present)
Cashbox (1963–1996)
Crawdaddy (1966–1979)
Creem (1969–1989)
Goldmine (1974–Present)
Hit Parader (1962–1985)
Melody Maker (1963–1999)
New Musical Express (1962–Present)
Rolling Stone (1967–Present)

Websites

As stated earlier, there are millions of websites that have a Clapton connection, and thousands that are dedicated to his story and music. The Internet is an always-changing organism, and I urge you to explore it as there are many treasures to be found.

The one website I will mention is YouTube, which has an almost unending multitude of Clapton performances and just about anyone else you can think of. Enjoy!

Index

THE FAQ SERIES